why
AFRICA
matters

why
AFRICA
matters

CEDRIC MAYSON

ORBIS BOOKS
Maryknoll, New York 10545

Founded in 1970, Orbis Books endeavors to publish works that enlighten the mind, nourish the spirit, and challenge the conscience. The publishing arm of the Maryknoll Fathers and Brothers, Orbis seeks to explore the global dimensions of the Christian faith and mission, to invite dialogue with diverse cultures and religious traditions, and to serve the cause of reconciliation and peace. The books published reflect the views of their authors and do not represent the official position of the Maryknoll Society. To learn more about Maryknoll and Orbis Books, please visit our website at www.maryknollsociety.org.

Library of Congress Cataloging-in-Publication Data

Mayson, Cedric.
    Why Africa matters / Cedric Mayson.
        p. cm.
    ISBN 978-1-57075-869-0 (pbk.)
    1. Africa – Civilization. I. Title.
DT14.M385 2010
960 – dc22
                        2009047807

Contents

Abbreviations   vi

Introduction   1

Chapter 1   The Five Horsemen of the Apocalypse   7

Chapter 2   The Earthling Matter   12

Chapter 3   The Liberation Matter   39

Chapter 4   The Ecological Matter   65

Chapter 5   The Political Matter   72

Chapter 6   The Economic Matter   95

Chapter 7   The Media Matter   110

Chapter 8   The Spiritual Matter   118

Chapter 9   The Crux of the Matter   153

Chapter 10   Something New Out of Africa   175

And in Conclusion   197

Notes   199

Index   209

Abbreviations

AACC	All Africa Conference of Churches
AAM	Anti-Apartheid Movement
AIC	African Independent or Indigenous Churches
AICA	African Independent Churches Association
ANC	African National Congress
BCM	Black Consciousness Movement
CI	Christian Institute of Southern Africa
CRA	Commission on Religious Affairs (ANC)
CWPR	Council of World Parliament of Religions
EATWOT	Ecumenical Association of Third World Theologians
EFSA	Ecumenical Foundation of Southern Africa
NGO	Nongovernmental Organization
NRLF	National Religious Leaders Forum
OAU	Organization of African Unity
PAC	Pan Africanist Congress
SACC	South African Council of Churches
SAFCEI	South African Faith Communities' Environment Institute
SASO	South African Students' Organisation
SB	Special Branch
TRC	Truth and Reconciliation Commission
UDF	United Democratic Front
UDHR	Universal Declaration of Human Rights
UNISA	University of South Africa
WCC	World Council of Churches
WCRP	World Conference on Religion and Peace

Introduction

Synopsis

Africa is older, bigger, and richer than most of us realize and has much to offer that is needed by the rest of the world. What some see as a basket case is in fact a treasure chest.

This book seeks to explore why Africa matters.

◆ ◆ ◆

We have here perhaps the most remarkable gathering of well-established moral wisdoms in the world — with our African, Hindu, Islamic, Christian, secularist, and other value systems. What have for thousands of years been separate streams of conscience in the rest of the world, and what are still largely and at times even totally separate, have come together here earlier than just about anywhere else, making possible a new and unique experience of ethical sharing.[1]

Most people see Africa through Western eyes. They have a one-eyed squint through the telescopes of explorers like Livingstone and Stanley; or the narrow-framed steel spectacles of missionaries they heard about in Sunday School; or the monocles, moustaches, and beards of colonizers like Cecil Rhodes or King Leopold of the Belgians; or over the sights of guns controlled by Queen Victoria's soldiers in their impressive colorful uniforms; or as TV commentators. They see Africans as savages engaged in brutal wars or witchcraft, ravaged by ignorance, famine, corruption, poverty, and HIV/AIDS, or as objects of exploiters, investors, academics, politicians, clergy, journalists, and film producers. Many Africans do the same. We present our continent and ourselves in pictures that we think sympathetic Westerners will find acceptable, because that destructive worldview still lingers.

But there is a deeper understanding of what makes Africa tick, and of why Africa's ticking clock matters to Washington and Westminster, the academics and housekeepers and workers of the world. History will tell humanity's time in terms of colonial liberation, not colonial conquest; the scientific and industrial revolutions of the twentieth century are being surpassed by the social transformations of the twenty-first; and the pursuit of globalized power from the top is being dislodged by the pursuit of globalized grace from below, as the majority world is heard. The headlines are moving from the West and North to the South and East, and listening ears are turning from the empires of the United States and the UK to China, India, Brazil — and Africa.

Africans come from the beginnings of time and the ends of the Earth, and their worldview often differs from that of the West. Hundreds of millions of us from blackest brown to whitest pink are seeking to relate our unique past and unique present to the united future. We are a mixed lot: humanity in a handful. From Cape Town to Cairo the bulging pockets of wealth walk beside the protruding bones of poverty; the heights of education and the depths of ignorance emerge in the same families; rural masses merge with urban sprawl; and human tongues and voice boxes anatomically the same produce over a thousand different languages. Nothing on Earth is older than Africa, but as the elder Pliny said two thousand years ago: there is "always something new out of Africa."

Many still think of Africa as the Dark Continent, which needs the light of Western civilization to survive, and certainly Africa has much to learn. Others fear that the world's ecological systems, economics, religion, politics, and media, dominated by the West, are ensuring that civilization will self-destruct this century unless we can find another way of life — and certainly the Dark Continent can shed some light on the matter of survival.

Africa is huge. You could put the United States or Europe into Africa several times without touching edges. There are almost a billion of us in thousands of tribes squashed by European conquest just over a century ago into fifty-three colonial states.

Fertile arable lands are the breadbaskets for millions, and crops are exported all over the world — apples, bananas, avocados, every sort of citrus, paw paw, pineapples, nuts, cloves, your morning coffee and night time cocoa, rice and rubber, sisal, paper, timber, tobacco, and wine by the barrelful. Thousands of feet above sea level, thousands of acres of coal reveal where long-lost forests stood. Oil is found under land and sea from Angola and Nigeria to Mossel Bay. The world's highest yields of gold and diamonds and gems are made here alongside vast resources of platinum, titanium, copper, aluminum, cobalt, asbestos, chrome, manganese, lead, tin, zinc, iron, and uranium. Coal and dams generate electricity for export, and Cape Town, having neither coal nor dams, is pioneering the quest for alternative nuclear power. Seas teem with fish from sardines to sharks but have been so plundered that the fish farming industry is growing rapidly.

The democratic revolutions that took hundreds of years to transform America and Europe have swept through Africa in a single generation, so a few hiccups are not surprising. But civilization, currently threatening us all, is actually a very recent development in the history of the world — the froth on the top. The secret of survival is to rediscover the essential experience of the power of human community that Africa knows as *ubuntu.* Africa still embraces those primal powers of humanity that drove evolution for hundreds of thousands of years before the quest for civilization cut many humans off from their roots. The West became besotted with what life could *do,* and lost the sense and power of what life could *be.* That is why we must explore Africa's ubuntu.

◆ ◆ ◆

I am a white African: a nonblack as the apartheid boys might have said. Most of my children and grandchildren live in Cape Town, where my great grandfather is buried. Penelope and I live in the bush by the Kruger National Park, where wild game roam as they have since before the time of humans, big as elephants and smaller than mosquitoes. Doing your being here is different from doing your being in New York or New Zealand, Moscow or Buenos Aires, London or Singapore.

My own experience runs from inside apartheid prisons to working with liberated governments; from dipping my feet in the Mediterranean of Moses, the sweep of the Nile, the Zambesi "smoking like thunder" over the Victoria Falls, to the massive rollers of the oceans from Antarctica pounding the continent's southern shores. It has been a lifetime of knowing people from presidents to paupers, bishops to agnostics, media producers to media fodder, women people and men people, young and old, black and brown and white, saints and sinners — and plenty who did not know the difference.

This book seeks to portray the comprehensive face of an Africa that matters to the world. Much of it looks north from south, for which there are several reasons. One is that I live in the south, as whites have done since long before the Pilgrim Fathers sailed for America. Another is that the struggle for religious, political, and economic liberation has older credentials in South Africa than anywhere else. The first African liberation movement, the African National Congress, was born in South Africa in 1912, yet South Africa was the last to win democracy, in 1994. A third reason is our mix: the dimensions of difference from which human unity must be forged are seen more clearly here than in many other places. The racial mix of "white," "black," "Indian," and "colored"; the mix of religions — African Traditional and Indigenous, Moslem, Hindu, Buddhist, agnostic, and every sort of Christian including some we invented ourselves; the mix of well-educated and ill-educated, of wealthy and impoverished, are all represented by great proportions of people, as they are in the wider world. And lastly, South Africa carries a lot of weight. We contribute much to the continent in terms of wealth and expertise, agriculture and manufacture, food and literature, education and culture, religion and politics. When the boundary walls of apartheid came down in 1994 and we came back into our own, the statistics of the continent as a whole changed dramatically overnight.

Some fear that the Africa of today has thrown away the legitimacy of the liberation struggle and accepted the domination of Western civilization. In any case, we have a lot to answer for, and Africa has to give an account of itself to the world. Sometimes our analysis and progress have fallen woefully short but at other times have been wonderfully good news.

This does not mean that Africa must now send missionaries to convert the rest of the world to "a better way of life": we suffered too much from that kind of missionary-ism in the past ourselves! This book is written as a contribution from Africa to a world seeking to rebirth itself.

Afterword

Recent struggles for liberation in Africa are far wider than political independence. Pitching the folk-memory of life against the oppressive practices of Western civilization makes Africa a matter of importance for the survival and enjoyment of all of us — West and East as well.

Chapter 1

The Five Horsemen
of the Apocalypse

Synopsis

The main areas of development, which many in the West see as signs of human progress, also herald our failure and destruction: religion, economics, politics, ecology, and the media culture. Africa helps us to see ways to confront their threats and dangers.

Like introductory clips on a TV program, with subtle soothing music, they appear first as five daintily trotting horsemen from the north and west and east, bringing Africa promise and blessing.

Religion trotted into the scene spreading gentle ways of peace and harmony and hope, with the sense of a Higher Power to care for us all. Economics entered as humanity learned to cultivate the land and breed cattle for food instead of subsisting on berries, nuts, and scavenging; to construct with wood, iron, and bronze; and invent villages, towns, cities, and, the great convenience, coins. Politics came in, prancing proudly with tossing head and whisking tail, as humans devised ways of organizing and governing themselves, bringing order and direction to their growing communities. Science stepped briskly up, well-shod hooves planting strong and certain steps to open up new transforming vistas and practices, solving so many problems, making so many possibilities. Finally, ambling into the human scene on the path laid out by those who brought together reading and writing, the printing press and radio waves, came the horseman of the media, to make a new educated Earthling* culture, informed and informing.

---

*Using the word "Earthling" startles us into realizing our reality as humble beings of Planet Earth and liberates us from the superiority often associated with the word "human."

Many in the West think these come to Africa as five horse-men with the aura of liberation, leading us from the fumbling uncertainty of early emerging evolutionaries into the power and promise of the modern world. But then, with the suddenness of a button pressed to change the scene from life to death, the five gentle horsemen of progress and peace change into the Five Horse-men of the Apocalypse. With gnashing teeth and slashing hooves, they become heralds of doom to Africa, advancing like mounted spearmen of the Middle Ages, protected by armor, lances raised to compel or kill, spearheading the destruction of civilization. The liberators became abusers, merciless oppressors and destroyers against whom neither Africa nor the Earth has any chance of continuing unless we can stop them. "The human race has only a 50/50 chance of surviving another century," writes Sir Martin Rees, the British Astronomer Royal.[1]

Our ecological systems are now under such pressure from their misuse that many scientists believe a collapse of the climate will happen this century. The simple ultimate fact is that we are filling and fouling Earth's atmosphere with carbon dioxide, the oceans are warming, ice is melting, sea level is rising, coastal cities like Cape Town, New York, and London, and countries like Bangladesh and many islands will be under water later in this century unless Earth-lings produce a massive ecological revolution now. "Ecology shows that unless humanity can learn to revere the whole of creation, and not just the human part, the entire world including our own species is in danger of extinction," writes David Tacey.[2]

Economics is dominated by international corporate and financial powers whose worship of the idol of the Market Economy is making more people more poor than at any time in history. The economic elite insists that private individualist possession of wealth is the key to economic success, not public democratic communal ownership, but we have frequently faced economic collapse because of the inherent failure and corruption of this privatized capitalist system. The West is currently being bailed out by vast economic packages from public communal government funds that will inhibit the world economy for decades, until it collapses entirely and does to the United States, the UK, Europe, Asia, and the world what Mugabe has done to Zimbabwe. Extant economics is suicide.

Politicians talk of world government, United Nations, and a united Africa for peace and prosperity but are ruled by the self-interest and violent competition of nation-states and destructive empires inherited from the adolescent colonial era. Good people in politics and government in many countries are undermined by incompetents positioned through favoritism, not ability, but the greatest threat comes because politics are controlled from behind the scenes by globalized self-centered economic empires. Joerg Rieger writes that "the post-colonial empire is marked by the fact that the direct exercise of power has given way to more subtly powerful and far reaching forms of exercising power. Direct political power has given way to economic influences."[3] It is, as Albert Nolan puts it, "the globalizaton of . . . neo-liberal capitalism, a thoroughly materialistic worldview . . . a culture that destroys other cultures and indigenous wisdom, making the rich richer and the poor poorer around the world," dominating everything by "the really oppressive power in the human world — the gun."[4] The political refusal of Earthlings to unite keeps us teetering on the edge of life-destroying violence, which can erupt into a fatal nuclear conflagration at any moment.

Another Horseman of the Apocalypse is the Media, the craftsmen of spreading culture, still producing millions of copies of print each day, but rapidly bursting out into radio, television, and the Internet. The theory of feeding the mind and will of an educated public has often degenerated into an advertising campaign to promote personal political and commercial interests. The media is rapidly becoming "the opium of the people," more destructive than the role Marx accorded religion, packaging the patchworks to warp minds, lauding the negative and antihuman influences of selfishness, elitism, killing, crime, and animal sexuality for the sole benefit of sales for the profit of its owners, the elite. Al Gore has written: "Now that the conglomerates can dominate the expression of opinion that floods the minds of the citizenry and selectively choose the ideas that are amplified so loudly as to drown out others that, whatever their validity, do not have wealthy patrons, the result is a de facto coup d'état overthrowing the rule of reason. Greed and wealth now allocate power in our society, and that power is used in turn to further increase and concentrate wealth and power in the hands of the few."[5]

Religion, instead of lighting the Way to life, salvation, and success, has led Christians, Jews, Muslims, Hindus, and other believers to threaten one another with destruction in the name of the God of Love, committed to centuries of mutual hostility, unable to break out of what Charles Villa-Vicencio calls "the iron cage of history." Solidly linked to political and economic oppressors, the religious elites endorsed and enhanced the conflicts of colonialism, the World Wars, and the Cold Wars in direct contradiction to their prophets. Religions today line up behind the wars in India and the East, in Israel and Afghanistan. They fear to contradict the global program of U.S. fundamentalist Christianity, instigating a Muslim terrorist threat to justify a U.S. military presence throughout Africa. In many parts of the world the quest for oppressive political and economic power is expressed in religious terms, garnished with promises of heaven or threats of hell, and inventing soul-myths to subvert minds and bodies and communities. Many spiritual people know this is false but continue to submit to the self-centered suicidal refusal of their institutions to unite together with an alternative spiritual vision to save Earthlings. They have talked of "ecumenism" and "interfaith" for over a century, but have no intention at all to actually be it, and enact the spiritual unity of Earthlings. Religions promote the Apocalypse.

Many people in Africa now realize that the Five Horsemen of the Apocalypse are real and devilish and destructive, controlled by poppycock religions, poppycock economics, poppycock politics, poppycock ecology, and a poppycock media. The supermarket notion that everything in humanity is gradually improving, trickling progress and prosperity down to all, is totally false. "Humanity has become a cancerous growth in the life of the world," reflects Professor Jakobus S. Krüger.[6]

Liberation and evolution come from confronting oppression and surpassing the claims of the respectable ruling powers of the elite. Basic changes have always taken place in humanity, and we should face them and make them without the fear inspired by false politicians or the superstitious folly spread by false preachers in America and Europe or by their sycophants in Africa. "Religious truth is evolutionary" wrote Gert Theissen. "It is not given once and for all in particular traditions. Rather, these traditions undergo decisive changes.... Modern men cannot view them in the same way as people from past times."[7] We have a prophetic mission to chase the Apocalyptic Horsemen away.

This is the context in which we ask why Africa matters. Chief Albert Luthuli, the great Christian who led the African National

Congress a generation ago, once said: "Somewhere ahead there beckons a civilization which will take its place in God's history with other great human syntheses: Chinese, Egyptian, Jewish, European. It will not necessarily be all black: but it will be African."[8]

And in a very real sense, we are all Africans.

Afterword

Human society will destroy itself in this century unless total change takes place. There is no possibility of "saving the situation" or "maintaining the status quo" in which these five horsemen of the Apocalypse do their thing. Like every empire in history they are collapsing, and massive suffering is inevitable in every community on every continent whether we like it or not . . . unless . . . unless . . . unless. . . .

Chapter 2

The Earthling Matter

Synopsis

Contemplating the stars enables us to grasp the wonder of being unique Earthlings that originated in Africa: body, mind, and spirit, in community. Earthlings spread around Earth a hundred thousand years ago in different patches, and civilizations later separated the spiritual from the secular. Africa did not do this but saw life as "all of a piece."

2.1. We Are All Earthlings

2.2. Cradle of Humanity

2.3. Patches

2.4. The Spirit of Earthlings

2.5. Belongingness

2.6. Prophets

2.7. Religions

2.8. The Rhinoceros and the God Question
      EARTHLINGS IN AFRICA

2.9. The Community of Earthlings in Africa

2.10. The Primal Reality of All Earthlings

2.11. The Lostness of Earthlings

2.12. Picture of a Continent

2.13. The People of Africa
       EARTHLINGS AND CIVILIZATION

2.14. The Debacle of Civilization

2.15. No Word for *Ubuntu*

2.16. The Religious Apartheid of Civilization

2.17. The Liberated Testimony

2.18. So Africa Matters

It is *"an unnerving thought that we may be the living universe's supreme achievement and its worst nightmare."*
— Bill Bryson[1]

2.1. We Are All Earthlings

We live in the bushveld of Africa. Our home is on the Crocodile River boundary of the Kruger National Park, where South Africa, Mozambique, and Swaziland stand shoulder to shoulder, and the wild game range is unfenced for hundreds of miles up into Zimbabwe. This is our world. But sitting on our stoep (veranda) one dark night, Penelope and I with our friends Horst and Christine were lit up by a sudden strong awareness of being Earthlings. Far from the urban glare of Johannesburg, London, and New York, the stars summoned us to a space view of reality. We watched for an hour with no one saying a word, the silence disturbed only by the distant cough of a lion, and the insistent rattle of the cicadas.

The sky was extravagantly speckled with stars, millions of miles away, putting us with our politics, economics, and religion into our proper context as Earthlings. First come the planets of our own solar system. We could see the shadows thrown by the mountains on the moon. The sun, illuminating everything from behind our backs, shone on airless Mercury, cloudy Venus, dusty Mars, massive Jupiter with its sixteen moons, four of them easily seen with good binoculars, the rings of rock and ice swirling around Saturn, Uranus, Neptune, and pipsqueak Pluto. This is our own solar system — but it scarcely starts our journey into space. By Pluto, we are hardly out of bed.

The first star we meet beyond the grasp of our sun is Proxima Centauri, 4.3 light years away, with nothing but space on the way: nothing else at all. It would take a space ship twenty-five thousand years to reach it. Going full speed. Light years beyond it again, but twinkling in the same skyspace, we could see countless stars of our galaxy, and beyond that, thousands more galaxies in the wider universe. The whole sky sparkled with the intense reality of star-filled space that was staggering to believe — *but as far as we know not one of those totally real spheres actually before our eyes could offer us a cup of tea, a glass of water, or the breath of life.*

Our Earth alone, it seems, has developed life and people, a human race, a global community. The Earthlings we call ourselves are a unique reality.[2]

◆ ◆ ◆

Several billion years of unprecedented events enabled humanity to happen, but it does not register. Like wild game, anxious only to mark their own territory, we are so obsessed with ourselves that we fail to grasp the wonder of inhabiting an Earth in space. It is understandable. We have often had newborn children in our home, and all they can comprehend at first is a breast with milk and a supporting hand. Then a blanket, a cot, a smile, a room, a place to crawl and walk and run, and so our consciousness grows into the patches of the world we knew.

John Anderson, one of Africa's leading paleontologists, has a pole about nine feet high on which he has marked the duration of the successive stages of the universe through billions of years: Earthling life is simply the dust on top of the pole. But there is what Teilhard de Chardin calls a "zest" for life in it, which Brian Swimme says we only catch in little glimpses and insights because we are in the midst of the process.

> The image that I like is this: you have molten rock, and then all by itself, it transforms into a human mother caring for her child. That's a rather astounding transformation. Of course, it takes four billion years. You've got silica; you've got magnesium. You've got all the elements of rock, and it becomes the translucent blue eye and beautiful brown hair and this deep sense of love and concern and even sacrifice for a child. That is a deep transfiguration. Love and truth and compassion and zest and all of these qualities that we regard as divine become more powerfully embodied in the universe.[3]

Such stories illustrate the extraordinary length and depth of preparation that has gone into our production as Earthlings and the arrogant infantile depravity of those who seek to wipe it out by violence, poverty, and pride. Oleg Makarov, USSR astronaut, spells out the Earthling understanding:

Those who have been in space realize that, in spite of the complete disparity between them, they are one in an important way, namely, an acute feeling of being an inhabitant of Earth, a feeling of a personal responsibility to preserve the only planet we have. They realize that any predicament, disagreement, or obstacle can be overcome.[4]

2.2. Cradle of Humanity

I came face to face with the Africa of a billion years ago in the North Sea port of Dundee, in Scotland. A dry dock there is home to the ship *Discovery,* in which Captain Robert Falcon Scott and his crew sailed on their way to the South Pole in 1911. The museum alongside houses many precious products of that epic journey including magnificent photographs of the icy continent, larger than the United States, where no tree or plant can grow. The relic that most fascinated me was a small white plaster cast of a fossilized tropical plant they found in the ice. How on earth could it have grown there, where temperatures are too extreme for any tropical plant to survive? Neither Scott nor his scientists had the faintest idea — but now we know.

When the fiery volcanic Earth thrown off by the sun had been drenched with rain and begun to cool and become the watery planet, land emerged as a huge primeval continent, which scientists have called Gondwana. At the center of Gondwana was Africa, with South America tucked up under the bulge, Brazil nudging into Nigeria. On the other side, India and Antarctica clung to the east coast of Africa, with Australia swinging on a different axis beyond. It is a fascinating children's game to cut up a map of the globe and see how the continents fit together like pieces of a giant jigsaw puzzle whose shapes we still recognize today. Millions of years passed as the plates on which Gondwana was cast drifted apart to form the continents we know. That fossil in Dundee came from the time when Antarctica was locked in the warm and fertile embrace of prehistoric Africa and Australia millions of years ago. That is the perspective of the time scale in which we see why Africa matters.

The energy of evolution produced countless varieties of life in the sea and air, in plants and trees, insects and animals, birds and game, and Africa teems with them. Evolution pressed on, providing different forms of chimpanzee and gorilla. Homo erectus appeared in Africa maybe 2 million years ago, and eventually homo sapiens sapiens, which is the technical name for Us.

Modern discoveries, backed up by DNA research, confirm that humanity first appeared on the high eastern side of Africa, stretching from the equator down to the Drakensberg. Anthropologists and paleontologists can be as disputatious as theologians and economists, but there is now widespread agreement on the "out of Africa" theory.

From Raymond Dart's 1924 discovery of the prehistoric skull, popularly named "Mrs. Ples," at Taung, in Botswana, through the discoveries of Louis and Mary Leakey in the Olduvai Gorge in Kenya, Lucy in Ethiopia in 1974, and numerous discoveries of bones here and fossilized footprints there two things stand out. One is that at "some time well over a million years ago, some new, comparatively modern upright beings left Africa and boldly spread across much of the world," writes Bill Bryson in his highly readable style. The other is "that something over a hundred thousand years ago a smarter lither, species of creature — the ancestor of every one of us alive today — arose on the African plains and began radiating outward in a second phase."[5] This was Us. We survived and spread throughout the world, and in this sense, all of Us, all global Earthlings, all humans, all are Africans.

With an Earth several billion years old a species of a mere thousand centuries seems unimportant, but the sapiens has kept the homo very busy. Humanity spread throughout the continent and quite quickly set out from Africa to foot it around Earth in the Greatest Trek of history. They went north into Europe, and east through India and Asia. In the north, they crossed into Alaska and down the Americas. In the south, they took the Indonesian link to Australia and New Zealand and rafted it, Kon Tiki style, to the islands of the Pacific. By ten thousand years ago they had established settlements, races, pigments, speech, tribes, nations, cultures, religions, and political and economic systems all around the globe. Yet most of them, like most of Us today, had no sense of being that unique and marvelous reality: Earthlings. Americans, Europeans, Africans — we tend to think that the height of humanity is to become American, European, or African, just like us. Truth is — the tops is to be an Earthling.

2.3. Patches

We grew up as patches of people. We lived in racial and national patches, doing the things of political and economic patches, dressing in the clothes of our patch, speaking the language and dialect of our patch, practicing the customs of our cultural and religious patch, believing in the god of our patch, strapped into our patch-work and vying with the Earthlings on the other patches. Most of us still are: scurrying around like ants in and out of our heap, doing our national, racial, religious, financial, competitive human thing. We are Americans or Afghans, Turks or Brits, Aussies or Zulus, Christians or Muslims, Catholics or Baptists, black or white, rich or poor, educated or neglected, believers, atheists, or agnostics, with no concept at all of enjoying together our unique role as Earthlings inhabiting this incredible planet.

Each patch was obsessed with its own piece of planet at the different stages of development: Canadians or Chinese, Joneses or Lumumbas, Methodists or Sufis, bosses or workers. We had a family patch in a tribal patch, a national patch in a racial patch, built our patch an army, gave our patch a culture, worshiped the god of our patch, and the economy of only our patch mattered. In real hard fact all of Us are Earthlings. But only some of us know it.

2.4. The Spirit of Earthlings

The early Earthlings in Africa became aware of their spiritual nature long before the development of religious institutions. They knew their physical nature because they needed food, and because they could clobber and be clobbered by one another. They knew their mental nature because they could work out where the food was and would be, and how to anticipate a good clobber, for or against. But they also became aware from a very early stage that there was a spiritual content in their community relations. They could love or they could hate, seek peace or persecute, and this was motivated not by body or mind but by their spirit: a matter of attitude, approach, relationships, which bound their human personality into one and made them "all of a piece." Such is the deepest consciousness of Earthlings, still seen very clearly today in those most ancient human survivors, the Bushmen of Africa.

For 90 percent of the time since humanity first arose until today humans made a living as hunter-gatherers, living in small groups on what nature offered.... Bushman religion is a prime example of the kind of religion that was associated with the hunter-gatherer existence. In such societies religion is not a separate institution at all but perfectly interwoven in the life of the group as a whole, and there were no religious specialists.[6]

This sense of spiritual reality in every part of the secular world is the root experience and hallmark of African spirituality. No one had to run evangelistic campaigns to promote their religion. "In primal cultures, religious alignments are regarded by all in the group as indispensable to social harmony and satisfactory adaptation to their immediate environment. Religion was an integral part of life itself. All aspects of life were interconnected so that there was little difference between the sacred and the profane."[7] Our precivilized ancestors had a mature awareness that we desperately need today.

2.5 Belongingness

Shared belongingness is a basic trait of all Earthlings and appeared in all primal people. The weight of the awareness may be in Africa now, but the witness comes from all Earth's ancient peoples — American "Indians," Inuits, Siberians, Maoris, and sea islanders. The primal people of America, the "Native Americans," sometimes dubbed "Amerindians," still appear in many parts of the Americas, and we learned much while staying with some of them some years ago, for they reflect so much of African belief. They have brought some of their ancient beliefs into the writing era.

Remain close to the Great Spirit. Show great respect for your fellow human beings. Give assistance and kindness wherever needed. Be truthful at all times. Do what you know to be right. Look after the well being of mind and body. Treat the Earth and all who dwell thereon with respect. Take full responsibility for your actions. Dedicate a share of your effort to the greater good. Work together for the benefit of all mankind.[8]

From north and south and east and west the voice of primal experience asserts similar truths from their sacred-secular experience, and for tens of thousands of years the Earthlings of Africa lived them, undisturbed.

2.6. Prophets

As Earthlings spread around the globe, among them there appeared visionaries who were inspiring people to know. The prophets probed into notions of more than they could see, proclaiming spiritual concepts and values behind the feelings and motivations of the community. Though working within their own patches, the initiators of this great prophetic tradition had similar visions and messages, particularly regarding the spiritual underpinning of the life of human beings.

Similar themes run through the proclamations of the East, Zoroaster, Moses, Isaiah, Amos, Jesus, and Muhammad. They also appear in the great scriptures from the Vedas and Upanishads to the Bible and the Quran. Because they were related to the actual circumstances of life at that time, these teachings may have come in the form of laws (such as the Ten Commandments) or expositions (such as Isaiah, Gautama the Buddha, or Lao Tse), but all proclaimed the essential harvest of spirituality at the heart of human being, which Jesus pictured in the Beatitudes and Paul saw in terms of love, joy, peace, patience, kindness, generosity, loyalty, humility, and self-control. It might have been Zoroaster or the Gautama or Lao Tse writing, for all the prophets are Earthlings using similar thoughts and turns of phrase to describe what Kofi Appiah-Kubi calls "participation in the divine economy of salvation."[9] It was often challenging. "Prophets are people who speak out when others remain silent," says Albert Nolan. "They criticize their own society, their own country, or their own religious institutions."[10] They are still challenging today.

2.7. Religions

But the prophets did not invent religions: that was done by people who came after them. Although they originated in the concern of the prophets for the spiritual roots and vision of Earthlings, religious institutions became firmly tied to the economic and political elites of their particular patch. The proclamations of the prophets were changed to the doctrines and superstitions of the priests. As civilizations developed and institutions and writing were invented, the focus moved from the lived reality of the spiritual experience of the prophets to adherence to the written form of the institutions. The religious hesitations and antagonisms that bedevil Christians, Muslims, Jews, Hindus, Buddhists, and agnostics today, glaring at one another from patch to patch, do not come from Moses, Isaiah, Amos, Zoroaster, Jesus, or Muhammad, but from the priests who came after them. There is no valid theological justification for religious conflicts based on the twisted, inadequate juvenile squabbles of materialist patches.

The spiritual life that all Earthlings share in their nature is quite different from the later divisive institutions of religious patches. Is that difficult to accept? We are all spiritual creatures: body, mind, and spirit in community. But we are not all religious and do not have to be. Religions have helped some, but the dismaying truth is that their priority is not to discern and develop the spiritual life of Earthlings. Religious institutions are designed to promote the activities, words, services, rituals, superstitions, beliefs, oppressions, subserviencies, structures, and finances of their own patches and are usually unwilling to rediscover themselves and become Earthlings. The religions of modern times need liberating.

The patchy spirituality of Earthlings grew worse as religions became more sophisticated and more closely aligned with political and economic growth. From about three thousand years ago primal oral religion passed into the great written and priestly stage that saw the emergence of the major religions of Hinduism, Judaism, Buddhism, Christianity, and Islam. The followers of influential figures like Moses, Abraham, Zoroaster, the Hebrew prophets, Gautama the Buddha, Lao Tse, Confucius, Jesus, and Muhammad all settled into this conflictual patchwork growth. Earthlings became Patchlings.

Religious institutions have been a mixed blessing for Earthlings. They have so often diverted people from the reality of the spiritual experience of Earthlings to the promotion of religious structures, which is not the same thing at all. Earthlings need spiritual systems that empower communities to develop the strong experience of the qualities of compassion and cooperation, of vision and values. But our religious institutions are dominated by cacophonous competing bodies, each claiming a unique hotline to God, and most of them have focused on life after death instead of the prophetic proclamation of the Way to live on Earth now. The basic primal beliefs of all humanity are swept aside as irrelevant — and in Africa, of all places, where it first began!

2.8. The Rhinoceros and the God Question

Archbishop Desmond Tutu shattered an interfaith audience in the Johannesburg suburb of Lenasia in 1993 by saying that God was not a Christian. "Why do you seem surprised?" he asked. "Jesus was born only two thousand years ago. Do you think God was doing nothing before that?"

Africans, like all humans, have puzzled over the origins of their spiritual reality and have come up with three answers:

- "God is."
- "God isn't."
- "God wants us to do our own thing."

The debate has been expressed in everything from the utmost ridicule and confusion, to the most profound and sublime literature, sometimes with an unexpected clarity.[11]

The "God is" argument arises because Earthlings know they have a spiritual basis and motivation. What they do with their physical and mental facilities depends on their spirit. From this, many sense there is a greater spiritual power behind the whole of life, the vision and values perceived by the prophets, enshrined in the religions, worshiped as God, and promised in heaven — to those on their patch.

This has led to so much confusion and dissatisfaction that others feel "God isn't." Who and what and where is this God? We cannot accept the idea of God being in the sky now that we know the world is round, for where is up? Is it nowhere or anywhere? Nor can we accept a God who has chosen and un-chosen people, who blesses slavery, the subservience of women, or apartheid — or enables people to live for centuries with religions that assert such nonsense. Similar unanswerable questions arise about the afterlife, and those who have "gone on before us." Where are they? Will we see them again? What is life in a body-less dimension? The notion of "God" has been so complicated by the religious institutions that many people find "God" an unnecessary factor of faith. They dis-cover it is *not* necessary to believe in a god in order to pursue love, joy, and peace as foundational formative factors that respond to and release transcendent liberating powers in human community. The vital force of traditional African belief does not have to be made in the image of Man, Woman, or Spirit.

The third answer, which is the practical faith motivating many people today whether African, American, European, or Eastern, is that those who ask if God is or isn't are looking in the wrong direction, for "God wants us to do our own thing." At a most funda-mental level Africans are aware that our quest for spiritual maturity is the most vital part of our being, whether set out by our ancestors, the mystics, or Dietrich Bonhoeffer.

The essential answer to these God questions is devastatingly simple: we don't know. It is like discussing decimals with a tod-dler or asking a man about birthing a child: we don't operate on that level. God and heaven are beyond Earthling know-how.

We have a photograph of a rhino stuck on our refrigerator door, poking a rather disapproving rhino horn at us, and the caption reads: "What part of 'no' can't you understand?" Sort of divine of him.

"God" is often used as shorthand for much that is crucial and much that is speculative, but that sort of argument falls easily into the disruptive patter of patchworks. Much of our unthinking and rethinking takes place because we were reared in a pre-scientific, premodern, preeducated, predemocratic, preliberation, pre-postreligious age. The patchwork generation did not realize how oppressed and oppressive it was. Finding the way from patchwork living to being Earthlings is at the heart of much of the African quest for liberation. Those who do not believe in God do not neces-sarily reject belief in the spiritual, either individually or collectively, and believers cannot reject unbelievers as unspiritual. Earthlings are spiritual beings.

EARTHLINGS IN AFRICA

2.9. The Community of Earthlings in Africa

Africans have had their share of the conflicts of patchwork living, but long isolation behind sea and sand kept them in touch with the primal spiritual experience of precivilized Earthlings. This does not promote the rosy romanticism of the noble holy savage, for Africans can be as blatant with brutality, corruption, and superstition as any other humans. The difference is in the community, not the individual, in the context, not the incident, in the collective, not the selective.

In the bush where we live, both game and people move freely from place to place. There is no question of welcoming visitors at our gate: there are no patches because there are no fences. Everyone belongs to everywhere, and everywhere belongs to everyone. Earthlings make free of the Earth. It is a difference of attitude and understanding in Africa that gives a greater grasp on the reality of human life. Steven Bantu Biko said: "The great powers of the world may have done wonders in giving the world an industrial and military look, but the great gift still has to come from Africa — giving the world a more human face."[12] It is the face of the Earthling community.

From a different part of Africa, and a different gender, Mercy Oduyoye of Ghana gives a similar witness:

> Africans recognize life as life-in-community. We can only truly know ourselves if we remain true to our community, past and present. The concept of individual success or failure is secondary. The ethnic group, the village, the locality are crucial in one's estimation of oneself. Our nature as beings-in-relation is a two-way relation: with God and with our fellow human beings.[13]

One of the reasons why Africa matters is that the human spirituality of ubuntu is far nearer the surface in Africa, and the liberation we require is buried less deeply under centuries of institutional dogmatic indoctrination and superstition than it is in many other areas. We can get at it more easily, because, as Methodist Bishop Ivan Abrahams says: "We brew our theology in African pots," close to the basic primal spirituality of Earthling communities in all ancient peoples. "The modern Western emphasis on individual rights has swung the pendulum so far in the opposite direction that many people are no longer aware of the interrelatedness of life." A concept of belonging to a community, to a family group, and to nature may go a long way toward combating many of the diseases of modern society.[14]

2.10. The Primal Reality of Earthlings

A foundational assumption of the traditional African experience of ubuntu concerns possessions, particularly the possession of land. Earthlings are land people: they were born on it, live on it, and die on it. However we sing about it, work on it, or argue about it, this land is our land, we belong to this land, and so does every Earthling. Nelson Mandela brought this into his defense at his trial in Johannesburg in October 1962.

> The structure and organization of early African societies in this country fascinated me very much and greatly influenced the evolution of my political outlook. The land, then the main means of production, belonged to the whole tribe and there was no individual ownership whatsoever. There were no classes, no rich or poor, and no exploitation of man by man. Africans were free and equal and this was the foundation of government. Recognition of this general principle found expression in the institution of the council, variously called *Imbizo* or *Pítso* or *Kgotla*, which governs the affairs of the tribe. The council was so completely democratic that all members of the tribe could participate in its deliberations. Chief and subject, warrior to medicine man all took part and endeavored to influence its decisions. It was so weighty and influential a body that no step of any importance could ever be taken by the tribe without reference to it.
>
> There was much in such a society that was primitive and insecure, and it certainly could never measure up to the present epoch. But in such a society are contained the seeds of revolutionary democracy in which none will be held in slavery or servitude, and in which poverty, want, and insecurity shall be no more. This is the history which, even today, inspires me and my colleagues in our political struggle.[15]

"Salvation, which for us means liberation," writes Jean-Marc Ela of the Cameroon, "is never the soul's salvation, but the world's salvation."[16] Joe Teffo says that "to the traditional African community God exists in all things and everywhere. . . . There is evident an all-pervading energy or Life Force which inheres in everything . . .

intellect, intelligence, reason, love and ubuntu."[17] We go beyond the fervor of national anthems and favorite hymns and know ourselves as a community of Earthlings.

It was out of this awareness of a reality in the unknown that people began to seek to communicate with those they did know who had gone into the unknown — their ancestors. Primal people in America or Europe, like Africans, do not worship their ancestors as gods, but venerate them. Africans communicate with them as "the authority that serves as the source of meaning, values, moral norms, and assigns roles and status," writes Archbishop Buti Tlhagale.[18] "They are believed to intervene in the daily affairs of their descendants. In situations of illness, conflict, and misfortune, rituals are performed in order to solicit the protection of the ancestors." Christians, Muslims, and many in the East warm to those links.

2.11. The Lostness of Earthlings

Sensible modern people find much inherited Western "religion" is de-inspiring. It has lost the sense of the Life Force — though people may be too indoctrinated to admit it. Most religions today have diverted us from spiritual strength to institutional order. People tend to become chilly agnostics, or overheated, superstitious fundamentalists, and many throw the spiritual baby out with the religious bath water.

They know they need spiritual integrity and strength, but find inherited religious packages give them neither: they may like the music and the friends, but the institutions are spineless, meaningless, and powerless. They find little solace in ancient rituals or modern superstitions: they want a postreligion reality that builds on the roots of human experience.

It often seems easier for Africans to accept that the battle of the patches failed to grasp the promise of unique Earthlings and has continued to plague us throughout the centuries, growing worse rather than better with human development and the escalating conflict of civilizations. The worst perpetrators of anti-Earthling, antihuman, behavior have not been located in "pagan" or "heathen" Africa, but in the great monotheistic religions of Judaism, Christ-ianity, and Islam, especially in the anti-Earthling

Christ-ian* civilizations of Europe and North America, which have
fought the most terrifying and destructive wars in history. The
invention of modern weaponry and the wish to use it for global
political and economic supremacy has led these "enlightened" and
"leading" patches to militarize the Earthling situation and is currently poised to bring humanity to an end altogether, writing *finis*
to Earthlings of this century.

These space-unique Earthlings, awesome epic of evolution, this
global human community appreciated so clearly from our stoep in
Africa that particular night of light, clings to the suicidal tradition
of pitching patch against patch until death Us do part. We are lost.

2.12. Picture of a Continent

This Cape is a most stately thing, and the fairest cape we saw
in the whole circumference of the Earth.
— Sir Francis Drake on board *The Golden Hind,*
off Cape Point, 1580

Drawing a round sphere on a flat piece of paper is a problem, especially if the globe is as large as Earth. If you draw a map with Africa
at the center, North America and Europe are streaks on the edge.
But putting the Northern Hemisphere in center stage does not help
either, because while New York, London, and Moscow can be shown
in their relative positions across the bottom of the page, the North
Pole cannot be spread across the top because it is a single spot. And
the shortest way from Moscow to New York is not across the page
but over the top. Maps can mislead us.

This was the problem when sailors discovered that Earth was
round. The sixteenth-century solution by Gerhard Mercator, still
the basis of many maps, has fooled us ever since. We learn history
and geography in school and newspapers from Mercator's projection, which draws the lines of latitude further apart as they near the
poles. This shows Europe, North America, and Asia as larger than
Africa, whereas in fact it is the other way around. China and India
together would fit comfortably into Africa, and the United States

---

*The hyphen in "Christ-ian" and "Christ-ianity" is an attempt to differentiate between the
original message of Jesus and the doctrinal developments that crept into later ecclesiastical
practice.

is only slightly larger than the Sahara Desert. If you put Cairo on New York, Cape Town would be in Argentina. We have inherited a distorted view of the world.[19]

The globe on my desk is "upside down" and shows Africa more accurately. The South Pole is at the top (to which astronomers have no objection) and Africa dominates the front view. The continent covers over four thousand miles from Cape Town on top to the Mediterranean at the bottom, and over four thousand miles across from Senegal on the Atlantic to Somalia on the Indian Ocean. You catch a glimpse of Europe, Asia, and the Americas around the edges. The continent is not level. The eastern side hitches up to high ground, and mountains run like a spine from Ethiopia down through Kenya and Tanzania, to Zimbabwe and South Africa. Much of the continent is several thousand feet above sea level, the thinner air demanding that aircraft runways in Johannesburg and Nairobi are longer than in London and New York. Until the recent onset of climate change tropical mountains like Kilimanjaro on the equator were permanently snow capped.[20] Icy cold still grips Lesotho in winter. Hot sandy deserts engulf much of Algeria and Niger, Libya and Egypt, Chad and the Sudan, and appear again further south from Namibia to Botswana.

Several African rivers are among the best that Earth can offer to feed the surrounding oceans, sweeping slowly and silently past in stately splendor for much of the year, maybe a hundred yards wide. The rainy season transforms them into roaring, rushing torrents with crested waves and scouring currents, several miles across, dispersed through deltas bigger than Belgium. The Nile (4,160 miles) thrusts into the Mediterranean. The Niger (2,600 miles), the Congo (2,900 miles), and the Orange and Vaal (1,200 miles) feed the Atlantic, and into the Indian Ocean, in addition to many smaller flows, comes the Zambesi (1,600 miles) after its mile-wide, ninety-degree left turn, and hundred-meter tumble over Victoria Falls. Few rivers are navigable for more than a mile or so from the sea, because they reach the coast from the high hinterland in tumbling falls, rapids, and gorges. Natural harbors are far apart.

It helps to register the reality of Africa by noting that although the mouths of these huge rivers were known for centuries, the sources of the Nile, the Niger, the Congo, and the Zambesi were not discovered until long after those of the Mississippi, the Amazon, and the Danube. The main deterrent was not hostile armies, or distance, or dangerous beasts, but mosquitos you could hardly see, and viruses you could not see at all.

The continent presents a kaleidoscope of cultures developed within the common life of thousands of tribes that still exist, despite developments that drove them into national, colonial, and urban consortiums. All had chiefs or headmen: some combined with kings; a few had woman rulers; some were dictatorial; most had democratic forms of government that permitted criticism and differences of view to be expressed by anyone. Within the African Union today fifty-three African countries gather this extended family of cultures and tribes into a combined continental concept.

Far from being the "dark" continent of heathen witchcraft that was presented to the world for generations, Africa is highly religious. Every creed of the modern world is represented here in profusion. The All Africa Conference of Churches (AACC) meeting in Maputo in 2008 represented 173 churches of every variety of Christendom from 40 different countries, many in membership with the World Council of Churches. They are outnumbered by innumerable independent African congregations. Perhaps a third of Africans face Mecca five times a day to say their Islamic prayers; millions light the candles of Hindu shrines in their homes or their temples; thousands of Jews attend synagogue on Saturdays; and both the World Conference on Religion and Peace and the World Parliament of Religions have branches on the continent. Behind and beyond and within all these, untold millions adhere to the traditional beliefs and practices, the worship and healing, the vision and values presented through primal African religion, as old as any human ways on Earth. Plus agnostics, many of whom are deeply spiritual people.

2.13. The People of Africa

Throughout it all are the people of Africa. No one knows quite how many of us there are, for the population explosion constantly blows up the census figures, but the unreal figures of hundreds of millions translate into the real flesh and blood of a woman here, a man there, and children playing the games of Earthling offspring everywhere.

The woman may be chairing a meeting of councilors in a city skyscraper; spreading her washing to dry on the hot flat sun-drenched rocks beside a river; piloting a jumbo jet into Abuja airport; planting sweet corn by hand, a few seeds at a time, on a scrap of land that has caught a scrap of rain; or welcoming the caresses of her man after a hard day teaching in the university.

The man may be seated on the floor in a mosque turning the pages of a huge hand-scripted Quran; burning through metropolitan traffic with fifteen passengers in the latest kombi taxi with horn blaring outside and gospel music blaring inside; flicking a twenty-foot whip to guide the oxen pulling his plough; holding his violin tight beneath his chin while his hands bring out the incredible beauty of Beethoven in D; or casting a seine into the sea for the family's supper.

The children — black or brown, pink or beige — will be playing at weddings or running in the Olympics; drawing with sticks in the sand or felt tip pens on writing pads; managing complicated games with a collection of stones or a computer keyboard; stamping their feet as they dance in time with a twig tapped on a hollow trunk, a radio tuned to America or Europe, or a circle of cowrie shells strapped around their ankles.

These are the people of Africa, the product of its history, geography, economics, and religion, the people of the cradle of humanity.

EARTHLINGS AND CIVILIZATION

2.14. The Debacle of Civilization

Iqaqa aliziva kunuka — Xhosa proverb[21]

When the Earthling wanderers who left Africa ten thousand years ago scrambled back five hundred years ago, the Europeans introduced many wonders — from ploughs to philosophy, quinine to fertilizers, and writing to cell phones — plus a spiritual disaster that is now proving fatal to Earthlings. Scattered around Earth, homo sapiens had been bleached and repigmentized, settled and bred and made into races, endured cold and wet climates that demanded housing with walls they could draw on and teach themselves to write, invented wheels and sails and compasses and education, organized themselves into nations, and became, in a word — civilized. They returned to Africa on camels or caravels: Portuguese and Dutch, British and Belgian, French and German, Muslim and Hindu, Jew and atheist pouring into the continent, with goodies and guns, to plunder, enslave, exploit, trade, and colonize. They brought much that was good — and the fatal debacle. Civilization had separated the spiritual from the secular.

That division has lacerated Earthlings. Establishing religious institutions as separate entities usurped the experience of a spiritual presence inside the spread of secular Earthling community, undermining the vital force in humanity and opening the door to oppression, conflict, organized superstition, fear, and fundamentalist heresy.

When ships from the north first visited Africa, following Vasco da Gama in 1497, anchoring their wooden hulls off the beach or in the estuaries before braving the breakers to come ashore, they saw no churches or mosques, no temples or synagogues, no priests or scriptures or theological colleges, and concluded that Africans were "heathen." It never occurred to them that the spiritual nature of the human community could be nourished in any other way than through religious institutions like their own. This was far from the truth and is crucial to our quest to see why Africa matters to the West today. Seeing no signs of religious institutions, European colonialists dubbed Africans "pagan." They failed to register the deep spirituality in Africa, pulsing through all Earthling life, giving vision and energy to evolve onward and upward, quite independently of any religious institutions. They were looking for a religious apartheid, a separate category of existence, and it wasn't there.

Instead of encouraging the comprehensive spirit of Earthlings, civilization had invented conflictual religions that subjugated the spiritual to material priorities, promoting competition instead of cooperation, and Self-centered oppression instead of Us-centered compassion. Religious institutions invariably cooperated with economic and political elites to evolve people backward into soul-less animals seeking to eat one another. This quest for power and control by individuals and elites in the political, economic, and religious institutions would be challenged centuries later only by the democratic growth of people power. Precolonial Africa had never lost it.

Civilization not only divided the "secular" and "spiritual" concerns of Earthlings, but put them in charge of different institutions.

Earlier Earthling leaders, whether European or Asian, like African chiefs, were accorded responsibility for spiritual and cultural activities of the tribe as well as political and economic matters, but civilization separated them. It removed the focus on moral and transcendent responsibility from everyday practical concerns. The breath of the spirit liberates: the dictate of religions confines and oppresses. Consigning spiritual approaches to specialists in religious institutions instead of incorporating them as political and economic imperatives is still the major curse of civilization.

This was a major concern of the South African Kairos document in 1985, which critiqued the failure of the "civilized" church attitude in the struggle against apartheid.

> Spirituality has tended to be an otherworldly affair which had very little, if anything at all, to do with the affairs of this world. Social and political matters were seen as worldly affairs that have nothing to do with the spiritual concerns of the Church. Spirituality has also been understood to be purely private and individualistic. Public affairs and social problems were thought to be beyond the sphere of spirituality.[22]

The depth and heart of liberation/salvation is that the secular and the spiritual are brought together again, and one of the main reasons why Africa matters is that it unifies them. Out of the current collapse of so much in the spiritual and secular worlds comes the reconciliation, the rediscovery, of Earthling unity in ubuntu.

2.15. No Word for Ubuntu

Many African languages have no word for "religion": it does not exist and does not need to be called anything. It is not a separate category but simply a way of handling life that everyone shares. Similarly, there is no word in European languages for *ubuntu*. Western words like "human-ness" are pressed into service to describe this fundamental relationship and acceptance of one another in the sacred-secular experience of Earthlings. "It speaks of the essence of being human," says Desmond Tutu.[23]

> Ubuntu means they are generous, hospitable, friendly, caring, and compassionate. They share what they have. It also means

my humanity is caught up, is inextricably bound up, in theirs. We belong in a bundle of life. We say, "a person is a person through other persons." It is not "I think therefore I am." It says rather, "I am human because I belong." I participate. I share. A person with ubuntu is open and available to others, affirming of others, does not feel threatened that others are able and good. . . . Harmony, friendliness, community are great goods. Social harmony is for us the greatest good.

"Ubuntu" is the human response to one another that all can experience. It does not have to be spelled out in religious terms at all.[24] For African Earthlings the spiritual and the secular went hand in hand; they were all of a piece. Those who remained in Africa after the Great Trek around Earth of ninety to a hundred thousand years ago developed a sense of the wholeness of life that was quite different from the divisiveness of civilization and still throbs at the heart of the African psyche and in all those who retain their Earthling roots.

"The African has a sense of the wholeness of life," writes Luke Pato. "In traditional African religion there is no separate community of religious people because everyone who participates in the life of the community also participates in its religion." Every commentator on African traditional awareness brings out this profound spiritual-secular understanding of primal belief, which defines the roots of Earthlings. All ancient communities still in touch with their Earthling-ness reveal it throughout the world. It is the crucial human experience that many civilized people have to rediscover.

African understanding does not cut spirituality adrift from other aspects of life. They are two sides of the same Earthling experience, and separating them causes immense problems. "The unresolved and omnipresent tensions in Western Christian culture between theology and science, religion and politics, worship and human life — become blatantly conflictual in Africa," writes Joseph Donders.[25] Africa knows in its depths that civilization has got it wrong. Trying to confine spiritual experience within the doctrinal commands of religious institutions is like trying to describe a car ride through the beauties of Africa by a lecture on internal combustion engines or geology. The prophets' concern to liberate and fulfill the whole life of Earthlings conflicts with the priests' concern to run religious institutions. Prophets sought to build holy people and holistic communities for this life: priests sought to make church members preparing for the next life

2.16. The Religious Apartheid of Civilization

Restricting morals and ethics to the personal life of individuals directed by religious institutions, and separating these from the secular life of the community, has been the disastrous root of much Western civilized oppression from which Africa is seeking to liberate itself today. It has had two major negative effects on the life of humanity in civilization.

First, it resulted in a neglect of the true and widespread spiritual concerns of Earthlings, because religious institutions are not primarily concerned for the spirituality, morals, and ethics of Earthlings at all. The priorities of religions are ecclesiastical, not spiritual. The awareness and commitment to spiritual matters was downgraded because the main thrust of those who ran religions was to maintain their power, prestige, privileges, and possessions. Many will deny this with the utmost sincerity, but dogma and power dominate. The provision of buildings, equipment, and facilities for the promotion of their segregated gods and historical bias takes precedence over concern for the shared spiritual, economic, and political needs of the Earthling community. "The church becomes wrapped up within the processes of institutionalization and defines itself in terms of its hierarchical and organizational structures," writes Des Van der Water.[26]

This is particularly clear when we consider the spiritual life of Earthlings as a whole. Ecclesiastical apartheid rules. Whatever their visionaries may hope, the religious bodies give no priority to working together for the spiritual enlightenment and empowerment of the Earthlings of the human community. Most Christians and Muslims, Jews and Hindus, Buddhists and agnostics are as separated today as ever they were; they want to remain that way and are only marginally interested in actually coming together to promote the spiritual vitality of the human community and the welfare of Earthlings. Many call it syncretism and dub it sin.

In the struggle against racial discrimination in Africa Christians were divided. Following the color bar example set by the churches of the British Empire, apartheid was invented by staunch Christians of the Reformed churches, and even the churches that criticized it were run on apartheid lines. For many years their awareness that apartheid was wrong was not allowed to interfere with the way the Catholics, Anglicans, Methodists, Presbyterians, and others ran their churches.

Despite the spiritual values of the traditional African understanding of spirit and ubuntu, this was abjured and rejected after Africa was "civilized" by the arrival of religious institutions. Writing only a generation ago in *Africa and Christianity* for the prestigious Oxford University Press, D. Westerman explained that "however anxious a missionary may be to appreciate and to retain indigenous social and moral values, in the case of religion he has to be ruthless.... He has to admit and even to emphasize that the religion he teaches is opposed to the existing one and the one has to cede to the other."[27]

The colonial conquest era believed that Africans and all other primal people were ignorant savages who had to be saved by professing a colonial religion. It was a central matter of faith for both the Christian and Muslim institutions seeking to establish their superiority over African Earthlings, but they were wrong. Civilization brought to Africa antihuman institutional forms of religion that missionaries sincerely believed would save the soul of Africa but in fact destroyed it. Many in the civilized West still maintain that Africa must follow in perpetual tutelage and servitude, but the real values of Earthlings are in everyone and are being rediscovered in the liberation struggle against the corruptions of civilization. This was the first tragedy of religious apartheid that befell African Earthlings when they entrusted their spiritual life to the management of religions whose priority was self-centered institutionalism, not community-centered spirituality.

The second tragic result of the religious apartheid that civilization brought to Africa was that the economic and political communities became a law unto themselves. They abrogated the sense of ethics and morals and subjugated it to the promotion of their own secular interests, inventing their own approach to what is good upon which to run the affairs of the world. This approach is still rife in the West, and has corrupted Earthlings to such an extent that only a major spiritual revolution in political and economic affairs can enable Earthlings to survive this century.

Land — and everything on it — became the personal possession of individuals instead of the communal site of Earthling fulfillment.

The mode of life became individual not collective; the focus was on Me, not Us. It was totally opposed to the principles of Earthlings, to the ways of humanity in Africa, and to the insights of the prophets from the earliest to Jesus and Muhammad. The whole a-moral, un-ethical, in-human anti-Earthling motivation and structure of modern civilized society took over as good and right. The patches prevailed. We laud a system that makes some Earthlings rich but condemns most to poverty. Many leaders make speeches about limiting poverty or aiding the needy but refuse to address seriously the obvious fact that it is our economic *systems* that impoverish most Earthlings. We deplore poverty but worship wealth and refuse to consider the structural systemic connection between them. Spirituality becomes a formal adherence to religious institutions unrelated to the lived expression and experience of how human beings enjoy life together.

Joseph Donders believes that this problem has a still more profound dimension.

> As long as people worship in nature they can easily see that nature and human life are holy in all their aspects. As soon as a church or temple is built a radical change takes place. The religious dimension is separated from the rest of life, caught and imprisoned in space and time. After this segregation nature and the rest of life are viewed as profane. After this secularization of the world and life, religion becomes an extra, something at the margin of life, a super-addition, something super-natural. At that point, priests begin to represent the other world which they themselves create — a world they will safeguard and defend by hook, crook and law, as their exclusive prerogative.[28]

So here we stand on our religious patch, wearing the clothes of our religious patch, speaking the language of our religious patch, supported by the people of our religious patch, waving the symbols and scriptures of our religious patch, reading the books and preaching the theology of our religious patch, and practicing our oppressive economic and political systems, in great need of liberation by people who know that the spiritual and the secular are not separate but two sides of the same experience of Earthlings.

2.17. *The Liberated Testimony*

Another testimony is emerging in parts of Africa. As the struggle for liberation from colonialism became clearer people from different faith and racial patches on the local level began to act together to defy the oppressive regimes and reenact their Earthlingness. They were rediscovering the spirituality of Earthlings. It was an awareness of which the Zimbabwean Gwinyai Muzorewa writes when he says: "In the teaching of love of neighbor, the concept of sharing, and the possibility of the ideal community of believers, the African traditional community serves as a theological background in which love and respect, rather than rules and regulations, govern human conduct."[29]

Rediscovering ourselves as Earthlings is difficult because it means liberating ourselves from our patches, in which we are so securely trapped that we think that is the way humans are meant to be. Many people in America and Europe today, like many unliberated people in Africa, sincerely and deeply believe in the priority of preserving and promoting their racial, religious, and national separateness, exactly as those who promoted colonialism and apartheid. Many see the structures of capitalism and the market economy as inviolable methods of human organization and well-being, as imperative and unchangeable as the law of gravity, to be defended as articles of faith, fought for, and if necessary died for.[30]

Nowhere are we Earthlings more trapped than in our religious patches. Not only are we nurtured to believe that our patch alone is correct and all others misled, but these same beliefs have been used to justify utterly inhuman and anti-Earthling wars throughout the history of civilization. In recent history alone, the international suicidal carnage of the First and Second World Wars, the so-called Cold War, and the current manipulation of Christians, Muslims, Jews, and Hindus, by political and economic oppressors, is producing the most serious disruption and destruction on Earthlings since homo sapiens first emerged in Africa a hundred thousand years ago. The vision of love and peace and harmony spelled out by all Earthling prophets is dashed aside by the institutions controlling our religious patches. Earthlings are afraid of these truths, but they need spelling out with the utmost clarity.

The type of Christ-ianity spelled out during much of the colonial period in Africa and during the far wider Bush-Blair regimes (not only in the fundamentalist churches), is clearly a major threat to world peace and the survival of Earthlings and brings into question the legitimacy of Christ-ianity. Are we promoting a corrupt patch of Christ-ianity from which Earthlings must liberate themselves? How should Earthlings treat the Christ-ianity of the West, the Islam of al-Qaeda, or the Judaism of Zionism? Like apartheid? There are alternatives.

In Gugulethu Township, Cape Town, a peaceful protestor had been killed by police and under Emergency Regulations attendance at his funeral on August 10, 1985, was heavily restricted. Nineteen leaders from different religious groups decided to ignore the restrictions, attended the funeral together, were arrested together, and taken to the cells together at Wynberg Magistrates Court. Despite their guard of twelve uniformed police they decided to hold a worship service in the cells. Allan Boesak read from scripture and Rev. Lionel Louw conducted the singing. Imam Gassan Solomon led prayers, Moulana Farid Esack preached, and they finished by singing "Nkosi Sikelel' iAfrika," the ANC anthem, which would become the national anthem of several African countries. One of them said afterward: "We discovered each other, different faiths but comrades in struggle. We nineteen people in a cold room waiting for a magistrate struck a blow for interfaith dialogue at the highest level and in a matter of hours years of suspicion were broken down."[31]

2.18. So Africa Matters

Africa intrigues us. From the first Earthlings we glimpse the genesis in our genes, contrasted with the competing and destructive patches of humanity that spread around the world we occupy today. Western civilization rejected what mattered most to Africa: the spiritual-secular unity of Earthlings and its expression in ubuntu. Despite the pressure from the West, many in Africa today are attempting to break through the centuries of religious, political, economic, and cultural indoctrination, transform the conflict of patch vs. patch, and rediscover the wonder of being these unique Earthlings. S. A. Thorpe writes:

> This awareness must still be created in all people so that it becomes a part of our "folk religion." The consubstantiality of life which is such an integral part of primal religious tradition

must become a vital principle in all religious orientation. As we open ourselves to embrace the world we must acknowledge how close knit our global village is. We cannot exist without one another. This principle must become embedded in our deepest religious approach to life.[32]

Africa matters to the West and the East, not because it knows all the answers, but because it looks in the correct direction. Africa gives us a new look at reality. Many no longer see things from the Western or Eastern or Northern points of view; we go beyond the Christian, Muslim, Jewish, Hindu, or atheistic outlook; our sight lines are set beyond black or white or Indian or colored; we are no longer defined by riches or poverty but begin to see ourselves as Earthlings. It is the quest of many today throughout the world. How do we return to the spirituality at the heart of Earthling reality? What can Africa contribute to the rebirth of humanity?

This vision is vital in enabling Us to unseat the Five Horsemen of the Apocalypse charging into the midst of the Earthling community, brandishing destruction in the name of Religion, Economics, Politics, the Media, and Ecology. Our survival depends on finding the answers. To do this we must examine a subject on which African Earthlings are experts: liberation. Our vision and values need liberating to find our way forward as Earthlings.

Afterword

The contrast between the spiritual/secular apartheid of civilization and the wholeness of *ubuntu* is the essential challenge faced by Earthlings in Africa, the West, and the world today.

Chapter 3

The Liberation Matter

Synopsis

The spread of Western civilization to Africa during the past five hundred years has illumined the clash between the oppressive colonialism of Western civilization and the primal ubuntu culture of Africa. This puts new light on the current global struggle for survival. We all have to ask ourselves if we are liberators or oppressors.

3.1. Conditioned to Liberation

3.2. The Experience of Liberation from Oppression by the Patches

3.3. Liberation Is Social

3.4. Liberation Is Spiritual

3.5. Liberation Is a Constant Living Process

3.6. Liberating the Mind of the Oppressed and the Oppressor

3.7. Liberation from False Assumptions

3.8. Liberation from Economic Oppression

3.9. Plunder

3.10. Slavery

3.11. Colonialism

3.12. Globalization

3.13. Liberation from Political Oppression

3.14. Liberation from Religious Oppression

3.15. The Courage to Question Religious Authority

3.16. The Heresy of Fundamentalism

3.17. Liberation from Religious Hostility

3.18. The Missionary Problem

3.19. When Liberators Become Oppressors

3.20. Liberating Our Vision and Values

If you follow my teaching you are truly my disciples, you will know the truth, and the truth will make you free Jesus.
— John 8:31–32

3.1. Conditioned to Liberation

People are conditioned by their circumstances. Penelope is conditioned to watch her step. She was mugged some years ago: they knocked her down, grabbed her handbag, jumped on her leg and broke her ankle, and ever since she has to watch where she puts her feet. My problem is deafness. I am conditioned to watch people's lips to see if anyone is talking to me, and always to check if there is a place at a table or in a room for me to be near the speaker. Many in the West are conditioned to think that West is best, period, and has no need to change.

Africa is conditioned to the struggle for change. Liberation from oppression lies at the heart of the whole African experience and is a major reason why Africa matters to all Earthlings. It underlines a critical factor of human life, for evolution has always meant liberating ourselves from one stage to enter the next. Africa has been oppressed in so many ways that the struggle for liberation became the way of life, a factor of people's being. Liberation did not gently lure you toward a distant dream; it drove you with a muscular intensity of conviction and commitment. It was not an intellectual attraction to an idea read in a far-fetched newspaper, a policy propounded in a faraway parliament, or a theology expounded from a far-above pulpit, but a daily direction of energy here and now. Because you are oppressed, you think and act liberation, which is why leadership invariably comes from the oppressed, not from oppressors.

Liberation is a two-way process, a "from the old" and an "into the new." At one level we have moved into the modern world, but "liberation" did not mean "Westernization." Until our daughter Bongi was five years old she hardly ever wore shoes because the African climate seldom made it necessary. But then we exiled to the UK, where people lived constantly in footwear — some even wore socks in bed! One day Penelope caught the youngster going out barefoot and asked her why she had not put on her shoes. The reply was simple: "I don't want to lose my African feet."

Liberation does not mean Westernization: we walked into the modern world on our African feet. Modernization had to be worked out in African terms that did not mean that people from the Ashanti to the Zulus would automatically reject the role of kinship, social status, polygamy, sexual division, age ranking, or religion from their past. Status under colonialism meant adopting European culture in dress, religion, schooling, and attitudes to land and ownership, but liberation meant reviewing these changes in African terms — which was more than inventing "Afro" shirts. It meant changing the picture and replacing the hierarchies of politics, trade, jobs, wealth, social relations, religion, and lifestyles, both in towns and in rural areas.

3.2. The Experience of Liberation from Oppression by the Patches

The experience of liberation in Africa has been from many different sorts of oppression: economic, political, religious, gender, and cultural attitudes and systems in society, and experiences that condition your mind. It is about people being free.

No one from the outside world could liberate us: it had to be an inside job, something we did ourselves. Even at the height of the Cold War, when the United States and the UK were backing oppressive governments and activities throughout Africa, and communist states were assisting the liberation movements by training men and supplying materials, no one in their wildest dreams imagined that outside forces could invade Africa, throw the colonial empires into the sea, and install liberation. Liberation comes from within people whether the focus is in their heads, their hearts, or the systems ruling their societies. Africa also knows that individual freedom can be obtained only within the collective of a freed society.

Long involvement in the dangerous secret world of the liberation struggle sometimes led people to suspect the credentials of comrades who came from a different background, and it was necessary to relearn this experience of working in a larger society. It was a major problem for some ANC members when the Black Consciousness Movement (BCM) emerged. They were oppressed by their own loyalty to the ANC.

Horst Kleinschmidt had known Steve Biko well in their university days and worked closely with different members of the Black Consciousness Movement before it was necessary for him to go into exile. Soon after that, Kleinschmidt wrote in correspondence with the author:

> My contacts in the ANC facilitated me meeting the ANC president, Oliver Tambo (Comrade O R as he was respectfully referred to in ANC ranks). Meeting him initially filled me with fear and trepidation. In my mind I was going to meet the man who should have been the South African president. . . . As I was of recent refugee vintage, Comrade O R enquired at length about Steve Biko and the Black Consciousness Movement "back home." It was not as yet outlawed. Comrade O R in a fatherly fashion calmed my nerves by holding my hand as he spoke. I recall his words to his advisers sitting with him: "What is so special about black consciousness? Ever since we formed the ANC Youth League in the 1940s we were motivated by such consciousness. We should not fight them — they are part of us.

O R was liberated from all the patches.

3.3. *Liberation Is Social*

African Earthlings know that liberation is social as well as personal: a struggle in community and not just in your own head and home. The struggle to free human society from oppression involves everyone whether they choose to be in it or not. It is a constant way of life, an attitude, not something to which you can contribute on your day off. You are on the side of oppression or of liberation, and there is no fence to sit on between them. Much of the world (especially those reared in the personalized systems of the West) sees humanity in terms of individualistic competition rather than with the collective view of humanity deeply rooted in Africa. People in the globalized Western world think in "me" terms, not in "us" terms. They focus on how much profit *I* can make, what will it cost *me*, how will *I* benefit, how can *I* be saved from my sins, which party will be best for *me*, can *I* win the talent contest, just watch *me!*

Africans know these things too, but the approach is communal. What can *we* do? What will this mean for *us*, for *our* families, *our* community, *our* village, *our* neighborhood, *our* land, *our* future? How can the needs and contributions of *our* people be represented? Many have pointed out that "African songs are group songs." Throughout the continent from the Sudan to Namibia, and Kenya to Gambia, people love choral singing; when you sit waiting for church or meetings to start it is not filled by an organist or a DJ: the people just sing together. It's natural. Children dance together, not on their own. Beneath all African competition is this liberated togetherness. Both the challenge of oppression and the vision of liberation have a unifying quality in society.

The actual social experience of gross human rights violations does something to the human psyche that simply hearing about them does not. In my youth I lived through the Nazi blitz on London, from the mass raids of high explosive and incendiary bombs of 1940 to the doodle bugs and rockets of 1945, with all their deaths, destruction, and excitements. Those early teenage years have long since gone and the detailed memory fades, but the experience of comradeship and hope, of threat and fear, of family and neighbors, of school mates and people in the bus queues, of fortitude and faith in ultimate victory — it was not just a personal feeling but a shared experience, a new dimension to living, for always.

Living through the struggle against oppression in Africa has done the same to millions: the guns and police and armies, the poverty and jails and detentions, the unending living-on-the-edge experience of the liberation struggle give an approach and understanding to life. Speaking in 1960, Julius Nyerere, the leader of Tanzania, recognized it: "Africans all over the continent, without a word being spoken either from one individual to another or from one African country to another, looked at the European, looked at one another, and knew that in relation to the European they were one."[1] They were not merely individuals, but a society being transformed.

3.4. Liberation Is Spiritual

Liberation is essentially a matter of the right spirit. It is the salvation at the heart of all religion. Naturally it requires organization, mobilization, funds, conferences, charters, books, programs — but all this is rooted in people with a lively liberated spirit, not those with oppressive conservative spirits. Liberation rediscovers the soul of humanity and often taps sources of vision and energy that lie outside the paradigms normally accepted by the ruling powers and the status quo. Colonial governments were so overwhelmingly powerful in terms of arms, money, education, the control of the media, and suppression of opposition that they seemed invincible, and thought they were, but none of it could withstand the people's commitment to freedom. When small groups of African students met, even in the United States and Europe, when clergy spoke to one another in their designated tea rooms at church conferences, when women toiled in the fields or at the missus' washing, when workers were hauling coal or gold far underground, and spoke to one another of African independence, it seemed a far-fetched dream, but they knew the deep determination in the spirit of their people far better than the mighty governments of Britain, France, Belgium, and Portugal knew it. Similarly, no one in the white-controlled state or church in South Africa ever dreamed that people would throw their passes in the face of the police at Sharpeville in 1960, that children would march to protest unjust schooling in Soweto in 1976, that several hundred preachers would prepare and publish the Kairos document without obtaining the consent of their ecclesiastical superiors in 1985 or defy the South African government by publicly supporting the liberation movements at the height of repression. A new spirit was unleashed.

This liberating spirit was crucial in banishing colonialism and envisaging a new humanity in Africa. South African Constitutional Court Judge Albie Sachs, on the centenary of the satyagraha program of Mahatma Gandhi, wrote:

> We had in this country an amalgam of cultural and spiritual ingredients that provided a profound philosophical setting for peaceful change. It was a case of ubuntu meeting satyagraha meeting an international tradition of struggle for revolutionary change. The result was something that has evolved and become deeply rooted in the temper of our people. As Gandhi showed through his life, idealism is sustainable in the real world. It needs only to be backed up by real commitment of millions of ordinary people.[2]

The spirit of liberation is an actual, real, spiritual power working in society like a mighty wind. Liberation can stumble and pick itself up again and go on in a constant living progress.

3.5. Liberation Is a Constant Living Progress

Human progress has not been planned out like a school curriculum to go from one positive development to another. It often goes sideways into a side track, which it turns into a major diversion, and another liberation struggle is required to get back on track and rediscover the way forward. Liberation is an ongoing process in many spheres of life.

A political example of the constant process of liberation is the way in which African states have sometimes started well, then been led astray into oppressive periods as many found from Idi Amin to Robert Mugabe, and then found their way back again at a new and higher level.

It is true of religion also. Under the surface of committed evolving Earthlings, there is a constant spirit to progress, to react against conservative elites who would hold humanity back, to rediscover and redeploy the vision and fervor of the prophets. It is the history of denominationalism — and now we are reaching beyond that into the postreligion era.

3.6. Liberating the Mind of the Oppressed and the Oppressor

During 1962 Nelson Mandela left South Africa secretly and spent some months touring the continent in support of the liberation struggle, traveling incognito from place to place and earning the name of "the Black Pimpernel." On one journey, he describes what he calls "a rather strange sensation."

> We changed to an Ethiopian Airways flight in Addis. As I was boarding the plane I saw that the pilot was black. I had never seen a black pilot before, and the instant I did I had to quell my panic. How could a black man fly a plane? But a moment later I caught myself. I had fallen into the apartheid mind-set, thinking Africans were inferior and that flying was a white

man's job. I sat back in my seat and chided myself for such thoughts. Once we were in the air I lost my nervousness.[3]

Many people in the West who are seeking the salvation of the world find it rings bells to hear that African liberation recognized the need to overcome the psychological submission of subservience to colonial oppression. People had been so indoctrinated to believe in their inferiority that the head misled the body. Journalist David Lamb, touring extensively in central Africa, wrote:

> The colonialists left behind some schools and roads, some post offices and bureaucrats, but their cruelest legacy on the African continent was a lingering inferiority complex, a confused sense of identity. When people are told for over a century that they are not as clever or as capable as their masters, they eventually start to believe it.[4]

Steve Biko, who led the Black Consciousness Movement in South Africa, identified the basic challenge as the acceptance by Africans of the white view that blacks were inferior people: liberation began by recognizing and rejecting this self-deception in the mind of the oppressed.

> There stirred within his consciousness the germ of an idea. This was to flower into a student movement which con-scientized blacks to analyze their socio-political situation by recognizing that they could be their own liberators through resisting their oppression with a different mental attitude. It was this attitude that became known as Black Consciousness.[5]

This assertion was so true that it spread with astonishing rapidity, despite the repressive acts of the apartheid regime, especially in the formation of a new student body, SASO. Biko said in court:

> SASO is a Black Student Organization working for the libera-tion of the Black man, first from psychological oppression by themselves through inferiority complex, and secondly from the physical one accruing out of living in a White racist society.[6]

Many in the West have the same problem today.

3.7. *Liberation from False Assumptions*

One of the crucial matters Africa brings to the attention of Earthlings is the necessity to liberate themselves from submission to a mass of false presumptions spread by the elites who claim that their views represent the correct and only route for humanity to travel. They do not. We have been hoodwinked by many of our politicians and editors, bankers and bishops who are given prominence in the media. Submission to inherited subservient thinking invariably condemns us to retreat into the patches of the past and miss the experience of the Earthlings of the present who hold the promise of the future.

Africa reminds us most poignantly that we do not have to believe like the erstwhile religious patches in order to be spiritual people. It is not true that humanity must follow the priorities of past centuries in the West as the sole route to Earthling success. Neither the West nor the religious institutions have the answers: it is deeper than that. The peace and prosperity of Earthlings come from compassion and cooperation, not from armies imposing greed and power. Liberated minds catch a new vision, a resetting, a confidence in themselves, the struggle, and the future. This moment of liberation may come in a flash of inspiration, a sudden awareness, a release from fear and pessimism, a rebirth, a conversion, the realization of entering a new world full of possibilities not seen before. Twenty-first-century Africans are not multicolored versions of eighteenth-century Europeans. Bokwe Mafuna saw very clearly that the false assumptions on which oppression was based would never yield to palliatives. "Africa (and the world) need a spiritual revolution: in politics, economics, culture, and social relations."[7]

3.8. *Liberation from Economic Oppression*

There is a fundamentally different approach to economics in primal Africa and the West. Africa, like all primal peoples and the prophets of all religions, believes the land belongs to all, to be worked for the good of all, and this affects the attitude to all possessions. Africa knows deep, firsthand suffering from the structures and systems that enable small elites to control the economy so that it belongs to them in violation of all ethical, spiritual, and Earthling principles.

The liberation of Africa from economic oppression has had to tackle four categories: plunder, slavery, colonialism, and globalization.

3.9. *Plunder*

Plunder was rooted in prehistory, when invaders with powerful ships or armies came, killed, captured, collected any treasures they could find, and took them home.

3.10. *Slavery*

Slavery, like apartheid, is a major learning curve for good Christians everywhere. It demonstrates how the interaction between the distinguished civilized economic, political, and religious leaders can produce a thoroughly evil and oppressive system and maintain that it is good.[8] The enslavement of one human being by another became common practice wherever civilization spread, and many accepted it as a necessary and godly practice. Some demurred if owners mistreated their slaves, but it never occurred to them that slavery itself should be abolished. After all, people in the Bible had slaves, and it was good for business. Lord Dartmouth, British colonial secretary in 1775 at the height of the slave trade, maintained that "we cannot allow the colonies to check or discourage to any degree, a traffic so beneficial to the nation." Slavery was a joint effort of warring African chiefs, "Arab" slavers, European ship owners, and merchants and slave owners in the West. From 1619, when the trade began in Virginia, hundreds of thousands of Africans were captured, bound, walked many miles to the coast, chained in ships' holds, transported thousands of miles over the oceans, and put on sale to produce profit for slave owners trading in tobacco, sugar, and cotton. Hundreds of thousands died.

From 1750 Britain became the major slave carrier in the world, with 130 sailings every year from British ports. In this extremely profitable triangular trade

> a ship sailed from an English port with a cargo of British manufactured goods, which were sold on the west coast of Africa. Slaves taken aboard were sold in the West Indies. The ships returned to the home port in Britain with a profitable cargo of colonial products for the English market. The growth in the

trade was a sign of its high profitability, which also made it almost impregnable.[9]

David Lamb, visiting the island of Goree off the coast of Dakar in Senegal, wrote:

> For millions of West Africans — the ancestors of what would become the United States' largest minority class — this is where freedom ended and serfdom began. It was here, in the dark dank slave house, that Arab traders bartered and bickered with European shippers, here that Africans spent the last weeks in their homeland, chained to a wall in underground cubicles, awaiting a buyer, a boat, and at the end of a long harrowing voyage, a master.[10]

Many nations were involved in aspects of slavery, but in the second half of the eighteenth century the leading slave trading nation was England. Although the UK Chief Justice Lord Mansfield had ruled in 1772 that the *possession* of slaves in Britain was illegal, the mammoth money-making *shipping* business continued for another fifty years. Millions of lives were smashed, and much of American and British wealth today is rooted in African lives of two centuries ago. The U.S. Civil War involved the emancipation of slaves; Denmark barred its citizens from slave trading in 1803, Britain in 1807, the United States and France in 1818. The ban on slavery was one of the reasons why fifteen thousand Boers left British rule in the Cape in the early nineteenth century on the Great Trek to open up what became the Free State and the Transvaal.

Opposition grew, often linked with the new liberating awareness prompted by the evangelical revival and political and spiritual developments, but it was a long process. A major factor in liberation from slavery was the Industrial Revolution, for machines were cheaper to run and easier to ship than slaves, and the slave trade was gobbled up by the commodity trade in the nineteenth century. Steam cost less than slaves.

Slavery was eventually ended, with all the consequent problems of how to rehabilitate and reroot millions of liberated people, but the endorsement of inhumanity for the sake of the enrichment of the elite has continued to this day.

3.11. Colonialism

Colonialism in Africa lasted less than a century, but it altered the face of the world forever. It was supported by the myth in the West that Western religious, economic, and political institutions were "good for the natives," which was totally erroneous. It spanned an encyclopedia of Earthling experience from King Leopold, who had the *London Times* delivered every day to his palace in Belgium to ensure that he missed no opportunity of exploiting Africa, to hundreds of thousands of African women tilling soil with heavy hoes, to courtrooms, boardrooms, and schoolrooms, imams and clergy, French gunners and Hehe spearmen, from missionaries in New York, Berlin, and London to Black Consciousness leaders who believed that accepting oppression was a sin.

Colonialism was about money making. It was not designed to enable African Earthlings to establish modern ways of life for their people, but to enable European nations with their guns and gadgets to invade and carve up Africa into juicy slices of profit and send all the proceeds home. The investment of capital from the home country was extremely lucrative in the exploitation of the resources and minerals found in other lands, to say nothing of the profits made from buying and selling the land itself. Even after slavery had been abolished, labor was cheap and was kept that way by a never-ending series of oppressive colonial regulations in every African country beyond the Mediterranean.

From the middle of the nineteenth century to the twentieth, incredible wealth poured into Europe to feed the money-making machines of industrial development, and build the magnificent commercial cathedrals of town halls, office blocks, factories, and shops whose foundations were not actually in the clay and gravel of Britain, France, and the Low Countries, but in the rocks and sands of Africa. There was no concern to develop African national identity: what counted were the bank balances in Europe. Colonialism began to decline immediately after the Second World War when the emphasis on liberation and human rights demanded that profits be invested in the colonized people rather than their oppressors.

Europe realized that the extraordinary profits of economic colonialism could not be maintained if their governments were politically responsible for introducing universal suffrage, housing, education, health care, workers rights, pensions, and modern amenities. The consciousness emerged that far from protecting economic exploitation, colonial politics were proving highly expensive, whether controlled by direct suppression as in West Africa or the Rhodesias, or by dividing and ruling as in supporting Tutsis against the Hutus in Rwanda. Responsibility for liberation and modernization therefore had to be moved to local African governments, while the West continued to reap the benefits of investment in business and aid for those in need (especially when given via their own NGOs).

Attempts were made to make colonies profitable by introducing new products and developing cash crop economies: cocoa in Ghana, groundnuts (peanuts) in Senegal, tobacco in Malawi, coffee and tea in Kenya, sisal in Tanzania, cotton in Angola. But these export crops were playthings for colonial profits on world markets. They often did not work for long—and fed no one in Africa.

3.12. Globalization

Globalization is colonialism wearing a bigger hat. Albert Nolan writes of "the globalization of neo-liberal capitalism, a thoroughly materialistic worldview based on the principle of the survival of the fittest, a culture that destroys other cultures and indigenous wisdom, making the rich richer and the poor poorer around the world."[11] Africa sees very clearly that the major global challenge is the systematic economic enslavement of the world by the owners of capital, and liberation from that oppression is the only path to life. It also sees that new black capitalists are ideal women and men to front the old financiers who still remain behind the scenes: pigment is marvelous stuff for disguising class!

Economic exploitation continues today, allowing a few African hands to put spoons into the pot, but the bulk of the profit still goes into the Western capitalist pockets, as Neville Alexander writes:

> The capitalist class can be said to have placed their property under new management and what we are seeing is the sometimes painful process of the new managers trying to come to terms with the fact that they are the managers certainly, but not by any means the owners of capital. Inevitably, a few individuals...who were paragons of radicalism in their day, have become pillars of conservative economics at the

same time as they have personally accumulated considerable wealth.[12]

Thabo Mbeki is even more dismissive:

> The dominance of the capitalist motive of private profit maxi-
> mization...has evolved into the central objective that informs
> the construction of modern human society. Nothing can come
> out of this except the destruction of human society.[13]

Many in Africa see the free market as the enslaved market from which the poor of the world, including Africa, are seeking to liberate themselves. Strong lessons are being learned from the antislavery campaigns of the past, by those seeking liberation from slavery to capitalist oppression today. It requires rejection by the slaves, but a major thrust must also come from strong action by liberated people in the capitalist countries, fortified by the globalization of a liberation theology. The problem is not the bad behavior of a few economic dictators, but an inhuman system. Just as apartheid was not a problem caused by a few naughty white racists but the inhuman system they devised, so the challenge is how can we liberate Earthlings from their blindness to the intellectual and spiritual pursuit of an economic system of crushing globalized greed? Western thinking and spirituality need to be liberated to replace the oppressive economic pattern centered on Me by the African ubuntu pattern focused on Us.

3.13. Liberation from Political Oppression

The heart of the liberation struggle in Africa was political, and it comes into focus more easily on maps. Among my treasures are some copies of early maps of Africa, which, until the nineteenth century, show only a sprinkle of coastal settlements, with large parts of the interior marked "unexplored" or "desert." Africa "was a coast, not a continent." It was widely explored by the people who lived there, but of this the Western cartographers knew nothing. Scratches on the rocks of time show that early empires existed south of the Sahara, from obscurity to obscurity, in Ghana, Mali, and the Songhai; huge stone structures in Zimbabwe were built soon after William of Normandy conquered Britain, and mine workings throughout the continent reveal those busy centuries on the other side of history. But we know little about it.

The African coast was first opened to Europe by the Portuguese as a place to take on water and vegetables en route to the profitable spice trade from the East. Other maritime nations followed. Dutch and Huguenots sailed and settled in South Africa, seeking freedom from oppressions in Europe, and as their empire and navy grew, the British came to establish their base at Simonstown. Africans did not figure as people, families, or individuals at all: only as slaves. In seven hundred pages in *The Scramble for Africa* Tom Pakenham mentions hardly any Africans at all except Livingstone's servants and a few chiefs: they did not figure.

During the nineteenth century the map of Africa was totally redrawn by European colonization. It was a period of crushing colonial political rule developed to protect and expand the lucrative economic exploitation. Africa did not belong to Africans, but to Europeans who spoke a great deal in the press of bringing light to the Dark Continent, from the pulpit of bringing salvation to the heathen, and in their board rooms of bringing profits home for themselves. The continent was chopped up into jurisdictions controlled from Europe. Britain ruled Egypt and the Sudan, much of East and Southern Africa, and the archimperialist Cecil Rhodes dreamed of a Union Jack that covered the continent and a British railway track from the Cape to Cairo. (He could do it today in a 4 x 4, but that was still a century ahead of him.) France dominated large parts of North and West Africa; Germany's footprint was planted in South West Africa; and Tanganyika; Central Africa was the enclave of King Leopold of the Belgians; Portugal possessed Angola and Mozambique; Italy claimed Ethiopia and Somalia; and Spain has had a toe on the southern side of Gibraltar for centuries. From the waters around, and in the banks, the United States watched the situation.

At the same time, it was the greatest period of missionary expansion and development that the continent ever knew.

> By the end of the 19th century, there may have been 8000 full-time missionary men and women, Catholic and Protestant, at work on the continent.... 90 percent of all African education in most of the territories was initiated, supervised, and developed by the churches.... In hundreds of locations across the

country there were clusters of buildings, a mission station, with flourishing fields and gardens, institutions, and training centers covering the wide range of missionary activities.[14]

But missionaries did not chop the chains of political oppression.

When John Gunther published *Inside Africa* in 1955[15] not a single African country was independent, but only forty years later everyone had political freedom by the time South Africa elected its first democratic government in 1994. Over fifty African countries were then politically responsible for governing themselves, which ushered in a new stage in the drama of oppression and liberation.

3.14. *Liberation from Religious Oppression*

Something new is groaning to emerge which will challenge the whole Church to the depths of its being. — C. F. Beyers Naudé

Although the African struggle for liberation from colonial political and economic oppression was headline news for many years, people seldom saw the necessity to liberate themselves from colonial *religious* oppression. The separation that civilization had made between spiritual and secular affairs meant that many ignored either one or the other: religion did not become involved in politics, and politics steered well clear of religion. Many of us still do not realize we were oppressed by our inherited religions. Only a few recognized that Africa was crying for liberation from the failures and diversions of Western theology and religion. When Bishop John Colenso arrived in nineteenth-century Natal, he found his main barrier was the false Christ-ianity that had been spread by his predecessors. "The great drawback is that the country is already saturated with a corruption of Christianity and the natives have acquired such a view of the character of God and of the Gospels as keeps them back from desiring to have a much closer acquaintance with it."[16]

Jean-Marc Ela of the Cameroons had the same insight a century later: "Many dioceses spend all of their energies and found all their hopes on precarious institutions that have no future."[17] So did Gwinyai H. Muzorewa of Zimbabwe, who also saw the positive alternatives:

In the teaching of love of neighbor, the concept of sharing, and the possibility of the ideal community of the believers, the African traditional community serves as a theological background in which love and respect, rather than rules and regulations, govern human conduct.... Sin against a fellow human being disrupts the smooth flow of community life. It upsets the communal status quo.... Against such a background African theology is reformulating new concepts of collective sin rather than focusing on individual sin.[18]

This quest to liberate Africa itself from the crushing restrictive approach of inherited colonial religions and discover a new spiritual identity for Earthlings is a liberated faith focus that the whole world sorely needs today. It is a postreligious approach that rediscovers the primal spiritual emphasis, with all the wealth of spiritual experience since, free from the corruption of ecclesiastical empire building.

It seeks to discover the meeting points of colonial religions, not their conflicts, and then go beyond them. It cannot be left to religious communities alone because many are still incapacitated by the spiritual sickness of religious superstitions that arose in the colonial era. Our spiritual acumen demands that we liberate ourselves from the oppressions of religious institutions. C. W. Du Toit expounds it:

The importance Africans attach to religion is indisputable. That is why the colonial strategy of using the gospel as a means of taking over the continent was so effective. Religion was to provide a transcendental basis for oppressing Africa. To the white South African government their statutorily entrenched values were synonymous with biblical guidelines. God had laid down the time and place (subordination) of nations. The whites' ethos was God's ethos and Africans would err if they failed to heed it. Arguments that apartheid policy was diametrically opposed to Jesus' ethos of an option for the poor, the sick, and the marginalized, that a Christian's freedom was non-negotiable, that people's person should be respected, and the like were dismissed as humanist philanthropy. The gospel that was brought to Africans so devoutly was to be the principal tool for breaking their spirit. Africans were emasculated with the sword of the gospel.[19]

This may seem an outlandish position for those who deeply and sincerely claim to be Christians but illustrates exactly how far adrift many Western Christ-ians seem to be from Jesus, and from a liberated African point of view.

Africans at the All Africa Conference of Churches (AACC) in Lusaka in 1974 faced this contrast between the corrupt apartheid-type religion brought by colonial missionaries with the comprehensive secular-spirituality of their own upbringing and belief.

> We must accept the real meaning of salvation in Africa today in the light of our own religious heritage, which sees the whole of life as religious without the classical distinction between sacred and secular. We recognize the task of evangelism as the total witness in word and deed to whole persons and communities, leading to liberation and fullness of life.[20]

Many Africans see clearly that the focus of both Jesus and Muhammad is totally different from the quest of the religious institutions that followed them, that saw themselves and their members as part of an elite. Bishop Manas Buthelezi commented: "The cooptation of the church to serve the interests of the ruling class and the power of the state came as a result of a long historical development that took centuries.... We can blame the church for having taken twenty centuries before exercising any effective resistance to halt the development."[21]

Muslims face the same problem of liberating themselves from officially sanctioned corruption, which some maintained was godly. Reza Aslan reports: "The Quran ... is invaluable in revealing the ideology of the Muslim faith in its infancy, that is, before the faith became a religion, before the religion became an institution.... Muhammad's revolutionary message of moral accountability and social egalitarianism was gradually reinterpreted by his successors into competing ideologies of rigid legalisms"[22] and uncompromising orthodoxy, which fractured the Muslim community.

Whichever focus of faith they follow, the spiritual life of African communities has demanded liberation from religious institutions that have become corrupt, divisive, and oppressive, however many good and sincere people remain in their ranks. Africa is currently swamped with ardent evangelists of different religious persuasions promoting fundamentalist money-making, power-seeking schemes to promote the so-called "prosperity cults," which buy much space on TV screens to manipulate fears and superstitions. Liberation from such oppression is crucial for the achievement of a mature society. It is the false type of spirituality that the Kairos document says "leaves religious people in a state of paralysis when faced with situations of crisis."

In order to recover and spell out the spiritual strengths and intellectual insight of human community revealed by the prophets in all religion, we need to liberate ourselves from the corruption and oppression which have crept into religious structures. Religious institutions dwell so much on how to get into heaven when we die that many believe this *is* the message of the prophets, who in fact said little on the subject. Instead of proclaiming the truths that make us free, many people in all religions propound superstitions that chain us down.

It is not only atheists and traditionalists but many believers in Africa today who know that religious institutions need liberating to recover the central message of Jesus, Muhammad, and all the prophets. There is a common ground of liberated humanity, the experience of salvation in this life not the next and of transforming powers in human community here and now, not a maybe in the sky in the future. Earthlings can find food for lively faith in all religions: it is from the oppressive falsehoods propagated by patchwork institutions that we need to liberate ourselves.

The postreligious era is not antispiritual: it revolts against oppressive, superstitious religion and is committed to rediscover the realities of liberated faith in Earthlings today. The corruptions of colonialism marched side by side with widespread dissatisfaction with inherited religions, which were increasingly unable to cope with the needs of Earthlings today. "The throne of global meaning fell visibly vacant," said Tom Nairn of Australia.[23]

3.15. *The Courage to Question Religious Authority*

Liberation has always required the courage to question religious authority, as is shown by the long history of disturbing prophets and denominationalism in all religious structures. According to Michael Scott, who was a British priestly champion of the liberation struggle in Africa (and once stayed with Nelson and Winnie Mandela in Soweto):

It needs courage to challenge the power of the State in the modern world, with its claim to be the exclusive arbiter of Right and Justice, and with the destiny of men and women under its control. But it also requires courage to question the authority and truth of Holy Scripture. Through centuries of belief in the infallibility of the Bible, the three great monotheistic religions have perpetuated the slander that it was through woman's thirst for knowledge about the meaning and origin of good and evil that evil gained entry into the scheme of things on earth. Perhaps we are standing at the threshold of a new reformation. But if there is to be a new renascence of learning for humanity, it will require women to play their part, both within and without the Churches, in helping to dispel the obscurantism on which some very powerful religious institutions have thrived for too long.[24]

This is also true of the matter of sin, guilt, and hell, where totally un-Jesus sentiments have dominated so much Western religion for centuries. No one questions that people can do wrong and harm one another, nor that God is good and wants us to be good, but the separation of the secular from the spiritual, and the individual from the social in civilized society has distorted the whole concept. Sin, guilt, and evil are also rooted in the political, economic, and religious social systems promoted by our ruling elites, who refuse to accept responsibility for social evils and use every stratagem of individualism to divert attention away from their own communal and social responsibility. People are indoctrinated to believe that everything bad is their fault and not the fault of wrong systems. Our religious systems put such constant emphasis on a God of vengeance and punishment, and promote such fear of everlasting banishment to hell, and demand such dependence on the efficacy of correct sacraments provided by correct methods to obtain the benefits of Jesus' sacrificial death, that all thought of changing the evil systems of society is driven from their minds. It is an approach from which we need to liberate ourselves, but it is not a new thought for people seeking liberation in Africa.

Bishop Colenso's God was not the God of vengeance who had to be placated by his Son's sacrifice for the sins of the human race. He reacted strongly against conventional ideas of the atonement, and his challenge was forthright. "Once for all let it be stated distinctly there is not a single passage in the whole of the New Testament which supports the dogma of modern theology that our Lord died for our sins, in the sense of dying instead of us, dying in our place, or dying so as to bear the punishment or penalty of our sins."[25] "There was no hell in our religion," said Steve Biko. We need liberating.

3.16. The Heresy of Fundamentalism

Driving through any of the myriad townships of Africa today you pass innumerable placards advertising right-wing churches. Some are local; many are part of major conglomerates funded from overseas with oppressive right-wing agendas. It is an oppressive religious approach that has been foisted on Africa recently with the full support of many economic and political bodies in the United States and Europe. Rejection of fundamentalism is at the heart of liberation today. Some religions have replaced prophetic theology by financial theology, and many religions have stopped doing theology at all. The field has been left wide open for any persuasive preacher who comes along. Right and wrong is displaced by profit and loss. The fat cats of faith present an emotional prosperity religion luring people to their church as the way to personal success, not social transformation. Major efforts are devoted to spiritual bribery that promises financial blessings now and eternal life to religious supporters, because "the power of all fundamentalisms lies in their persuasive effect, not in their truthfulness."[26]

Earthlings evolving toward a spiritually powerful community have always had to struggle against those who would use superstition as a means to oppress people, in Africa as everywhere else, but the struggle for liberation from fundamentalism in this continent has dimensions not widely known. Fundamentalism is big; it is false; it is strongly associated with and supported by the oppressions of Western capitalism. Throughout the continent fundamentalist churches have been promoted at a fantastic rate, whether based on a charismatic individual, or a forceful overseas organization, or both; its invitations for support rely almost exclusively on emotion and superstition, not a genuine theological basis; beginning in the Reagan years and brought to full power under the G. W. Bush administration, major U.S. private and government resources have been used throughout Africa's right-wing charismatic churches to promote un-Christian anti-Muslim propaganda and the claim of legitimacy for U.S. military aggression. And the major bodies of the Christ-ian churches do nothing about it and ignore the longing in their ranks to be liberated from all fundamentalist heretical superstition. The spirit of Africa is being undermined by religious bodies that are reluctant to tackle the inroads of fundamentalisms, because it would mean tackling their own failures.

3.17. *Liberation from Religious Hostility*

Religions also need to liberate themselves from their historical hostility to one another — and the strangely associated refusal to unite in opposing the antispiritual. The self-centered refusal of religious institutions to work together is one of the most offensive aspects of modern society. It is almost incredible that in the long, long struggle against oppression in Africa and apartheid in the south, with outspoken opponents of the oppressive regimes evident in every religious community, never once did the Christian, Jewish, Muslim, Hindu, and African traditional religions come together to criticize racism and apartheid, or work together to remove them. Here in Africa, where for most of the life of Earthlings spirituality was a part of life, communities of colonial religious sensibilities deliberately lived as worlds apart. They were patchwork humans with patchwork gods, and many still are. Their prime concern is not to liberate the people from oppression and ignorance, but to maintain their own institutions within the oppressive systems, and many of them continue to think and act that way today — worldwide.

Will the national and international structures of our religious institutions work together on the positive political, economic, and ecological issues relating to rescuing Earthlings from extinction later this century?

There is a strangely related issue: *all* our religious institutions, of *all* religious persuasions, agree that the fundamentalist groups supporting antihuman, anti-Earthling, activities are wrong, whether they claim Christian, Jewish, Muslim, Hindu, or agnostic roots. Why do they not come *together* and say so? What are they scared of?

Can we have faith in our religious bodies at all — for good or against ill? Can we liberate our souls and our communities only by writing off religion?

3.18. The Missionary Problem

The missionary movement played a major positive role in Africa (chapter 8.7) but it also received some of the strongest demands for liberation, culminating in the plea from twentieth-century African Christians at the highest level that the missionary enterprise from overseas be closed down. A major conflict developed between those (mostly in the West) who wanted to recruit more missionaries and money to extend their activities in Africa and those (mostly in Africa) who wanted a moratorium on sending either people or money, to enable Africa to discover itself. The AACC said: "If Africa is to find the liberation which the Christian gospel promises . . . can it discover a relevant Christian understanding and culture with such a heavy non-African presence?"

An essential problem in all churches was the motivation to measure success in the numbers of supporters recruited rather than their quality of life and the transformation of society. Churches concentrated on preparing individuals for the next life, which was facilitated by accepting a faith, rather than transforming their approach to this life, which had been the concern of Jesus. Instead of being deeply involved in the whole of life, churches left that to political and economic institutions: their own work was about winning souls for heaven. The input from the prophets and scripture was simply pushed to one side. Elliott Kendall, after years as a missionary in Africa and China, was convinced that "excessive concentration on church growth seems to be out of harmony with the New Testament understanding of Christian mission. . . . To limit Christian mission in terms of 'gospel-proclaiming, church-multiplying' missionaries is to depart from the fullness of the New Testament, yet this describes a large section of world mission today."[27]

There was a long period in many areas when missions were considered quite separately from church and run by different organizations. Missions were led by expatriates and were not interested in recruiting local people as missionaries: the converts could look after the kitchens, the cleaning, the vegetable garden, driving the vehicles, and running the offices, but the preaching, teaching, doctoring, and leading came from whites. The AACC said in 1963: "The lamentable truth is that after centuries of Christianity in

Africa, the Church, on the whole, cannot be said to have attained true selfhood."[28]

This spiritual isolationism brought even more serious calls for religious liberation in political circles. "In South Africa the Christian Church has probably been one of the most powerful instruments in making possible the political oppression of the black people. While the white colonialists were busy with the process of robbing the people of their land and their independence, the Churches were busy, however unconsciously, undermining the will of the people to resist," wrote Basil Moore of the South African University Christian Movement.[29]

But, but, but...for all their mistakes and problems, no one denies that the missionaries did marvelous things and changed the face of Africa. In the course of a century a few thousand people pioneered the coming of schools and colleges and technical training, doctors and clinics and hospitals, ploughs and plants and fertilizers, and the commitment to follow a vision.

3.19. When Liberators Become Oppressors

One of the warning bells that Africa sounds (for itself as well as for East and West) is that of self-delusion. In many countries throughout Africa those who began by heading the liberation forces ended by becoming oppressors: through their own volition in seeking power and privileges, or through the manipulation by oppressive forces from outside. It is well attested that "liberators have often turned into oppressors, victims into perpetrators," writes Henning Melber. "It is not unusual for a new regime to quickly resemble an old one. This has happened time and again around the world.... In this light, the 'anti-imperialist' Robert Mugabe turns out to be merely the final executor of the policies of the racist colonists Cecil Rhodes and Ian Smith."[30] It has not happened everywhere, but the pressures are everywhere, and only a constant struggle can resist them. It is not surprising. If the democracies with long experience and traditions like the United States and the UK are constantly threatened with collapse by economic and political corruption within their ranks, it is hardly surprising that young states in Africa from Ghana to the Congo, Kenya to Nigeria, and Algeria to Zimbabwe must fight a constant battle against the corruption of continuing oppression.

3.20. Liberating Our Vision and Values

The essential challenge facing Earthlings lies deep beneath any political, economic, or religious policy: it is the question of moral, ethical, and spiritual values, spelled out clearly by South African president Kgalema Motlanthe in June 2007: "The struggle against apartheid was not only about the transfer of political power from a minority to a majority...but about a fundamental shift in the dominant values of society.... From a society characterized by the relentless pursuit of individual enrichment, we are seeking to build a society that promotes the common good. From a society driven by greed, we are trying to build a society driven by solidarity and generosity"[31] — a secular-spirituality, the ubuntu of original Earthlings.

Many of the new elite of democratic Africa have allowed themselves to be picked up on the lances of the Five Horsemen of the Apocalypse and are being roasted to death like chunks of braaivleis (barbecue) on the fires lit by the civilized religious, political, and economic empires, whose media tell the public what to think and do, and whose policy of ecological destruction roars on, ashes to ashes. Many of those upholding the patchworks bringing destruction to the Earth are as deeply sincere and committed as were the supporters of the slave trade and apartheid. And as wrong.

Liberated people, whether in Africa, America, or Europe, find the pangs of theological hunger are not satisfied by the junk food of traditional religious imperialism, emotional evangelism, or superstitious fundamentalism. Scholars show that their basis in scripture is precarious, and many find them irrelevant in today's secular, interfaith, postreligious world. There is a spiritual restlessness, a yearning for purpose and spiritual power in secular affairs requiring the salvation of society for Earthlings in this life, not only for individual souls in heaven: sanctification, not evangelism, community regeneration, not self-centered individualism. We need the liberation of religious revolution. We need to liberate ourselves into Earthling thinking. Jesus called it rebirth.

Afterword

Colonial civilization was thrown over Africa like a heavy quilt, decorated with the rich and heavy embroidery the West wanted to see, crushing everything beneath it. Liberation has kicked off the covers, and underneath is the squirming movement of awakening emancipated life, flexing its muscles to get up and go. It is our vision and values that need liberating to find that way forward.

Chapter 4

The Ecological Matter

Synopsis

Life has been destroyed several times during the history of Earth, and Earthlings must clearly handle ecological systems correctly to survive. West and East and Africa have sometimes attempted to deny the urgency of the problems we face, but denial spells doom. The African quest for renewal assists us in spelling out the real problems and tackling the real answers.

4.1. Extinction

4.2. The Problems

4.3. The Answers

4.4. The Real Problems

4.5. The Real Answers

4.1. Extinction

Flying light aircraft was always a dream for me until my middle years brought the unexpected reality. The church moved me to a small town, with a small airstrip, two small aircraft, a small club fee, and a part-time instructor, who happened to be small. But my new assignment opened a very large door for me. For hundreds of hours after that I sat in the sky with a bird's eye view of Africa: thousands of miles of beautiful beach and breakers from a few hundred feet; seemingly endless lands of crops and grazing, fruit and forests; over the summits, in the valleys, or alongside mountains built in the beginnings of time; people under smog and smoke in the cities; innumerable whitewashed rondavels (huts) speckling the rural areas; fascinating changing rivers and dodging around and through the beauty of billowing clouds that kept them flowing; winds and air currents, factories and cathedrals, schools and hospitals, parliaments and highways: all brimming with people — and all doomed to extinction this century unless we do something never dreamed of before.

South of Africa stretch thousands of miles of very liquid water becoming colder and colder until it hardens into the ice of Antarctica, and that is one problem. The globe is warming up so rapidly that the ice at the poles is melting, the water level of the oceans is rising, and our grandchildren will need snorkels to reach the beaches we cavort on today. Every millisecond, we Earthlings are subject to powers so potent and huge as to be incomprehensible. Why does the moon not crash into Nairobi or New Orleans, or fly off into space? What makes space work?

It is not satisfactory to talk airily of the Big Bang or Creation, because these powers do unexpected things to us. We have all seen "shooting stars" when rocks from space burn up as they plunge into our atmosphere, and some of us have held in our hands the hard remains of small meteorites that survived the fiery journey and landed on Earth. Several billion years ago Africa was devastated by a massive comet that plummeted to Earth when it was still part of Gondwana, causing disastrous change and making the crater nearly twenty miles across that thrust up the ridge of hills around Vredefort. Better known is the comet that plunged into the Western Atlantic 65 million years ago, making Earth so uninhabitable that it wiped out the dinosaurs, and the power of life had to start all over again (this time including Us). On the other side of size, are the powers locked up in atoms, these specks of almost nothingness that can destroy cities in seconds. The spiritual and social powers that threaten the survival of Earthlings today are just as lethal: they only sound less dramatic.

4.2. The Problems

We all know the problems. Population is booming (especially in the poorer parts of Earth where children mean care for the elderly), health care makes more survive, and there are now more people over sixty than the whole population of Earth a few centuries ago. Most people in the world are hungry and poverty stricken; disease grows.

Smog is a fact of flying and breathing. The use of coal and oil to make electricity and run the engines of industry and transport are shrouding Earth in exhaust gases that trap the sun's heat like the glass of a greenhouse or a car left in the sun with windows shut. Like fumes in a furnace Earth's atmosphere is steadily warming, and the climate of a choking Earth is an un-support system for humans.

Forests are being destroyed to make wood chips and lands for agriculture, denying refreshment for land and air. The scenery of our journey from the cities to the bushveld has changed drastically in the past fifteen years. Areas of bush as large as countries have been planted with bananas, oranges, grain, and cane for sugar and fuel with little concern for the future of the land.

Fresh water is in short supply, and pollution is growing rapidly in every country; the seas are being fished out.

Every problem is made worse by the demands of war, which owes no allegiance to Africa or Earth, no reverence for life, no concern for culture and compassion, no support for cooperation and growth. Yet Earth is riddled with nations of fighting soldiers more terrible than fighting beasts, exterminating justice, peace, and hope, not to satisfy the hunger of humanity but the greed of those who would be demi-gods worshiped by evil. The United States has been driven by the killing culture of war almost continuously since its independence two centuries ago, and many countries in Africa seem headed the same way today.

Religions seem to have nothing to offer Earthlings except "don't believe it," "concentrate on heaven," or "Armageddon." The verdict of most scientists is that humanity is finished.

4.3. *The Answers*

We are provided with a host of answers. Africa's greatest source of power is sunshine, and solar lighting and heating instead of fossil fuels can provide for much of our energy needs. Domestic consumption of electricity is a major user of the central grid system that depends on climate-killing coal-fired power stations. Pollution could easily be reduced by switching to small-scale local solar generation. Commitment to local solar power could provide 90 percent of domestic production, at far less cost than building coal or nuclear power stations, which takes more than ten years. Providing solar power throughout the continent will provide work for tens of thousands.

Our greatest rivers are underused, and hydroelectric works at Ingo on the Congo alone can provide all the electricity Africa needs, with some left over for Europe too. Currents and tides in the seas provide much power in Europe, and Africa has plenty of sea. Denmark and Germany make much electricity from wind power; the systems are spreading to the Netherlands and the UK, and the mountains and lakes and coasts of Africa are simply waiting to be used, with no negative effect on ecological systems.

How can Africa possibly be short of food with such vast agricultural land? Why is it not used? Vast riches reside under the soil, and vast possibilities exist in the manufacturing and financial institutions to remove the pain of poverty. From heart transplants to pebble-bed nuclear reactors we know there is plenty of scientific ability for Africa to explore alternatives to the cars and trucks and jet planes with which we are killing ourselves off.

Poverty figures conceal wealth figures, but there are vast funds in private and government hands to raise the levels of education and retirement to remove the mind-set that we know fuels overpopulation.

Why does it not all happen? The hesitations over enacting the answers to our ecological challenges show that we are facing a different set of problems altogether.

4.4. The Real Problems

Africa helps us to see that the real problems behind the ecological disasters confronting humanity are quite different: our problem is the greed of the rich whose money is invested in the systems of ecological destruction. They will not put money into solar, water, tidal, and wind power, because they own the coal mines and power stations. The economic structures are such that the feelings and opinions of millions of citizens and shareholders are brushed aside by the handful of people who control governments and boards of directors. The real problems are economic, political, and, at heart, spiritual.

The essential difficulty Earthlings face is that both the ecological problems and their solution are directly linked to economic systems designed to benefit the rich elites next year, not to serve the interests of humanity in the next century, and this oppressive approach is accepted as right and proper by the political and religious powers. The money goes the wrong way.

The first priority of the elite is to protect and enlarge the possessions of the wealthy. If our economy was designed to provide for all humanity, as it was in precivilized Africa, we would have a different system, but when "riches for me" ousts "enough for us" we are involved in a people-killing process. Once profit is seen as the right and proper priority of the economy, as it is in the West and much of modern Africa, the method of making a profit becomes secondary, and the support of different routes of antihuman activities becomes acceptable, including want and war.

The second priority of wealth-worship is that it justifies spending money on luxuries for ourselves, rather than necessities for the poor, which is truly idol worship. One of the main reasons for the development of democratic politics was to ensure that the will of the people was heard and honored to ensure that wealth was spent correctly for all. It was a taken-for-granted principle of African ubuntu culture.

But it was *not* honored by Western civilization, which is designed as a tool for the care and promotion of the elite. This change of economic objective became the priority of many political parties in Africa as they were brought into the Western colonial mind-set. The blessings of civilization were bestowed on an elite class, but for the great majority civilization carried a curse.

Throughout the continent and the world the vision and values changed. Many sought political power not to serve the people, but for the people to serve them. The owners of Western power calculated they would make more profit out of oil and internal combustion engines than from railways; more profit from power stations and coal than from solar panels; and more votes in the United States and Europe by subsidizing Western farmers to outprice third world farmers. The real problem in addressing the ecological matter was not the Earth but the economy. There was no longer any doubt that the debate was about ethical and spiritual matters and must be resolved in the spiritual realm. But the religious institutions were petrified that if they laid their lives on the line of spiritual rectitude in economic affairs, they would lose the contributions they needed to keep their religions going. Simple as that. The real ecological problem is not what to do, but the readiness to do it.

4.5. The Real Answers

"There are huge financial interests in both nuclear and coal generation, but it will be a small minority who will be in control, whereas thousands could be involved in renewable energy. We cannot allow the vested interests of capital intensive energy generation to jeopardize the future health of the planet," writes Bishop Geoff Davies of SAFCEI.[1]

Africa helps us to see that the real answer to the ecological matter lies in liberating the self-centered demands of other spheres in economics, politics, and religion, that is, change.

Two things are made abundantly clear in considering why ecology matters to Africa. The first certainty is that ecological systems and climate have an impact on everything that matters to Africa and every other country on Earth: economics, politics, media, and religion: we are all in this together. Is the answer for the poor to bring pressure on the elite to deal with the matter? Is it to overthrow the elite à la Cuba? Do we hope to survive and leave our children to do the dying?

The second certainty is that the revolution to liberate Earth's ecological systems will be accomplished only through the vision and values of social-spirituality seen in the African matter of ubuntu. It is a moral, ethical, spiritual issue.

◆ ◆ ◆

Flying an airplane is much easier than driving a car: point the nose, set the throttle, and off you go: no curbs or corners or traffic lights. The main problem is knowing where to go, and what to do if storms and winds get in the way. Ecology is the same. We can work out where to go, but the storms of economics and politics can blow us off track, slow us up, or threaten to bring us down. The real problem is not ecological systems: it is politics and economics that have to be changed. Do we have the spirit to change them?

Afterword

The main problem about the ecological threat to human survival on Earth is that we don't want to believe it. We know why: the answers demand fundamental changes in the way we handle our economics and our politics. The West is a crucial part of the answer because it is a crucial part of the problem. Do we have the spirit to measure up to the answers?

Chapter 5

The Political Matter

Synopsis

The countries of modern Africa were invented by Europeans in the nineteenth-century scramble to make colonies. African politics thus emerged in the context of resistance to the oppressive practices of Western greed that had separated the secular from the spiritual. America and Europe remained committed to using violence as the means of political progress, but Africa (like Mahatma Gandhi, who lived there for twenty-five years) also sought a strong nonviolent philosophy and practice. Political liberation has now swept through Africa, but the negative effect of civilized pressure in all the patches has militated against peace and prosperity. The nonviolent commitment was crucial to the liberation of Africa, especially in South Africa in 1994. These experiences provide major political insights for the world community today.

5.1. The European Invention

5.2. The Context of Politics

5.3. Resistance

5.4. Liberation

5.5. The Way of Nonviolence

5.6. Has Liberation Failed Africa?

5.7. Seeking a New Political Vision

The most striking of all the impressions I have formed since I left London a month ago is of the strength of this African national consciousness.... The wind of change is blowing through this continent, and, whether we like it or not, this growth of national consciousness is a political fact. We must all accept it as a fact, and our national policies must take account of it. — British Prime Minister Harold Macmillan, Cape Town, 1960

5.1. The European Invention

In 1884–85 great political figures from Britain, Belgium, France, Germany, Portugal, Italy, and Spain, traveled by horse coach and train to a conference in Berlin. They met to invent Africa. They were there to decide the boundaries and centers of the countries that would serve the interests of European colonialism and capitalism. The whole continent was subjugated, with the partial exception of Ethiopia and Liberia. Its agreement that the countries concerned must "effectively occupy" the territory meant, in practice, that they must exercise military control. There were no Africans at the Berlin conference.

In a few short years the thousands of tribes of Africa discovered they were controlled from Europe, redesigned as part of countries they had never heard of, where they had no political rights, with boundaries that frequently ignored their traditional lands. These boundaries went through the middle of tribal territories, sundering ethnic and historical unities or forcing together tribes that had never been together before, with different languages, customs, structures, and beliefs. It made no difference to the gentlemen in Berlin who wanted a neat manageable system for exploitation, but it built in major problems for generations to come for those who actually lived there.

Guns ruled. Africans were forced to pay taxes on which they had never been consulted, contribute money and lives to wars in Europe, America, and Asia that had nothing to do with them, adopt clothes and customs that seemed quite unnecessary, and worship gods they had never heard of, while their land was systematically stripped of its resources. It was the politics of dictatorship. Neither Africans nor their oppressors were allowed any thought of being an Earthling community within which evolution was an ongoing process, within which injustice and oppression cannot survive and prosper. Those thousands of discredited African tribes with a common ubuntu base knew that the motive power of all humanity, the true ground of political order and progress, arose from the bottom up. It can never be imposed from the top down.

This was something that Nelson Mandela learned of political leadership in his early years in the rural area of Qunu, where he was brought up:

> As a leader, I have always followed the principles I first saw demonstrated by the regent at the Great Place. I have always endeavored to listen to what each and every person in a discussion had to say before venturing my own opinion. Oftentimes, my opinion will simply represent a consensus of what I heard in the discussion. I always remember the regent's axiom: a leader, he said, is like a shepherd. He stays behind the flock, letting the most nimble go on ahead, whereupon the others follow, not realizing that all along they are being directed from behind.[1]

5.2. *The Context of Politics*

Politics is always greatly affected by traditions that arise from the past and embrace the present and are often classified as good or bad. This judgment adheres to their proponents, and often to their descendants also, which can prompt sheer prejudice, injustice, and unnecessary barriers. Traditions are part of the context of politics, which affects all endeavors to move from the politics of patches to the politics of Earthlings, such as moves that encompass socialism and capitalism, communism and democracy, nationalism, racism, education, gender, and religion. Africa illustrates very clearly that politics arises in the context of change, which should be acknowledged and welcomed, not despised and denigrated. People can have wrong views very sincerely, change their views very sincerely, and hold new views very sincerely. It does not mean such people were bad or fickle: they were alive and growing up. Much of colonialism was wrong in principle, but those reared with other principles did not see it that way. You could be brought up to believe deeply that Queen Victoria was a right and good Christian ruler with a benign approach to the British Empire in India and Africa, and you could later realize with equal sincerity that you were wrong, which changed your politics. That did not make it necessary to believe that everything connected with the past must now be condemned, nor that everything your new colleagues thought about the future was entirely correct. The progress of Earthlings is alive, moving, progressing, with purpose in the community, and we move with it. We can be understanding, grateful, and glad of our forebears (or ancestors) and equally glad that we have been moved onward. I was born and brought up a Methodist and learned much from the writings, history, and people of John Wesley. If ever I go to London again I am sure to go with thankful delight to visit his house/museum in City Road — but please don't tie me up in his politics or his theology! We move on: the context changes.

The political dynamics of any society have to be seen in the context of other disciplines, which on this continent includes religion, for Africa is highly religious. Politics is rooted in the basic primal beliefs of all human beings, which survive in different forms of "traditional religion," often held alongside other and later concepts of faith. It includes the whole breadth of religions received during the colonial era, from Hinduism, Islam, and Judaism to the many forms of Christianity that run divisively through most denominations. Colonial forms of Christianity, often distinguished by strong racist attitudes and interpretations, were widespread and sincerely held not only by whites in Africa, but by those in Europe and North America also. The idea that religion should keep out of politics (which could be a political ploy or a cop-out) was for many a deep conviction of faith while, for others, the involvement of religious communities in state affairs was of central importance.

Russel Botman, while president of the SACC, made this clear, citing the call of Jesus to "Go and make disciples of all nations" (Matt. 28:19).

> Instead of the church making disciples, it has been making members of congregations. Instead of making disciples of nations, we have established a discipleship of denominations. ... We thought our main interest was to baptize individuals so that they would become members of the church. The text does not call us to make members of the church but disciples of the nation. The terminology "disciples of the nations" refers to the citizenship of a people. When we use words such as "nation" or "state" we are referring to the political community. ... We

are interested in making disciples of the nation. We are not
interested in turning the state into disciples ... or claiming the
power of the state ... nor to christianize the state. We are quite
happy with a secular state. We are interested in the politics as
it affects the nation.[2]

From earliest times Africa has understood religion in political terms
of its corporateness in community, not just a personal relationship
with some form of spirit. As Jean-Marc Ela of Cameroon writes:
"Religion is not reducible to a relationship with the supernatural.
It emerges as a social force as well. It provides the wherewithal for
a protest against the established order" — or support for it as the
case may be.[3]

People in the West need to consider that in "un-Westernized"
Africa there is no question that faith entails involvement in politics, and those who use their religion as an excuse for not becoming
involved in politics must question whether they are truly involved
in religion either. Such political discipleship has both positive and
negative connotations. Brigalia Bam, who was involved for years in
the programs of the World Council of Churches (WCC), said that
discipleship undergirded "the hope for a transformed society, a caring community of mutual commitment to one another, a people
working for the common good."[4] A critical component is also necessary, as Molefe Tsele points out. "Our faith should compel us to
witness God's will for a better world and the possibility of a better
economic system than one founded on the acceptance of the finality of human greed, natural competition, and the drive for more
and more profit."[5]

The apartheid concept of Western civilization, which keeps the
spiritual separate from the secular, was never an African understanding. It is in this secular-spiritual context that the political
situation in Africa has to be considered, and the story of Africa's
political contribution to the Earthling community assessed. The
antispiritual political struggle that has caused uncounted millions
to suffer and die in Africa, affects the world like the immoral
killing sprees of Western arms manufacturers on every continent.
This story of the struggle to enact spiritual power for the political
liberation of Africa falls into three phases: resistance, the liberation movements, and the liberation of the continent that is still
ongoing.

5.3. Resistance

Visitors have often remarked on the unusual birdbath in our garden, which is associated with an unusual history of interest to those who wonder why Africa matters today. The flat rock containing the water, scooped out by rural people scraping mealies, rests on a pile of smooth round stones as large as soccer balls, which obviously came from a river bed — but surely not from our local rivers in the Lowveld? Truly. They came from a river in Kwa Zulu Natal that runs through Bambata's kraal. They are a memorial to Bambata, the last of the African chiefs to rebel against the British colonial occupation in 1906, who was strongly supported by Paramount Chief Dinizulu. Many African people resisted the European invasions from the beginning, especially when colonialism began to bite, and Bambata stands in the long line from the Ashanti of Ghana, Tshaka, Sekukune, the Ndebele-Shona, Lobengula, Mzilikazi, the Maji Maji and the Hehe in Tanzania, Nandi and Giriama and the Land and Freedom Army (Mau Mau) in Kenya. The British killed Bambata, but we need to remember and honor him.

It was a far longer, more protracted, and violent struggle when significant numbers of white settlers were involved, as in Algeria, Kenya, Tanzania, Zimbabwe, Angola, Mozambique, Guinea-Bissau, Namibia, and Zaire.

The situation in South Africa was sometimes referred to as "colonialism of a special type" because the colonists were residents. Whites of Dutch, British, German, and French descent had been there for centuries, and the government was not in Europe but in Pretoria with parliament in Cape Town. Resistance was essentially focused against racism in all branches of society, but this resistance included a significant number of Colored and Indian people, and a growing number of whites.

5.4. Liberation

The first liberation movement in Africa and, as it was to prove, the last to achieve its object, was the African National Congress of South Africa (ANC). Four years after Bambata was killed the South African Native National Congress (later African National Congress) was convened on January 8, 1912. Long before the days of cars or aircraft, they traveled over six-hundred miles from Cape

Town in the south, well over six hundred from Beitbridge in the north, and hundreds from Johannesburg, Durban, Port Elizabeth, and innumerable rural dwellings to the geographically central city of Bloemfontein. It was an event of the utmost significance for the continent and the world. The conference followed a series of meetings in the provinces, several calls responding to the unjust aspects of the Act of Union of 1910 (which excluded blacks), the circulation of writing by clergy and academics who had studied or attended conferences overseas, and representations from chiefs who were the sole link to colonial authority for millions of rural people.

Leading figures were Sol Plaatje and Pixley ka Isaka Seme, who said: "We have called you to this Conference so that we can together devise ways and means of forming our national union for the purpose of creating national unity and defending our rights and privileges."[6] The proceedings began and ended with prayers and hymns, and the first National Executive Committee included four ministers of religion (which is one reason why Oliver Tambo emphasized the involvement of people of faith from the beginning of the ANC.[7])

The first half of the twentieth century was like a period of pregnancy in which the world was preparing for new life to emerge after the Second World War ended in 1945. Colonialism still ruled. The South African War between British and Boer ended in victory for the British, who rejected any thought of democratic voting rights for nonwhites in 1910, confined them to 13 percent of the land in 1913, and restricted them to prescribed urban areas with no franchise in 1923 and 1936. West and East spoke of the League of Nations, while no African anywhere on the continent had the franchise. American capitalism was challenging the supremacy of European markets; socialism was challenging capitalism in many places; the supremacy of the British Empire was under threat; agnosticism was decimating religions and becoming respectable; new theologies were afoot; black Americans of the postslavery generation were discovering a distinctive approach to the world in terms of emancipation, liberation, and freedom; and deep down out of sight the roots of humanity in Africa were being reborn.

There were great political changes in the world during the brief thirty years of the First and Second World Wars (1914–18 and 1939–45). The British suffragette movement was put on hold during the Great War, but by 1918 voting rights for women were inevitable. Many sectors of society previously reserved for men began to be open for women, and the voting age came down for everyone. Full-time education at schools provided by government became compulsory throughout Europe. Workers organized themselves; some countries became socialist or communist, and the right to employment at a fair wage with comprehensive benefits became an issue for everyone. Health services and pensions were established, and the issue of justice, which was high on the antifascist agenda of the Second World War, became an issue of human rights for all.

But that was Europe. What would an agenda of democratic rights in a just and classless society do for Africa? Winston Churchill, the great democratic leader of the fight against fascism and co-founder with Franklin D. Roosevelt of the Atlantic Charter, was an arch-imperialist. That charter, signed on a British warship in American waters, set out some of the war aims of the United States and the UK to "respect the rights of all people to choose the form of government under which they will live, and . . . to see sovereign rights and self-government restored to all." But not to Africa. Churchill was rooted and reared in the British colonial school with a well-worn pith-hat view of Africa. In his journalistic youth he had been in Omdurman and taken part in the last hectic, jangling, pounding charge of British cavalry; he later made a quiet, silent, creeping escape from captivity in the Boer War. When Africa hailed the Atlantic Charter as a step toward freedom, Churchill told the British House of Commons:

> At the Atlantic meeting we had in mind primarily the restoration of sovereignty and self-government . . . to States and Nations in Europe under Nazi yoke . . . so that this is quite a separate problem from the progressive evolution of self-governing institutions in the regions and peoples which owe allegiance to the British Crown. (September 1941)

Europe could be liberated from fascism — but not Africa from colonialism. Even Ernest Bevin, Britain's foreign minister in the 1945 Labor government once defined Britain's policy of decolonalization as "Give — and keep."

Although the Second World War brought to a head the worldwide clamor for liberation from oppression in terms of money, work, health, education, freedom, votes, and prosperity for all, Europeans with stakes in Africa had no intention of allowing their profits to be diverted to such egalitarian progress. Political liberation would enable this responsibility to be placed on the shoulders of the liberated people, while investments in commercial matters kept the profit for the Europeans.

Few people today have heard of a suburb of Manchester, England, with the improbable name of Chorlton-cum-Hardy. It was here, in 1945, that a meeting was held of the Pan-African Federation. It was chaired by W. E. B. Du Bois, the black American pan-Africanist, to ensure that "the principles of the Atlantic Charter be put into practice at once." Participants were mainly from West Africa, and included Jomo Kenyatta of Kenya and Kwame Nkrumah of Ghana. It was a clear announcement that after the war was over the struggle for the liberation of Africa would come to the front of the stage. Observers have often noted that all the problems in the world seem to have taken up residence in Africa, which seems like a steaming cauldron. So we must be a bad lot. On other hand, the sometimes unique nature of our struggle has produced some significantly different answers in the quest of evolution. Apartheid was not defeated by invading armies, bombing by aircraft, or bombardment from ships at sea. Despite many years of violent oppression of the people by government police and soldiers and some small military-type resistance, the thrust for liberation at home and abroad came through the mobilization of ordinary civilians. Apartheid was not defeated by the Great Powers of either West or East, but by a million actions of peaceful political pressure by ordinary people. So we must be a good lot.

While the struggle was essentially defined in terms of white-black and rich-poor, it was also infused by large scale crossovers between such groups. The British vs. Boer wars of the late nineteenth century riddled white politics until well after the National Party came to power with its apartheid policy in 1948, but the opposition United Party was similarly steeped in racial discrimination. The church was deeply divided on political grounds. Many white Christians supported apartheid as the purpose of God: some rejected apartheid in theory on the theological ground of being One in Christ, but practiced it in its congregations, district synods, circuits, and the training, stipends, pensions, and appointments of its clergy.[8] Many wanted to bring change in church and state but were scared that struggle would mean suffering.

The whites-only South African election of 1948 brought the National Party to power, which many saw as the culmination and reversal of the South African (Boer) War of the previous generation, a victory of Afrikaner over English, but it was essentially a victory for apartheid in the whole of southern Africa. The whole continent saw South Africa as the heavy hand of oppressive white colonialism. Three million black citizens were forcibly removed from areas now designated for "whites only." The 1950 Suppression of Communism Act sounded acceptable to a Western world dominated by the anticommunist rhetoric of the Cold War, but it defined communism in such broad terms that it could embrace almost anyone. Although education had been begun and run by the churches, it had long been accepted as a responsibility to be financed principally by the state. It was taken over entirely by the Bantu Education Act of 1955, which redesigned the curriculum to educate blacks only up to the level required to fulfill a servant role.

Until this time, opposition to apartheid had been mainly in the form of political protests and deputations presented to government at high levels, but from 1949 the ANC engaged in a new Program of Action to include boycotts, strikes, and civil disobedience. Throughout the period from 1912 to 1960, when it was banned, the focus of the ANC was to build local branches of politically conscious and emancipated people, toward establishing a responsible electorate. Partly inspired by Mahatma Gandhi (who had practiced law for twenty-five years in South Africa and developed the Satyagraha program here) the Defiance Campaign of 1952 organized thousands to deliberately break the apartheid laws and go to jail. 1955 saw an ANC led nationwide campaign to discuss the type of new South African society that people envisaged, which produced a program accepted by three thousand people at a mass meeting in Kliptown, Soweto. The "Freedom Charter" affirmed that "South Africa belongs to all who live in it, black and white."

Later that year 156 were arrested and charged at the Treason Trial, which dragged on for four years. Peaceful protests reached their height in action against the Pass Laws, which forced black men and women to carry passes constantly to confirm their right to be in any area. Thousands of people burned their passes in protest, going to jail, and when several hundred women and men sought to hand them in at the police station in Sharpeville, south of Johannesburg, the police opened fire. Sixty-nine were killed and hundreds wounded, mostly in the back as they sought to run home. Within days, the regime had detained eighteen thousand people, banned both the ANC and PAC, and no one was allowed to speak of them except as terrorists for over thirty years. Not a shot had been fired or a person killed by those seeking political liberation.

Then that changed. The ANC rejected civil war, but decided that since people were being killed in peaceful protests, it was morally legitimate and politically necessary to engage in selective sabotage, and the military wing, Umkhonto we Sizwwe, was formed to advance political objectives. Its leadership was discovered and arrested in Rivonia, outside Johannesburg in 1963, and it was at his trial, facing the death sentence, that Nelson Mandela made one of the best known and definitive statements in the quest of liberation in Africa:

> During my lifetime I have dedicated myself to the struggle of the African people. I have fought against white domination and I have fought against black domination. I have cherished the ideal of a democratic and free society in which all people live together in harmony and with equal opportunities. It is an ideal which I hope to live for and achieve. But, if need be, it is an ideal for which I am prepared to die.[9]

He was imprisoned on Robben Island, off the coast of Cape Town, for twenty-seven years. Twenty-seven years. With many others.

Under the apparent quietness of the 1960s, imposed by the rigid clampdown of the apartheid regime, the political struggle grew deeper and wider. Small radical movements in the churches and in the student bodies began to develop. Overseas concern began to turn into pressure. Then, suddenly, a new political dimension appeared. The Black Consciousness Movement emerged first among students, focused on Steve Biko, Barney Pityana, Mamphela Ramphele, and their colleagues. Its central theme was that black people must throw off their psychological submission to subservience, stand on their own feet, and go forward with a new consciousness of black humanity and citizenship. It was not anti-white, but a truly liberated movement. Despite attempts to drive wedges between BC and ANC, they were expressing a fundamental agreement on the evolution of human community across the spectrum of races, classes, and ages. On June 16, 1976, the baton was grasped by children in black secondary schools in Soweto. Beyond primary school, most teaching in "Bantu" schools was through the international medium of English, but new government regulations now decreed that certain subjects be taught and examined in Afrikaans. "No way!" said thousands of students in Soweto who set out to march to the center of Johannesburg to protest. The police shot them down. In the next few days, thousands of other students across the country marched in protest also, and police bullets flew again. Hundreds were hit, and the parents, who had originally been shocked into silence by the "naughty children," were transformed into activists overnight.

The liberation struggle in South Africa had now reached a new and definitive stage. Throughout Africa countries were being liberated, but South Africa was still involved in this extraordinary war. On one side were the political rulers and their armed forces, elected by a few whites, backed by white finance, and supported by the white leaders and majorities of most of the Western world, who refused to support the struggle, saying it was "communist inspired." On the other side was the huge mass of the African population. They had not the slightest intention of toppling their oppressors by force of arms: they did not have the arms, the money, or the vote, but they were going for justice, truth, and right in the human community. They had a united commitment to cooperation; they believed that care and compassion for the people would prevail, for the answer was not in guns but in ubuntu. It was a straight political contest between the Earthlings and the patches.

In 1983, despite the constant bannings, the United Democratic Front (UDF) sprang into being, bringing together groups from across the whole spectrum of politics, religion, economics, and the media who sought liberation. In 1989 the ANC issued the Harare Declaration, spelling out the conditions for talks with the National Party. P. W. Botha was replaced by F. W. de Klerk; the Berlin Wall came down and the Cold War ended. And in February 1990 F. W. de Klerk unbanned the South African liberation movements, Nelson Mandela and hundreds of prisoners were freed, and peaceful negotiations for a liberated South Africa began.

So it was that year after year, decade after decade, the people of Africa were seeking fundamental, just, evolutionary growth by peaceful change, despite the violence they faced. One of the greatest demonstrations of this attitude came in South Africa when the struggle was over, when democratic power was in the hands of the majority, and the decision was made by the victims to handle the perpetrators of these decades of apartheid horror, suffering, imprisonment, violence, and death with the Truth and Reconciliation campaign.

5.5. *The Way of Nonviolence*

Visitors to the British House of Commons are intrigued to discover that the Government and Opposition parties do not sit side by side, but facing one another across the chamber — with a gap between to keep them two sword lengths apart. The question of violence has always been at the heart of political discussion. Many modern people, especially in "Western" and "Christian" countries, still retain the colonial view that violence is part of the African culture, although violence had fortunately been civilized out of the Western Christian way of life many centuries ago. But this is simply not true. The colonial presence in Africa was imposed by violence. This obliterated resistance, not because guns killed better than spears, for dead was dead, but guns did it at a longer, safer range than spears. Shells, bombs, and rockets are the same, but more so. Yet Africa has an interesting view on violence.

Africans realized long ago that although violent reactions are understandable (especially in animals) they do not work for humans in community. Violence is built in to the competition for power and riches, designed to glut the greed of oppressors over their victims. Violence has been the methodology of the West, Europe, and the United States, and Africa knows it well, but this continent's approach is far nearer the Earthling concept that human problems are not solved by pitching patch against patch, but by learning the skills of care (respect) and cooperation.[10]

Human problems are not solved by the fear of, nor desire for, violence. Strife between clans and chieftainships has been part of Africa, but the priorities of ubuntu were not abrogated. Conflicts ended with the ceremony of the Washing of the Spears, followed by interaction, intermingling, and intermarriage — in contrast to many Western and Eastern cultures where conflict is nurtured and inflamed for centuries.

People nurtured in Africa have a vision beyond that of those brought up in colonial Western civilization. This comes into clear focus when we contrast the ending of the World Wars in Europe with the end of the apartheid system in South Africa. When World War I ended the Allies imposed horrendous reparations upon Germany and the poverty that followed was a major factor in the rise of Nazism. It was even worse after World War II. Although Hitler had shot himself in his bombproof bunker below Berlin, many of his leading colleagues were jailed, brought to trial, and judicially exterminated. The world spoke very clearly and forcibly against those responsible for Nazi and Japanese atrocities (including the Holocaust) and invented special laws and special courts in Nuremberg and Tokyo to bring them to justice and to sentence them to long terms of imprisonment or death.

The struggle against apartheid, during which unknown millions suffered and innumerable people were killed by the apartheid forces, sought a *political* victory for people to live together, not a *military* one to destroy them. The objective was not dead bodies but live votes; not guilt and revenge but confession and forgiveness. The achievement of political liberation in South Africa brought with it challenges that many countries had never had to face in quite the same way. The first time that millions of black and white people had stood side by side in the same queue was at the polling booth in 1994. Before that everything had been Black, White, Colored, or Indian. The challenges were many. How do you handle several million white people who have been brought up to believe in and practice separate development as the only way to peace and prosperity? What do you do about thousands of whites who have legally bullied, jailed, tortured, or killed other citizens — and how do you treat the millions who have suffered? How do you deal with a situation where hundreds of thousands of white civil servants, mainly Afrikaners, suddenly feel threatened because the new government would be expected to find jobs for millions of black citizens? And how do you cope with churches that, despite the prophetic pronouncement of a handful of people, are solidly dominated by a church theology as rigid and colonial as the state theology of the apartheid regime?

This situation required a new development in world community to agree that certain actions rejected the fundamental rights of human beings. They should be seen from a deeper perspective than that of national conflict and defined as "a crime against humanity." This understanding was basic to the Universal Declaration on Human Rights (UDHR) of 1948, which had the insights of many nations and religions behind it. In 1967 the UN General Assembly declared that apartheid was "a crime against humanity" and in 1977 imposed sanctions on South Africa — which many in the West ignored. The general failure of the UN to actually act on questions of human rights moved Mary Robinson, head of the UN Human Rights Commission to say in 1998: "It is a failure of implementation that shames us all."[11]

When South Africa was liberated it had different ideas about the way to peace, justice, and human rights. It required a pragmatic, realistic response to a real and tense situation, a response rooted in the quest for ubuntu, not violence. On the one hand were hundreds of thousands who had suffered oppression and death from apartheid all their lives; and on the other hand were thousands with arms, who had passions poised to oppose the fact that the apartheid government had "given in to the terrorists." Both sides consisted of sincere people rooted in traditions they had been taught were right and good and Christian.

The first part of the response came from Joe Slovo, the leader of the South African Communist Party, who proposed what became known as the "sunset clause." This was the commitment by the ANC that the thousands of whites working in government offices throughout the country would not be thrown out automatically and replaced by blacks; they would be allowed to remain at their posts, and find their own place in the new nonracial society.

The second was the epoch-making Truth and Reconciliation Commission (TRC). The commission was empowered to listen to the evidence of those whose human rights had been trampled by the apartheid regime, and to those who had inflicted their suffering, and to recommend amnesty, not prosecution, for those who admitted their crimes.

Justice Richard Goldstein put the position clearly:

The decision to opt for a Truth and Reconciliation Commission was an important compromise. If the ANC had insisted on Nuremberg-style trials for the leaders of the former apartheid government there would have been no peaceful transition to democracy, and if the former government had insisted on a blanket amnesty then, similarly, the negotiations would have broken down. A bloody revolution sooner rather than later would have been inevitable. The Truth and Reconciliation Commission is a bridge from the old to the new.

Hearings were held in many parts of the country, and the horrendous tale of apartheid atrocities was told by many who had suffered and survived. There was no question of wiping out the past as if it had not happened, but those who admitted their crimes and were remorseful could be forgiven. These TRC issues presented by political liberation were essentially matters of the spirit demanding a nonviolent response.

They were one of the most important facts learned in Africa, particularly in contrast with the medieval approach still practiced in the United States and much of Europe and the rest of the world. Liberated Earthlings believe in reconciliation with adversaries, not destruction.

Nonviolent action also dominated many antiapartheid actions overseas. Support for the liberation struggle took various forms, many involving political activism against such conservative regimes as Britain under the government of Margaret Thatcher, which did much to support the apartheid government. There was wide support for the Anti-Apartheid Movement in Europe, particularly when the ANC called for sanctions against commercial, political, academic, and ecclesiastical bodies that supported or cooperated with the apartheid regime. Protests were registered by leading politicians, academics, businessmen, and bishops, but the weight of the pressure came from ordinary people. The major banking concern of Barclays, which had financed much of the apartheid regime, was forced to pull out of South Africa by its most impecunious members — British students. Their strategy was simple: because the British government pays study grants to students and all banks know that clients seldom change their banking institutions, all banks seek to "catch them young." British students simply said to Barclays: "We are moving our grants to other banks until you pull out of South Africa." It took ten years — but the students won, and Barclays withdrew.

Throughout Europe ordinary housewives from stately homes to working-class flats refused to buy South African clothes, food, fruit, nuts, and wines. Cashiers at supermarkets in Liverpool and Belfast refused to ring up purchases that were breaking the sanctions, and when they were sacked thousands of colleagues threatened to walk out too unless they were reinstated and the goods taken off the shelves immediately — now, this afternoon. Once a week, every week, in all kinds of weather, women from German churches demonstrated at travel agencies, South African Airways offices, embassy and consulate offices, and against people traveling to support South Africa. International cricket, soccer, and rugby boycotted South Africa. From Canada and the United States to India and Australia ordinary people heard the message of the ordinary people of South Africa and brought pressure to bear. The politicians and financiers heard the message. Nelson Mandela and Walter Sisulu and hundreds of others on Robben Island heard the message. The last apartheid president, F. W. de Klerk, heard the message very clearly indeed. He unbanned the liberation movements, released Nelson Mandela and other political prisoners, and began negotiations.

So political liberation happened. One by one the colonial flags came down, new African flags were unfurled, and new national anthems sounded from ocean to ocean. Ethiopia had never been colonized; Liberia had been established for freed slaves in 1847. Egypt (1927), Libya (1951), Morocco, Sudan, Tunisia, and Western Sahara (1956) had followed, and then came the flood (see the accompanying table).

5.6. Has Liberation Failed Africa?

In 1790, shortly after the beginning of the French Revolution, Edmund Burke wrote a far-seeing book (*Reflections on the Revolution in France*). He was sympathetic with that struggle by the French people to free themselves from the oppression of the aristocrats, but he predicted it would fail, descend into violence, and finally collapse into dictatorship. Disasters and war followed the American Revolution, which expelled eighty thousand British loyalists, monopolized the executive and legislative powers, restricted the franchise, practiced slavery, and has been involved in war almost continuously ever since. Throughout the world the pattern has taken different forms, but it has been constantly repeated, and Africa has found the same. It is one thing to break free from the chains, but quite another to land on your feet.

Liberation in Africa was often followed by a series of disasters. International outrage was raised by horror stories like those of

AFRICAN INDEPENDENCE DATES

| 1957 | Ghana | |
| 1958 | Guinea | |

1960   Mali   Somalia
       Chad   Mauritania
       Nigeria   Senegal
       Cameroon   Zaire
       Togo   Cote d'Ivoire
       Central African Republic   Burkina Faso
       Benin   Madagascar
       Gabon   Congo

1961   Sierra Leone   Tanzania

1962   Burunda/Rwanda   Uganda
       Algeria

1963   Kenya
1964   Zambia   Malawi

1965   the Gambia

1866   Botswana   Lesotho

1968   Equatorial Guinea   Swaziland
       Mauritania

1973   Eritrea

1974   Guinea-Bissau

1975   Cape Verde   Cameroon
       São Tomé   Mozambique
       Zaire   Angola

1976   Seychelles

1977   Djibouti

1980   Zimbabwe

1993   Eritrea

1994   South Africa

Idi Amin in Uganda (1971–79), Jean-Bédel Bokassa of the Central African Republic (1966–79), Macias Nguema of Equatorial Guinea (1969–79), Sudan, Liberia, Somalia, Rwanda. Dictators flourished. Western weapons materialized everywhere. The civil wars of Angola, Mozambique, Namibia, Zimbabwe, and Rwanda ran into rebellions throughout the 1990s. In Ethiopia (1991), Algeria (1992), Burundi (1993), Nigeria (1993), Congo-Brazzaville (1993 and 1997), The Gambia (1994), Lesotho (1994 and 1998), Niger (1995), Central African Republic (1996), Congo-Kinshasa (1997), Sierra Leone (1997), Comoros (1998), Côte d'Ivoire (1999 and 2002), Guinea-Bissau (1999), and Somalia (1999), the struggles seemed to go on forever.

Writing in 2004 Sipho Buthelezi says that "the post-colonial state, after political independence, inherited the essential characteristics of its predecessor and only changed the composition of the managers and functionaries of the state, but not the form, content and character of the institutions anchored in the colonial era."[12] There were several reasons. Africa is not naturally the home of a couple of dozen of ex-colonial countries committed to antagonism, but to thousands of tribes with common ubuntu aims on a developing continent.

One of the great stalwarts of the South African Black Consciousness Movement (BCM) was Mamphela Ramphele, who is now a prominent and renowned academic. Long before liberation happened she observed: "A serious and costly error of the BCM was its failure to recognize that not all black people are necessarily committed to liberation and that the poor are not inherently egalitarian." Stephan de Beer comments that "the assumption that all blacks are committed to the ideals of liberation and therefore to the kind of communal solidarity that will facilitate liberation is erroneous."[13]

For the past century, its inexperience manipulated by the sophisticated pressure of influence and investments from overseas, Africa has continued to be exploited, and many of its own leaders have succumbed to those "civilized" pressures. Western weapons appeared throughout the continent, and no one asked if the payment was in stolen gold and diamonds, drugs, or bribes handed in at the back door.

The 1963 Organization of African Unity Charter included the principle of noninterference with the internal affairs of other member states. After the ousting of Amin, Bokassa, and Nguema in 1979, this restriction was softened by the Banjul Charter in 1986, but the main change came with the transformation of the Organization of African Unity (OAU) into the African Union (AU). The essential political problem has embarrassed international circles for years, since the post–World War I attempt to establish a League of Nations and the post–World War II establishment of the United Nations Organization: How do you control the bad boys? Nkrumah's dictum "Seek ye first the political kingdom and all else will follow" proved inadequate. Colonial authoritarianism was so embodied in economic dependency and neo-colonialism that it was beyond the ability of political empowerment to overcome.

The challenge in Africa was how to relate the sovereignty of a liberated independent state with the concern of the continent when a state appears unwilling or unable to protect its citizens from unacceptable suffering. The situation becomes more complicated when the question of the viability of an alternative government is in question, or when the political or economic policies of members of the international community are involved.

◆ ◆ ◆

Life is threatened by the misuse of politics when governance emulates animals seeking prey, with rapid movement from multiparty states to one-party states to military rule. The body-mind-and-soul human communities evolved over millions of years to make these stupendous Earthlings, but rather than planning the success and wellness of humanity, civilized politics has promoted the antagonism and destruction of patches, manipulated by personal ambition.

Turmoil has been inflicted on Africa by colonial invasion and division, religious competition, the demands of international capital, lack of education, and Western influence, and this has demanded that Africa discover and apply a new vision and values. It has required a reassessment of Africa's needs, an African focus on the demands of life, and a change of priorities. Authoritarianism must give way to democratic decision making, as in the original ubuntu life of Africa, with the just redistribution of wealth on lands owned by all. These are the crucial matters for Africa that are provoking new thinking in Africa today.

Education was originally to make black Westerners, but we have decided that the priorities are different. The focus is on African priorities, on spiritual and communal health, on the research and practice of agriculture, justice, and community welfare rather than individualistic Western academic traditions. We rediscovered that manual labor is dignified and productive and vital and admired, not a subject of contempt. Refugees can be welcomed as victims of the liberation struggle to which we are committed, and it is strength not weakness when leaders happily step down at the end of their term.

Claire Robertson, who is no doubt familiar with the centuries of turmoil that occurred on other continents, has said: "It takes time to make one nation out of many cultures, languages, religions, classes, and interest groups, and sufficient leisure to develop it. For many, the struggle to survive allows neither time nor leisure for anything else."[14] The distribution of power on the basis of economic linkages, shared monetary systems, military treaties, and financial aid is based on the colonial inheritance, not the African tribal ubuntu community sense of nationhood. Party systems were Western inventions that appear to have much to commend them, but the issues are different. Concentrating on the major issues rather than competing for power to establish different systems led to one-party states in which the priorities were clear, the policies were similar, and the competition was about who would represent the people. Tanzania, Kenya, and Zimbabwe are examples of those who originally retained voting independence within a ruling party, but this often succumbed to the quest for power. Power became focused in the central committee of the party, not in parliament or government, and dictatorship lifted its head. Communal conflict was promoted as a consequence of manipulation by political demagogues in and out of government, who exploit real or imagined grievances or fears to mobilize supporters and gain political advantage. This marginalized the input of trade unions, universities, religions, the judiciary, and independent newspapers as in Ghana, Malawi, and Uganda. It often led to military takeovers because the military were the best organized. But they were not the best politicians or economists. The need of a vigorous civil society became clear, coup d'êtats were common, and another stage of civilian rule regained democracy in Upper Volta (Burkina Faso), Ghana, and Nigeria. Throughout those early years of liberated Africa, it was a continuing quest for personal power vs. people power, a tense experience to discover the way to go for Earthlings who had not been subject to civilization. What has failed is the attempt to make

Africa think and act like a Western satellite. It has been at the cost of much African suffering, and many feel lost, but we know another future lies ahead. Thank goodness.

5.7. *Seeking a New Political Vision*

The quest for a liberated united continent constantly grows. The present dispensations can be seen as a stage in political life moving toward the renaissance of the continent in an extended African family, despite all attempts by political, economic, and religious elites to lure us back into patches. Africa is seeking a new political era, a new way of doing politics rooted in its traditional Earthlingness rather than emulating the West and the separation of its patches.

The development of the African Union reveals the commitment of the African people to reestablish their Earthling experience and vision. Communities need motivating to produce the answers. Throughout these periods of political change and development three features have emerged. First, Africa is still deeply rooted in its original base of thousands of tribal families that were never well served by being reconstructed as fifty artificial countries designed by and for colonial rulers. Second is the widespread realization that only an African political unity, built from an ubuntu-driven democratic base, can serve the needs of Africa today, or the world, as it moves toward the evolution of Earthlings. Third, the influence of Western finance, politics, and religions is disastrous.

The South African "miracle" of 1994, providing a lesson in compromise and political maturity to the world, has retained an aura of uniqueness up to the present.

A comparison with ethnic cleansing in the Balkans, genocide in Rwanda and Congo, intractable politics in Ireland, and ongoing conflict and one-sided power in the Middle East over the past decade underline the achievement. Looking back, one sees that the relatively peaceful transition from apartheid to democracy was, in fact, not a miracle but the outcome of a long-focused proactive struggle over many decades, which came at a high cost with many casualties.[15]

As the world becomes increasingly international it is vital for those [Western] agents involved in negotiating the political and economic future of African nations to recognize that the culturally specific character of African social organization is not an artifact of the past, but a vital cultural resource that has the power to consolidate community identity and mobilize community action in modern Africa.[16]

Visions of a world government and a United Nations that could provide a structure for peace and prosperity have been proposed from time to time, from Jesus' proclamation of the Basileia to modern calls for political unity and ethical and moral understanding. Liberation from the suicidal commitment to our present political patches is the only way forward, and only such political leadership can embrace the economic and religious leadership required to enable Earthlings to save their planet.

Owen Sichone puts this consciousness in Africa in a wider focus that makes sense in the present situation of the world:

> The last two decades of the twentieth century were described as lost decades. . . . For African people in particular the lost decades were a reversal of the social gains won by the liberation struggles of the past. And the question must come to mind: Do the economic and social inequalities we now see all around us warrant a new social struggle for change? The answer must be "yes" because there are already numerous social movements across the globe involved in this struggle.[17]

The "wind of change" bringing the growth of African national consciousness, which Harold Macmillan recorded as a potent political reality in 1960, has been followed by a veritable tsunami demanding the consciousness of an Earthling political reality. That is a matter of the human spirit. It is our vision and values that need liberating to find our way forward in politics.

Afterword

A major item on the Agenda for Earthlings is a liberated global political landscape. The politics of patches offers no future for Earthlings but tension, disruption and disaster. Africa has learned that change does not come from conquest but from cooperation, but the world is swamped by politicians, economists, religions, and newspapers who need to be liberated. There is a new struggle for change.

Chapter 6

The Economic Matter

Synopsis

How to organize an economic system to provide for Earthlings is a major problem. Many think the needs of the poor must be met by building empires of wealth that will trickle down to all. On the other side is the testimony of primal people in Africa and elsewhere, of the prophets in all religions, and of intellectuals who sit with the poor that we need a new system, an ubuntu economy. What does that mean in terms of hunger, homes, hopes — and Western involvement?

6.1. Africa and the Earthling Economy

6.2. The Earthling Economy and the Prophets

6.3. The Colonial Economy

6.4. Socialism

6.5. Liberation from Economic Exploitation

6.6. The Collapse of Capitalist Empires

6.7. The Development Economy and Africa

Words of three South African prime ministers before liberation:

Paul Kruger on the discovery of gold: *Instead of rejoicing you would do better to weep: for this gold will cause our country to be soaked in blood.*

D. F. Malan: *The Negro does not need a home: he can sleep under a tree.*

C. R. Swart: *The white man cannot survive if the black man is allowed equality of opportunity.*

6.1. Africa and the Earthling Economy

One of the most ancient human rites in the world is still practiced a million times a day throughout Africa, and proclaims a profound theology. I recall some memorable occasions.

- going to visit a remote kraal when I lived and worked in the Transkei, people pouring out of the huts in welcome, one of the youngsters dashing out to the hens and the great burst of squawking as our lunch was secured and brought into the kitchen, the time of greeting and welcome and news, and then as we readied for the meal — this little ceremony.

- or another time at a Sunday braaivleis (barbeque) lunch with one of Nelson Mandela's cabinet ministers and his family, a Catholic whom I knew had been to Mass an hour or so before, and when the food came out — the little ceremony.

- or again, an evening here at home in the bush when the whole family came together to celebrate some birthdays, and as everyone stood with raised glasses and much calling and laughter to toast our health — the same small ceremony.

The ceremony is simply to spill a drop of drink on the ground, or cast down a scrap of food, as an acknowledgment offering to the spirits of the ancestors — a sort of grace, a thanksgiving, a grateful recognition of dependence and gratitude as Earthlings of the Earth. No one would call it a sacrament, but it carries a deep theological significance for our economic life. It is a different worldview that the whole world needs if it to save itself from self-destruction.

Africa sees very clearly that our livelihood and economy belong to the Earth, not to enslavement by wealthy elites, and this is an essential element of liberated belief. An ubuntu economic system promotes neither poverty nor wealth and recognizes that the love of money is indeed the root of much evil.[1] This understanding is rooted in the earliest Earthlings who subsisted on the fruit and products they took from the Earth or scavenged from the remains left by bigger beasts. It survived when they learned how to grow crops and domesticate animals, and, no longer having to move constantly to new hunting grounds, they developed villages and divided tasks between them. It was a shared endeavor, for an ubuntu economy is for all, from all, to all, based on exchanging goods and services to one another's benefit, and there were neither poor nor rich.

Then came civilization. In much of the world communal ownership gave way to private ownership, a wealthy class took precedence over a poorer class, competition ousted cooperation, Earthlings became oppressors or oppressed, bribery and corruption emerged. Africa's means of production and finance were taken over by the Western system, but this has not changed either the heart of Africa nor the core of ubuntu economics.

6.2. The Earthling Economy and the Prophets

As on so many subjects, the wise men of the East, Israelite prophets, Jesus, Muhammad, and primal believers worldwide, including in Africa, had another understanding.

Jesus told a most devout young man, highly obedient to the religious demands of the day, that his need was not to study the scriptures or say his prayers or support the synagogue but to dispose of his wealth and give to the poor. He made it very clear to Zaccheus that the key factor of justice and honesty was to turn around the system in which the rich were stealing from the poor. John the Baptist had a similar view: conversion to godly living was not focused on going to church but on "he who has two coats let him share with him who has none; and he who has food let him do likewise." Jesus did not choose the rich and comfortably well off elite to spread his message of liberation; rather he chose twelve poor workers and fishermen, having been brought up as the son of a carpenter himself. His response to hopes for eternal life did not spell out what people had to believe or give to religion: it was whether or not they were identified with the poor and needy. Jesus was quite clear that the approach to economics should be on the basis of our common humanity, giving to each in terms of their needs not according to their deserts.

The *zakat* tithe introduced by Muhammad "was not an act of charity but of religious devotion: benevolence and care for the poor were the first and most enduring virtues preached by Muhammad in Mecca. Piety lies "not in turning your face to East or West in prayer . . . but in distributing your wealth out of love for God to your needy kin: to the orphans, to the vagrants, and to the mendicants: it lies in freeing the slaves, in observing your devotions, and in giving alms to the poor" (Quran 2:177).

The key to Earthling spiritual success was not in holy books and prayer but in how you handled the economy. Duchrow states:

> The perspective of the common good fundamentally starts with the weakest, most threatened members of the community. If they can live, all can live. Justice and life are the basic perspectives and golden thread of biblical traditions. There is no neutral place for knowledge, ethics, and action, along the lines of "neutral" scholarship. In every situation people are faced with the decision whether to adopt the stance of the status quo, or a critical constructive position of liberation.[2]

6.3. The Colonial Economy

All the prophets reject as un-Earthling constructs the economic systems that structure the wealth of the world into the hands of the few. This ensures that one person or group exploits another person or group, that there be an unfair and unjust distribution of social wealth, and that the great majority are poor and remain poor.

The primal beliefs expressed in the African approach of ubuntu — the communal ownership of land and the common fruit of the Earth, the ruling power of unity, compassion and cooperation, are entirely in harmony and deeply aligned with the prophets. It is a worldview that will work, opposed to the Western worldview, which keeps people poor. The communist dictum of "from each according to his ability, to each according to his need" is similarly rooted in both the primal and prophetic understanding of the only way that Earthling economic communities can operate with success. The Ecumenical Association of Third World Theologians meeting in 1985 saw this very clearly:

> The present economic system, like an immense idol, the beast of the Apocalypse (Rev. 13), covers the Earth with its cloak of unemployment and homelessness, hunger and nakedness, desolation and death. It destroys other ways of life and styles of work which counter its own. It breeds pollution and hostility to nature. It imposes an alien culture on peoples it has conquered. In its infinite greed for wealth it sacrifices persons,

mostly of the Third World, but increasingly of the First, as a bloody holocaust to itself. The beast has become a raging monster armed to the teeth with tanks and cannons, nuclear bombs, warships with computerized missiles and satellites, bringing humanity to the brink of total and instantaneous death. But in the struggles of the poor and oppressed throughout the world against all forces of dehumanization there is a sign of life and victory. There is faith and confidence in the God of life.[3]

It was this consciousness of the experience of both poor and rich that prompted Bishop Manas Buthelezi to comment at the Fifth Assembly of the WCC at Nairobi in 1975: "There was apartheid and discrimination in the Church long before it was introduced in the rest of society as a deliberate government policy. . . . Can poor people really belong to the same Church with those who have made them poor?"

The economic challenges that confronted the people in Africa as they sought liberation were in many ways new and strange to Africa, raising basic questions that all Earthlings face about the form of a liberation economy. Was it to be a form of top-down capitalism? Some thought they could clean up and "Africanize" capitalism, removing racism, imposing a benign and beneficent rule in the hands of blacks and dependent mainly on aid, loans, and the assumption of white positions, as they sought in Kenya and Ghana. Was it to be a form of Afro-Marxism? Liberation began to happen before the end of the Cold War and some countries like Ethiopia, Mozambique, and Angola saw their future in Marxist terms. It showed promise, but faltered with the end of the Communist bloc and the Cold War. Or would it be through a new bottom-up socialism that could emerge only with the pace of African liberation? This was Nyerere's vision of a modernized version of what became known as "African socialism." Tanzanian Ujamaa would not be imposed from the top but rise from the commitment and reorganization of the people from the bottom. But could that occur without an investment of capital that was locked up in the West?

Each of these systems found that their hopeful expectations stumbled over the sheer scale of poverty and underdevelopment, economic dependency on others, a lack of skills and education, ethnic and class rivalry, weak and inexperienced democratic and economic institutions, a failure of vision and values, the Western control of the world's wealth, and above all, the world's failure to attend to what ubuntu meant in a modern economy.

The adapted colonial economic agenda was designed and enforced by the rich to increase their riches, saying it would trickle down to the poor, but the trickle down was only to the very few whom they had coopted. Greed so legitimized oppression that it became clear that the real problem of humanity was not poverty but wealth. Wealth brought to civilized people bribery, corruption, crime, and suffering beyond anything endured by the uncivilized precolonial people of Africa, who still believed in an "uncivilized" economy designed to serve all the people, not an economy designed to make profits for some. They discovered that Africa — like the world — needed not only independence from oppressors, but interdependence of the oppressed.

6.4. Socialism

Although civilization had in many respects rejected the spiritual and collective concerns of humanity and concentrated on the secular and individual, it could not destroy the basic ubuntu nature of Earthlings. Like having two legs and big brains, that's the way we are. This has continued to assert its reality throughout history, noticeable examples appearing in Britain long before the British Empire sought to enfold Africa in its colonial grip. It had prompted much of the conflict in the struggles between the Catholic and Protestant churches focused on Henry VIII and Elizabeth I and the later English Civil War with Oliver Cromwell. It was clearly seen in the emergence of the Levellers in the sixteenth and seventeenth centuries, who were the forbears of socialism. They campaigned for universal suffrage (even though limited to males), and they sought a sharing of wealth and power, free education for all, and public welfare. They brought into focus the conflict between property rights and human rights, which is still a major factor in modern Africa.

Once there was political freedom to address the needs of the ordinary people, there was widespread agreement throughout the continent that some form of socialism was the answer. Very few in Africa imagined that capitalism could liberate the human community, but the socialism they explored was not the product of Marxist insights or European politics either: it arose directly from an African understanding of society. This shines out clearly from the vision of the prophets of those years.

During his 1962 journeys Nelson Mandela passed through Dar es Salaam and was invited home by the newly independent country's first president, Julius Nyerere. "It was not at all grand, and I recall that he drove himself in a simple car, a little Austin. This impressed me, for it suggested he was a man of the people. Class, Nyerere always insisted, was alien to Africa: socialism indigenous."[4] Nyerere believed that "socialism — like democracy — is an attitude of mind. In a socialist society it is the socialist attitude of mind, not the rigid adherence to a standard political pattern, which is needed to ensure that the people care for each other's welfare."

The basic difference between a socialist society and a capitalist society does not lie in their methods of producing wealth, but in the way that wealth is distributed.

Our first step, therefore, must be to re-educate ourselves; to regain our former attitude of mind. In our traditional African society we were individuals within a community. We took care of the community and the community took care of us. . . . And in rejecting the capitalist attitude of mind which colonialism brought into Africa, we must reject also the capitalist methods which go with it.

One of these is the individual ownership of land. To us in Africa, land was always recognized as belonging to the community. Each individual within our society had a right to the use of land because otherwise he could not earn his living, and one cannot have the right to life without also having the right to some means to maintain life. But the African's right to land was simply the right to use it; he had no other right to it, nor did it occur to him to try and claim one.

The foundation, and the objective, of African Socialism is the extended family. He . . . regards all men as his brethren — as members of his ever extending family. *Ujamaa*, then, or "family hood," describes our Socialism. . . . We, in Africa, have no more need of being "converted" to socialism than we have of being "taught" democracy. Both are rooted in our own past — in the traditional society which produced us.[5]

For Tom Mboya of Kenya:

When I talk of "African Socialism" I refer to those proved codes of conduct in the African societies which have, over the ages, conferred dignity on our people, and afforded them security regardless of their station in life. I refer to that universal charity which characterizes our societies, and I refer to the African's thought processes, and cosmological ideas which regard man not as a social means, but as an end and entity in society.... When I think of African Socialism I also have in mind those ideals and attitudes of mind in our tradition which have regulated the conduct of our people with the social weal as the objective.... These ideals and attitudes are indigenous, and they spring from the basic experience of people in Africa and Kenya....[6]

Kwame Nkrumah of Ghana asserted that socialism

is the only pattern that can within the shortest possible time bring the good life to the people. For socialism assumes the public ownership of the means of production — the land and its resources — and the use of these means for production that will bring benefit to the people.... If this new economic and industrial policy is to succeed, there must be a change of outlook in those who are responsible for running our affairs. They must acquire a socialist perspective and a socialist drive keyed to the socialist needs and demands.[7]

George Padmore, a fascinating character, formerly Malcolm Ivan Meredith, was born in Trinidad in 1903. He lived in London and Moscow before his extensive sojourn in Ghana, where he wrote:

The revolution taking place in Africa is threefold. First, there is the struggle for national independence. The second is the social revolution, which follows the achievement of independence and self-determination. And third, Africans are seeking some form of regional unity as the forerunner of the United States of Africa. However, until the first is achieved, the energies of the people cannot be mobilized for the attainment of the second and third stages, which are even more difficult than the first. For it means the total elimination of the economic and social heritage of colonialism, such as bribery and corruption, ignorance, poverty, disease, and the construction of a society in consonance with the aspirations of the people for a welfare state with their well-being at heart. The socialist objective means the scientific planning of production and distribution, through the common ownership of the means of production and service, so that ultimately all people regardless of race, color or creed or social origin will be able to enjoy exactly what they want to fulfill their needs.[8]

Centuries of theological, political, and economic thought and experience in Europe had led to the emergence and growth of various forms of socialist theorizing and anticipation as the way ahead for humanity, and in Africa this was part and parcel of a wider consideration. Writing in 1964 the editors of *African Socialism* had a clear understanding of what Africa was saying at that stage. "The form of consciousness which has emerged with enormous significance (albeit with little organizational power for the moment) has been that of *African-ness*. If there is little consciousness of being a Ghanaian, a Togolese, or a Nyasalander, Africans are nonetheless conscious of being African, and it is this sentiment that political leaders have sought to mobilize."[9] They saw political freedom as providing the liberty to chart the way to total liberation including economic independence and fulfillment, but it did not happen that way for one simple reason: capital.

There was little disagreement about what ought to happen (and could have happened in theory). Africa had plenty of land and resources and people to develop from prehistory to a modern educated and productive state in a century, as the United States and Australia had done. The original root of Africa's wealth was its agricultural potential, which could be developed to provide support for the vast move to the urban centers, where an industrialized population could turn Africa's mineral and manufacturing potential into the full experience of a people enjoying economic and cultural liberation. But it needed money for machines, equipment, training, buildings, and transport through cash, credit, or investment, and Africa did not have money. To buy modern agricultural equipment and material and train people to use them and grow and sell and profit from what millions of others need means *capital*. Factories can make the million requirements of a modern liberated civilization and equip people with education and jobs to make them and use them to bring great profit to all: but it needs *capital*. To provide transport which people will pay to use while they move about needs *capital*. Politics can lead to huge developments and transform the lives of millions: but *politics costs*. Education is an essential aspect of socialism. The heartbeat of it, like love, requires no learning, but the development of socialism transforms every aspect of life and demands a growing knowledge and expertise in schools and colleges and training establishments, but they need *capital*.

> There were a number of exciting experiments undertaken by African politicians, such as Julius Nyerere in Tanzania. However, these became bogged down in the quagmire of inadequate funding, increasing dependency on foreign aid and domination of the industrialization process by the local subsidiaries of transnational corporations.[10]

Socialism can liberate serfs and transform a country from the Middle Ages to a modern state within a generation: but socialism needs *capital*. And those who possessed the capital of the world had no intention of using it in Africa. Some might use it for white farmers or white-owned factories but not for blacks. They would use it to take the profits back to Europe or America but not to develop African people. Economically and socially it was possible, but the racism of the white West made it politically and theologically impossible.

The money Africa needed to develop the continent was held in Western hands in Western banks, and the Western capitalist patches still saw anything African as heathen, dangerous, and risky. In addition, Western financiers became the greatest bribers of the modern world. Much has been said about the rapacity of African leaders accused of taking bribes, corruption, fraud, and deceit, especially since the emergence of political independence. Nothing is said about the real initiatives of iniquity in the consistent Western activity to bribe and twist the African leadership to do the Westerners' will, so that oppression after liberation became greater than ever: highly respectable, "the way civilization works." Not only were the outside boundaries of African countries decided by the West at the Berlin Conference of 1885, but the internal architecture of the economy has been designed by the West ever since.

It carried all before it, and within a century, with the collapse of the Cold War, the new global order was supreme, the United States the only superpower, and capitalism the only successful model of development to set before the Third World. Except that many

Africans knew in their depths that the Western way was not the answer.

6.5. Liberation from Economic Exploitation

The deep inner meaning of the liberation struggle is now seen by many as freedom from the acceptance of economic exploitation that has seeped into the warp and weft of society, so that instead of the economy being a wedding garment it becomes a shroud. Dr. Molefe Tsele, when secretary of the SACC, wrote that: "Our faith should compel us to witness God's will for a better world and the possibility of a better economic system than one founded on the acceptance of the finality of human greed, natural competition, and the drive for more and more profit."[11]

We need a movement to promote the moral use of possessions, where the root problems of poverty are correctly defined as the problems of riches and religion. Colonial development was focused on the interests of the banks, trade, shipping, mining companies, and white settlers and the demand for markets for Western manufactured goods. But since political liberation occurred Africa has seen little of economic liberation. After centuries of civilization and decades of liberation we are still ruled by economic systems that make most people poor; the media, the banks, and politics give little attention to the impoverished and are ruled by the wealthy; the focus of commitment is to satisfy personal greed, not community need; and the comfortable say with the utmost sincerity: "But that is how it is! You can't change human nature!"

The elite economic classes just *rule:* they do not have conferences to give their reasons or justify their actions, nor do they conscientize their followers. They carry everything before them by domination, doing in matters of money and possessions what religious leaders do in terms of religion. They are quite blind to any other course of action and feel no need to justify themselves. Some African leaders have been carried away and bought into this right-wing economic ruling power, which is the total opposite of ubuntu culture. They fail to see they cannot justify their acceptance of inhuman, self-centered attitudes. Traditional African societies have run on community values since long before civilization was invented and know that positive personal values can thrive only in societies bent on positive community values.

Thabo Mbeki, when asked to steer an ANC socialist ship on a globalized Western capitalist ocean, told the Mandela Foundation in 2006:

> The capitalist class to whom everything has a cash value, has never considered that moral incentives are very dependable. ... Within the context of the development of capitalism in our country individual acquisition of material wealth, produced through the oppression and exploitation of the black majority, became the defining social value in the organization of white society. Because the white minority was the dominant social force in our country, it entrenched in our society as a whole, including among the oppressed, the deep seated understanding that personal wealth constituted the only true measure of individual and social success. The new order, born of victory in 1994, inherited a well-entrenched value system that placed individual acquisition of wealth at the very center of our society as a whole ... get rich! Get rich! Get rich![12]

Since liberation came to Africa, the oppressive global economic empire has continued to grow and has been dominated by those who own and control the wealth of the world, and by government workers who are frequently incompetent, inexperienced, or victims of corruption. At the heart of inequality, poverty, and underdevelopment is the continued ownership and control of the economy by a small unelected and unaccountable elite. Addressing Africa's social deficit means transforming the balance of forces on the market, transforming ownership patterns, and thoroughgoing structural transformation of our economy, but it is not done by revolution. The quest for riches, the fear of confronting the powerful, and the clever ruthlessness of Western oppressors and their acolytes have defeated any attempt to bring real liberation to Africa and the world.

6.6. The Collapse of Capitalist Empires

Empires collapse. "They puff themselves up in their power alone, and when the bubble is full blown, and everybody supposes them to have won, God pricks the bubble, and it is all over," said Martin Luther. Because morality is the basis of successful humanity, immoral systems and practices will not work for Earthlings. They produce oppression and then collapse, which is happening to capitalism now. The British Empire, Cold War, and apartheid were not overthrown by enemies: they were false and collapsed from within. History demonstrates that oppressive systems do not survive.

Earth is currently discovering that a global economy based on profits for a few lurches from crisis to crisis and is not sustainable. Africa must seek to establish an ubuntu economy that will continue when the market economy collapses. Ulrich Duchrow has traveled widely and reports an increasing worldwide confirmation of the African experience of the inadequacy of the empire controlling the world's capital and the necessity of an alternative answer. He says that resistance is flaring up among many people. "They all come up against the same causes: an economic system geared purely to profit maximization and thereby having no regard for the life of human beings and nature."[13] "Globalization has the sole goal of liberating the accumulation of capital from all social and ecological barriers. The result is the total market, which is in the process not just of destroying life on earth, but with it its own foundations."

From the East there has been similar confirmation. Bishan Singh seeks "an economic culture in which our economic lives become a part of our ethical and spiritual practice... which in our present context is a profoundly revolutionary act."[14] "Communities all over the world are struggling to restore ethics to their economic practice, to become critically aware and socially responsible for the way in which they may organize, use, consume, and manage their resources. They are advancing the practice of voluntary simplicity, creating livelihoods for the unemployed, adopting alternative ways of producing and distributing goods and services to reduce resource use, recycling waste into reusable resources, undertaking sustainable agricultural practices, and providing credit for the poor."

The crucial question is not how to enable the present system to survive, because its days, like feudalism and the preindustrial age, are evidently over. But how do we prepare for the emergence of alternatives? Former South African president Kgalema Motlanthe put his finger on the answer when he said: "If we are to change our economic and social relations... we also need to fundamentally transform the values which they have relied upon to survive."[15] These are the vision and values of the postreligious development revolution, which Martin Prozesky calls "the values of global flourishing."[16]

6.7. *The Development Economy and Africa*

Today's debate on the liberation of people from poverty into prosperity goes beyond the conflicts of recent centuries between the dictatorial owners of capital (who claimed to be religious but often were not) and the working-class socialists (who were driven by a spiritual acumen their words often denied). The debate today is focusing on a hard-nosed and comprehensive agenda of development economics that demands that the economy be liberated from the domination of oppressive financial institutions concerned only for their own profit. The vision of the prophets, both theological and political, has to be translated by the skills of economists into an ongoing program. Only such a liberation struggle against economic oppression by the owners of capital can enable Earthlings to follow the vision of the prophets, and the roots of Africa. "The love of money is the root of evil." An ubuntu economic system is not dominated by the love of money; it sees beyond both poverty and wealth. It also requires a deep review of the role of government and the role of religion.

S. de Gruchy, seeking the role of the religious community in the quest for a developmental economic system in Africa, says that, "We lack a coherent vision of development that will enable us to talk with and walk alongside African civil society as it seeks to engage in transforming the worlds in which we live."[17]

Africa has problems in heaps. It currently does not produce, and must import, vehicles, machinery, pharmaceuticals, fertilizers, electronic equipment, and much else from ships to jumbo jets. It pays by export of primary commodities — agriculture and minerals — but the West has pushed prices down so that debts soar. When the Cold War ended, international attention and investment focused on "rebuilding" the Soviet empire, and now focuses on the rise of China, India, and Brazil. The blind age of globalization has made people aware that converting land use from food production to cash crop production leaves local people hungry. Pouring government funds into failed, inefficient capitalist enterprises increases the victims of collapse and does nothing to birth a new economy. The potential market of the world's poor is breathtaking, but short-term Western industrial control and the failure of government planning drastically limits it. Can Africa bring any of its vision and values to point the way forward in economics, where the real challenge is not how to find profits for our industries and agriculture, but how to find jobs for all our workers, whose subsequent spending power is the only way forward?

In his address to the Chris Hani Institute on January 28, 2009, Jeremy Cronin emphasized that the key indicators of progress are not arbitrary figures of growth, but decent work and sustainable livelihoods, which "will require the marshalling of our resources around a state-led industrial policy that prioritizes the transformation of our productive economy." It begins by "breaking the suffocating grip of private monopoly cartels in the mineral, energy, finance, chemical, and agro-processing sectors in order to ensure a more balanced development of small and medium enterprises with a capacity to create jobs." He identifies four areas requiring systematic transformation to ensure sustainable transformation — heathcare, education, rural development, and community safety — as integral components of a developmental path to systematic transformation.

This pulls the economic emphasis back to basic elements of being Earthlings in the modern world, and Africa knows that this means recovering the essential factors of ubuntu. Sara Berry has written that "the very complexity and ongoing struggle for power and privilege and their importance for the pursuit of economic resources, means that sustained development will come about only if Africans play a leading role in transforming their own economies."[18] That is certainly true, but it appears to mean that Africans must learn how to transform their economies to fit in with the priorities of the Western world. There is an increasing awareness, not only in Africa, that the self-centered capitalism of Western society is the main reason for the approaching extinction of human community on Earth. We need different economic systems altogether.

Afterword

The economic worldview of the West, trying so desperately to take over Africa, is based on making profits. Repeated failures demonstrate that this approach does not work. Africa knows that the only profitable path is an economy based on shared, compassionate, cooperative, collective democracy. The alternative is extinction.

Chapter 7

The Media Matter

Synopsis

The ability to share information and inspiration by writing and reading led to profound developments beyond the oral era, which had both losses and gains. Africa recognizes the media as a major tool of liberating culture, but also of oppression and subjugation. Some in the West find this difficult to understand, but the liberation of the media and of culture is a crucial matter for us all.

7.1. History

7.2. The Influence of the Media

7.3. The Seduction of Sincerity

7.4. The Liberated Media Agenda

7.1. History

Africa has an interesting connection with the media. Hieroglyphics were invented by Africans in Egypt about five thousand years ago. The Kushitic civilization had a form of writing five centuries before Jesus, and Ethiopia developed its own, but writing and reading as we know them today developed later in the Earthling story. The apparent reason is ecological.

Students of architecture have noted that people who lived in climates that were frequently cold, wet, and dark were forced to build shelter from the weather for much of the year. Buildings had walls; walls could be drawn on in the long winter months; drawings could carry meaning; and this led to the invention of writing. Even the worst weather in most of Africa was not bad enough for long enough for people to need permanent buildings with walls, so most early African culture was oral, or in dance.

The ability to influence others has always been a key factor of progress and power. From Moses and Aaron, the prophets of Israel, Hinduism, and China, the Pharisees and Jesus, the letters of Paul and Caesar, kings and rulers, preachers, popes, and denominational reformations — all depended on news and views dispensed by voice or paper. As civilizations and writing developed and institutions were formed, many people adhered more to written forms than to the lived reality of spiritual experience. People need information, and inspiration.

♦ ♦ ♦

There is more to the mediation of culture than saying your ABCs — whether you use a South Efrican, Amurican, or fratefully Bretish accent! Expressing vision and values in words, putting faith, hope, and love into sentences, can be restrictive. The media can be good or bad: they can present truth or twist it to promote false understanding and action; they can liberate or oppress; counsel peace or war; inform, instruct, and heal, or stir up antagonism; deepen division or promote transformation to unity. Africa is poised between oral theology and written theology. Oral tradition is usually given a back seat, as if it were only an elementary step on the way to the proper exposition of meaning in printing, which would present "the gospel truth." Writing takes precedence.

In earlier days in Africa when agreements were made between colonial settlers and the nonwriting local inhabitants, these were written down as treaties signed by the Europeans, to which the African chief signified agreement by making a cross, or touching the pen, as a sort of sacrament, the written word carrying more weight than the spoken word. But there was and still can be a major difference between "a piece of paper" and what is "written on a person's heart." "Accepting" something does not necessarily mean "experiencing" something, just as "believing" a theology does not mean "living" a theology.

Oral tradition and oral theology carry a deeper and wider experience from one person to another than written words can describe or convey, and it is the meaning, the experience of a culture that has to be mediated, not a form of words. Oral tradition, whether of custom, law, or theology, carries with it the living experience of those who express it. The words may vary, the methods may vary from speech to song to dance to chant to response and interchange between speaker and hearers, but the heart of it is mediated from one to the other.

Traditions confined to written words can easily become something to be learned instead of lived: a statement, constitution, or code of conduct, rather than a way of life. And this is why the media can so easily be misled and misleading. The media can distort truth, propound lies, and divert attention to emotional factors that have no value for the emancipation of Earthlings. They can serve the oppressors instead of the people and can undermine or destroy democracy, especially when its owners, directors, and staff are assembled with this intent. There can be no doubt at all that much of the media in Africa, as in the West and East, does in fact serve the interests of oppressive political, economic, and religious institutions.

But the struggle to liberate society from oppression is strongly present in the media too, and it is this that requires our strongest support. All the early struggles for liberation in Africa used small local newssheets or newspapers, which were limited in size but of major influence. Then came modern printing, radio, television, cell phones, and e-mail, which enlarged the influence and changed the focus. The African media today are dominated by Western interests. The ownership and control of much African media are held by those seeking to sell the products and politics dictated by the West. The oppressive input infiltrates so many areas of life that the media have been called the opium of the people.

Communications were designed to facilitate colonial rule and economics, not to serve Africa. Roads and railways were built to connect mines, minerals, and agricultural and political centers to the ports linked to the West. From Morocco communications ran around the bulge of West Africa, not through it, around the Cape, not through it, up the coast to Somalia and Egypt, touching at ports but not going through Africa. Until the age of air travel there were few viable cross-country routes, so people traveled hundreds of miles to the coast and went by sea. (Even today you can drive easily from Halifax to Vancouver or Chile, or from Marseilles to Moscow or Korea, or from London to Tibet or Singapore, but driving from Cairo to Cape Town or Dar-es-Salaam to Dakar will give you problems.)

When communications developed and the mass media arrived, they frequently emphasized Western ways rather than the interests of Africa.

7.2. The Influence of the Media

Liberated Africans attempting to retain or recover their status as Earthlings have learned to be especially careful of the media. For all its protestations of its quest for truth, much of the modern media throughout the world has become dependent on financial and political directors who represent oppressive forces. Many readers do not trust the media. In many cases stories are not properly investigated, and the media have no hesitation in presenting a false point of view to steer opinion in the way their leaders desire. Censorship is rife for political or commercial reasons. Western influence is exerted throughout the media to convince Africa that Islam is the big danger to peaceful progress, and only a major U.S. military presence can protect the continent. Many journalists have descended into cynicism or subjugation because they have had to choose between telling the truth and losing their job or writing what they're told to write and keeping their job. The need to liberate ourselves from submission to the media's ability to tell us what to think and do applies to those both inside and outside Africa.

"The image of Africa is distorted in the western mind by the concentration of the mass media on coups and conflict. There is such an emphasis on reporting coups and outrage that the whole presentation becomes a lie," wrote Elliott Kendall,[1] and the position has become immeasurably worse since liberation. When the West gave up making profits by controlling colonial political oppression and diverted its attention to making money by colonial economic oppression, the media became a major weapon.

At a University of the Witwatersrand workshop in 2008, a journalist asked: "Why was not a single financial journalist anywhere in the world able to predict that . . . the current economic crisis . . . was going to happen? The reason is that they severely compromised themselves by becoming too involved with the industry they were reporting on. . . . We need to have a democratization of the media. It should not be in the hands of a few oligarchs as it is now."[2]

Al Gore has written:

Now that the conglomerates can dominate the expressions of opinion that flood the minds of the citizenry and selectively choose the ideas that are amplified so loudly as to drown out others that, whatever their validity, do not have wealthy patrons, the result is a de facto coup d'état overthrowing the rule of reason. Greed and wealth now allocate power in our society, and that power is used to further increase and concentrate wealth and power in the hands of the few.[3]

Many believe it to be true that the media of Africa are controlled not by the quest for truth, information, and a truly liberated humanity, but by those who wish to sell their policies or their products. We are in urgent need of liberation.

Joerg Rieger suggests that a major objective of the media is to undermine our understanding. "There is no word here about the temptations presented by the advertising industry which incites the consumer spirit in order to explore new and greater markets."[4] This has an even wider connotation in Africa, and there is no doubt that the guilt lies largely with those who flood the continent with cheap TV films from the United States. The minds of the people of Africa — especially the young people, of all races — are filled with images of powerful American or European people who never have to work, who live in palatial mansions with every modern gadget, who drive expensive cars and wield expensive guns without any concern for law or order, whose motivation is possession, who kill at will, who indulge in constant sexual affairs, and in whom there is not the slightest sign of the depth of happiness that comes from the ways of the prophets or the spirit of ubuntu. Releasing such media is doing more to undermine the liberation of the people of Africa than all the evil dreamed up by political potentates or military dictators.

7.3. *The Seduction of Sincerity*

A matter of great concern brought to a head in the media industry is the question of sincerity. In the Genesis myth of Adam and Eve, taught to Jewish, Christian, and Muslim children for centuries, much blame is heaped upon the serpent for beguiling Eve, and upon Eve for beguiling Adam, but they were quite sincere about it. "The woman saw that the tree was good to eat and pleasing to the eye, and it was desirable for the knowledge it could give" (Gen. 2:6).

She truly believed she was doing a good thing, but the lesson of the myth is exactly the opposite, and it is a simple fact that sincerity is not enough to prove that a proposition or an action is right and good. They can be absolutely sure that a certain course is correct, willing and ready to die for it as innumerable people have done, totally sincere and totally wrong.

Sincerity is a most seductive sentiment. To claim "we meant well" is no excuse because sincerity is not enough. People are often sincerely wrong. The South African premier Malan's belief that natives did not need as much income as whites because they did not have such a high standard of living, and that housing was not really a problem because they could sleep under a tree, was as sincere as Marie Antoinette's famous response to the complaint that the people did not have bread: Let them eat cake. Those people operated on a level that was very sincere and very wrong.

Matthew tells a tragic tale of the seduction of sincerity when Pilate washed his hands as a sign of his rejection of responsibility for the execution of Jesus (Matt. 27:15–31). Pilate sincerely believes that Jesus is guiltless of any crime; he sincerely believes his wife's plea for clemency; he sincerely believes the Jews supporting their priests will riot if he does not sanction the execution. The Jewish priests sincerely believe that Jesus had blasphemously claimed to be the Son of God and the King of the Jews (though he had done neither) and sought his death for stirring up the people against authority. Both Pilate and priests sincerely believed their way was the best for their society. So they crucified him.

Sincerity is not enough. This is painfully clear in the history of Africa, where countless people have given their lives for false beliefs and inhuman motives. Time and again we commit wrong actions because we adhere to false beliefs "with all our hearts."

Africans of all colors are as susceptible as any human beings to greed, selfishness, pride, and manipulation by the powerful pressures of tempters to believe they are right, when they have actually been seduced by sincerity.

7.4. *The Liberated Media Agenda*

Earthlings of the twenty-first century face untold riches of cultural development and resources as the means of communication have flourished. On the one hand the means of communication enable people from every culture in the world to share their insights and experience, and on the other they are a major challenge to ensure the liberating value of the cultures we spread.

What is the task of print and screen in a liberating ubuntu culture, where electronics have usurped the pens of Mark and Paul and the angels? There is a great media future in the transformation of humanity. Compassion, cooperation, and commitment will sell newspapers and television programs because people cherish these values. The media can be highly informative about values and methods to challenge evil and liberate community, but their paymasters demand a commercial, antihuman emphasis. This is the challenge of the spiritual revolution.

"True Christian presence . . . needs comprehensive and sustained participation in the political community. The church needs to participate in the full process: setting the agenda, making the rules, and critically examining the outcomes," writes Russel Botman.[5] So where are the theologians in the media? Does being religious remove our responsibility? Where are the interfaith media instilling a new vision and dispensation? Where is the postcolonial vision with the verve and values to lead the continent to maturity? Who will put together interfaith theological consultations on the role of the media in rebuilding humanity? Where are the small, alternative, independent media that chart the way? The liberation of the media is a vital matter for Africa today. We must counteract the Western influence on so many facets of life and rediscover the basic African approach to humanity. The initiatives are not coming from the big boys at the top, but from small independent movements keeping up the pressure.

The essential work of all the prophets was proclamation. From the early prophets of the East, through the great teachers of the Middle East, and on to Jesus and Muhammad, they had a message to be mediated to the people. How do we do that today?

Afterword

A major difference between the twentieth-century struggle to liberate Africa and the twenty-first-century struggle to liberate the Earth is the communications revolution. You do not need a newspaper or a TV station or an army or a fortune to do what you can do with your e-mail or your cell phone. The action can start at your finger tips.

Chapter 8

The Spiritual Matter

Synopsis

Africa has everyday experience of the wide range of human spirituality summed up in the word "ubuntu," which is the key to the life and progress of Earthlings. The unhappy witness of human religions prompts Africans to pursue the search for a spiritual evolution that is desperately needed by both West and East. We must move beyond our inherited religious institutions to a secular spiritual revolution.

PRERELIGIOUS SECULAR SPIRITUALITY

8.1. Traditional Beliefs

8.2. Primal African Spirituality

8.3. The Vital Life Force

8.4. *Ubuntu*

8.5. The Prophets

RELIGIOUS INSTITUTIONS

8.6. Christianity in Africa

8.7. The Missionary Era

8.8. Colonialism in Africa

8.9. African Indigenous Churches

8.10. Ecumenism

8.11. The Interfaith Era

8.12. Fundamentalism

8.13. Have Religious Institutions Failed Earthlings?

8.14. So Where Are We Going?

Religion was one of the motivating forces in everything that we did. . . . Religion will have a crucial role inspiring humanity to meet the many enormous challenges we face.
—Nelson Mandela to the World Parliament of Religions in Cape Town 1999[1]

PRERELIGIOUS SECULAR SPIRITUALITY

8.1. Traditional Beliefs

Professor Jakobus Krüger of the University of South Africa, who is a quiet and not particularly demonstrative man, describes a day when he suddenly found himself overwhelmed by a deep consciousness of the human spirit. He writes:

> I was studying some exquisite Bushman engravings in the Upper Karoo. There they were, strange animals like phantasmagoria on large black dolomite boulders strewn over a brown koppie (a small hill) in a vast, flat, hot, barren, forbidding landscape. This had obviously been a "place," in the full, religious sense of the word, for its inhabitants or for those who sought physical or spiritual refuge upon its bare slopes; not merely a locality, but a source and center of meaning and power. Standing there in the hot sun I could not resist the urge to go down on all fours and press my forehead to the dry soil in an act of homage and communion with those who had frequented that place and been driven out. It was a deeply humbling and at the same time an illuminating experience to stand in a seemingly empty landscape and realize that in fact it is filled with a human presence thousands of years old. They were here, and in a sense still are. I was standing on "holy" ground.

He felt caught up in an experience permeating "the long perspective of evolutionary time, in the context of the emergence of humanity as a species." His quest became a pilgrimage. Jakobus was recognizing and "establishing solidarity" with the spiritual awareness of Earthlings in Africa from before time was invented. We "cannot live except in this sort of sacred space."[2]

Diarmuid O'Murchu knows the same awareness:

The ancient Spirit-world remains largely incomprehensible to the crude rationalism that governs a great deal of contemporary research.... Long before formal religion evolved, about five thousand years ago, our ancestors danced and drummed, chanted and meditated, prayed and ritualized — all in tribute to the divine life force they intuitively knew to be loving yet awesome, near yet all-encompassing, benign and at times inexplicably capricious. When it comes to spirituality, our graced ancestors could embrace paradox to a degree largely unknown in the congealed religious world of our time.[3]

When liberated African Earthlings consider religious institutions today they seek to do so without the unwritten political and economic small print of the West. They seek the message of Jesus or Muhammad without the necessity to support the empires of Constantine, Queen Victoria, Paul Kruger, the United States, or Muslim regimes. Their beliefs are not beholden to the necessity of supporting the finances of overseas-based religious institutions. Such African spirituality is liberated from many of the constraints placed upon those in the West or East who use religion to support their political or economic conflicts, and sees the spiritual matter of Earthlings from a different perspective.

Many modern people have been so indoctrinated by the sweep of material progress that they degrade the spiritual progress through which Earthlings have found life for centuries. Songs of love and joy, dances of exuberance and processions of grief have been around for thousands of years and mean more to our spirits than many modern wonders. Our ability to send a few people to the moon is on a lower level than the wonder of millions who have enjoyed its beauty as "Slowly, silently now the moon / Walks the night in her silver shoon" (Walter de la Mare). The ability to make bicycles and internal combustion engines gropes millennia behind our ability to experience the ways of faith, courage, or compassion. We have wandered from wonder, spurning the things that make Earthlings powerful and forgetting we have been spiritual creatures for a long, long time.

The traditional religious orientations in Africa were coextensive with their societies. Like all religious systems they were taken up in processes of change and will certainly not remain unaffected by the shock of modernity. Yet among the religions of the world, African religion retains a unique position and makes a unique contribution.[4]

Africa knows that spirituality is not "otherworldly." Spirituality is an experience of secular Earthlings.

8.2. *Primal African Spirituality*

We noted earlier that the Western explorers who came here five hundred years ago found no signs of spiritual life because they were seeking the wrong things in the wrong places. Many of us still do the same. In his study "Concepts of God in Africa," John S. Mbiti of the WCC examines the beliefs of nearly three hundred African tribes. It is fascinating that although many tribes had little contact with one another in earlier periods, they all held to the existence of a Supreme Being and believed that God was One — although a few, like some world religions, believed there were lesser spiritual beings also, good and bad. Some thought the God they did not know was too high above them to be addressed directly, so they approached him through their ancestors whom they did know.

African children in a thousand tribes are fascinated by the myths of creation that abound and come in great variety. God makes humans from clay, brings them out of a hole in the ground, or from reeds, or a marshy place, or God lowers man and woman from the sky, or from a cloud.

A fascinating factor in all these creation stories — including those in the book of Genesis, which Jews, Christians, and Muslims revere — is that they are secular myths, not religious myths. They are about human people doing human things, not priests doing religious things. The foundations of spiritual beliefs are laid in the material world. The supernatural is a facet of the natural. This was a feature of all primal religion, and "because traditional religions permeate all the departments of life there is no formal distinction between the sacred and the secular, between the religious and the non-religious, between the spiritual and the material areas of life. Wherever the African is, there is his religion," wrote John Mbiti.[5]

When South Africa's 1996 Constitution says we are "united in our diversity," it is referring to the depths of life in which all humanity is rooted, based on our primal cultures where "religious alignments are regarded by all in the group as indispensable to social harmony and satisfactory adaptation to their immediate environment. Religion is an integral part of life itself."[6]

The spiritual awareness of African traditional religion is ecumenical in essence. It is not based on doctrines and creeds and catechisms that people have to be taught, but on the human experience of spiritual reality in the world around them. "Religion among Africans is not treated as an isolated entity," says Professor Joseph Lesiba Teffo. "Traditional African life and practice is characterized by the motif of wholeness. In traditional African religion there is no separate community of religious people because everyone who participates in the life of the community automatically participates also in its religion. There is no separate day of worship because the whole rhythm of daily life is a continuous liturgy that permeates such commonplace things as eating, drinking, ploughing, and working. As Archbishop Desmond Tutu so aptly puts it: 'The African worldview rejects popular dichotomies between the sacred and the secular, the material and the spiritual. All life is religious, all life is sacred, all life is of a piece.'"[7] An important insight that Africa has to offer to the West is spelled out by David L. Mosoma: "In the African world, the distinction between religion and politics did not exist. The African world-view emphasized the wholeness of life. For this reason, religion and life belonged together."[8] "It is an example of a worldly religion with a secular spirituality," concludes his colleague C. W. Du Toit.[9]

This is related to the fact that humanity originated in Africa, for as Diarmuid O'Murchu writes in his study *Ancestral Grace:* "Most of the great discoveries related to early humans come out of Africa, particularly the countries along the eastern seaboard. Africa is our birthplace as the human species. It is our primordial home, the place where we struck deep roots and laid the foundations for the evolutionary trajectory that has brought us to where we are today."[10]

8.3. *The Vital Life Force*

When the French colonized much of West Africa the perspicacious discovered that the Africans there had exactly the same sense of a spiritual driving force within human (Earthling) society as others in Africa, which all the prophets had recognized. They called this *la force vitale,* and the response to it, through many different languages, was ubuntu.

Whether they come from the ancient seers of Northern India, the Middle East, the plains of America, or Africa, the wise and perceptive among all primal peoples recognize there is a spiritual energy in human beings quite distinct from their physical and mental equipment. According to Mbiti:

> Religion is part and parcel of this African heritage which goes back many thousands of years.... Through the ages religion has been for Africans the normal way of looking at the world and experiencing life itself. For that reason it is found wherever people are. It is integrated so much into different areas of life that most African languages do not have a word for religion as such.... African religion functions more on a communal than an individual basis. Its beliefs are held by the community; therefore it does not matter much whether or not the individual accepts all these beliefs.... African religion is an essential part of the way of life of such people. Its influence covers all of life.[11]

Barney Pityana recognized it in the legacy of Steve Biko, which "infused blacks with a spiritual fiber, a mettle and a fighting spirit. It is the inner soul-force seen to be invincible."[12]

The experience was shared by many different sorts of people. Nelson Mandela writes:

> My father remained aloof from Christianity and instead reserved his own faith for the great spirit of the Xhosas, Qamata, the God of his fathers. My father was an unofficial priest and presided over ritual slaughtering of goats and calves and officiated at local traditional rites concerning planting, harvest, birth, marriage, initiation ceremonies and funerals. He did not need to be ordained, for the traditional religion of the Xhosas is characterized by a cosmic wholeness, so that there is little distinction between the sacred and the secular, between the natural and the supernatural.[13]

Another facet of the traditional African approach to spirituality was strongly related to the fact that it was not part of a political or economic quest to establish an empire. A. A. Mazrui writes:

> Indigenous African culture is religiously tolerant, partly because African traditional religions are not universalist in

ambition. Yoruba religion doesn't seek to make the entire human race belong to Yoruba religion. Kikuyu religion, Ganda religion and Zulu religion don't seek to convert the human race, so they are not universalist in commitment and conversion. They are not evangelical or competitive. They therefore have a built-in toleration of other religions.[14]

Many people brought up under the evangelistic pressures exerted by inherited Western religions and the agnostic pressures of modern commercialization tend to write off this concept of vital force in the human community as an immature, uncivilized African concept from a bygone prescientific era. Albert Einstein would not agree with them. The great scientist wrote:

A knowledge of the existence of something we cannot penetrate, of the manifestation of the profoundest reason and most radiant beauty, which are only accessible to our reason in their most elementary forms — it is this knowledge and this emotion that constitute the truly religious attitude: and in this sense, and in this alone, I am a deeply religious man.

8.4. Ubuntu

This sense of the spiritual in the life of the human community, independent of any institutional religious connotation, lies behind the African attitude to one another and the concept of community basic to Earthlings, which is caught in numerous African expressions related to the word *ubuntu*. Desmond Tutu admits that: "Ubuntu is very difficult to render into a Western language. It speaks of the very essence of being human. When we want to give high praise to someone we say, 'Yu. u nobuntu.' Hey, he or she has ubuntu."[15]

Pobee studied the subject of "blessedness" in the Akan people of Ghana. The notion proves insight into an African understanding of human relationships.

Among the Akan the key term is *ahoto*, which literally means rest and peace of the self. It means well-being, which speaks of rest, peace, and contentment both within oneself and in harmony with the world outside oneself.... The Akan understanding of well-being or blessedness is very complex, at once material and spiritual, internal and external, human and non-human, individual as well as communitarian. The highest good is what is best for the happiness of the individual and the community.... The biblical message that "blessed are the poor" cannot be experienced as good news until this traditional African understanding of blessedness is engaged.... Blessedness is enjoyed as a community or by a person in community. Here we reach the heart of the African self-understanding.... Interaction, inter-dependence, and bearing one another's burdens become the marks of this sense of community. The sense of community demands recognition by word and deed of one another as persons.[16]

This experience of "ubuntu" is a major reason why Africa matters, because it has been largely neglected or lost in the civilized West.[17] It preserves the original sense of community, of wholeness, the primal trait of Earthlings that civilization threw away, but the spiritual capital of which they can recover with a bonus of gladness and relief. It is the depths of communal fulfillment in life, bursting into song together whether at a funeral or a marriage, dancing to the altar in church or dancing at a political rally, to welcome a president, or to support a strike.

Ubuntu is not only African: it is a human attribute, a warming, embracing reality of being Earthlings together that civilizations rejected with their emphasis on competing with their neighbors instead of cooperating with them. Many who may be called saints or prophets in the West are simply expressing their basic human wholeness: ubuntu. Jesus and Muhammad were ubuntu people. We have been so pressured to be successful individuals that we have forgotten how to be successful communities. The elite of the civilized world taught their people to forget ubuntu, but Africans, as a people, did not.

African individuals were no different from other humans, but they had a wider concept and handled life differently, conscious of their wholeness, not merely their separateness. Africans can be as selfish and cruel as anyone else and can follow the same negative, self-centered, antihuman path as Idi Amin or Robert Mugabe. But deep within the human nature of all of us lies this vital community awareness that all Earthlings so badly need to recover.

It is the world's communal persona that has so much to learn from the primal people of the world, especially Africans, but it is human, of Earthlings, not only African. Many Western individuals already enjoy a well-developed social consciousness: it is part of our heritage as Earthlings, and there is nothing to stop everyone from delighting in and spreading ubuntu.

◆ ◆ ◆

At the height of the apartheid era in the 1970s, when the national government was determined to enforce separate development on every aspect of society including the church, the annual Methodist Conference was held in West Street Church in Durban. The president that year was Alex Boraine, who led the Youth Department, so the Youth Rally had special prominence. The church was packed, including hundreds of boys from Kearsney College (white) and girls from Inanda High School (black), all in their school uniforms, sitting on either side of the central aisle, all very proper. The service began normally enough with hymns and prayers, guitars and drums taking the place of the organ, and Ernest Baartman preached.

The finale was a ballet. To soft music from the group, the dancers ran down the aisles without warning, and made two circles, hand in hand, gyrating on either side at the front of the church, one black group and one white. Then one of the girls broke from her circle, and though the others tried to hold her back she began to dance on her own. It was a riveting performance as she mimed discovering herself, her hands fluttering over her hair, her face, her body, and then the pulpit, the communion table, and the cross. Suddenly, she saw the black group, and began to dance around them. Now the same thing happened to one of the boys in that group: he began to dance on his own and tried to break out of the group, but others held him back.

By now the whole congregation knew what was happening and were singing along with the music. The boy broke free, and after some hesitation, the two began to dance together in what seemed like a magnificent denouement of apartheid — but no. They realized that their original groups were still dancing on either side of the church in their separate racial circles. So the two went to their groups, still dancing, and one by one pulled them out, until the front of the church was filled with dancing, singing, laughing, joyful people enacting ubuntu together. Again, it seemed like the end, but was not.

I never knew if what happened next was part of the original script or the enthusiastic response of the dancers to the enthusiastic response of the singing and clapping congregation. Still singing and dancing, the dancers burst down into the aisles, and began to touch people on either side. Within seconds the huge congregation was on its feet, moving into the aisles, white and black together, old and young together, singing and dancing too. That was where they sang the last hymn and the blessing was given. Singing and dancing again they poured out into the street, lined with security police from the Special Branch, who still had twenty years to go. But the SBs were to go, not ubuntu.

◆ ◆ ◆

One way of appreciating ubuntu is by its opposite. Throughout the years of colonial oppression in Africa, thousands of people were detained in prisons, and many were kept in solitary confinement for long periods. The grill clanged shut, the outer wooden door banged shut, the keys clanged in the locks, and that was it: no one else was there; no one knew where you were, alive or dead; there was no one to talk to, no one to hear; the light was never switched off; there was no bell; a plate of food was pushed under the door by the warder's boot; the outside was cleared of others for thirty minutes once a day for you to take a shower and empty your shit bucket, and then another twenty-four hours: that was "solitary." There was nothing to read, but when it happened to me, I found an old sheet of newspaper on a shelf, the adverts page, and read it many times. My friend Horst Kleinschmidt has reflected that more than anything solitary proved what the absence of community means. You cannot talk, touch, hear, or interact with other people, and you gradually break down. To have no possibility of contact with others destroys your own humanity: it has sent many people mad. That is the opposite of ubuntu.

Yet that is what our modern Western society does to people. Handling everything only from an individual point of view means we lose the skills of Earthlings, build fences around our patches, and peep through holes to watch others building fences around their patches. Potted entertainment destroys the enjoyment of entertaining one another. We have been bought into a system where instead of enjoying doing our ubuntu thing together, we pay others to do it for us. In the 1960s the kids made music on their own guitars and sang and danced to it: but now we sit and watch others do it for us on DVDs, isolate the sick from those who care for them, seclude the aged and infirm, watch on TV as others play games, visit game reserves, and theater, instead of doing it together ourselves. Many brought up in the West have not realized the limitations imposed upon them by their individualistic self-centered lives, or how much their suppressed Earthling nature pines for the joy and shared-ness of ubuntu.

It is not a matter of education or wealth, for the poorest and least educated can live by ubuntu; it is not a question of being religious, for people can be extremely religious and not show the spirit of ubuntu, and others can be bursting with ubuntu and have no religious pretensions at all. It is a matter of attitude and approach, of being in relationship with people.

This is why many people have found major wars so enjoyable. Parts were terrible — the wounds and deaths, the bombings and slaughter, the breakup of families, the shortages and restrictions — but for most people, most of the time, there was a daily fulfillment of ubuntu, the togetherness, a doing things together from shopping and queuing, entertaining in your home, regular work with jointly occupied others, friendships with the neighbors, and such dancing and games and entertaining one another at parties even in an air raid shelter: it was the togetherness that mattered!

Ubuntu provides an interesting understanding of religious worship. Worship together provides great ubuntu experiences for Earthlings, which people find deeply satisfying and enjoyable: throwing their voices into the harmonies, performing the familiar rituals together, standing and sitting, kneeling and handholding, sharing the food, the cadence of voices following the rituals together, happy for your place in the group, your group in the congregation. The experience of ubuntu is very hands on and real and natural and fulfilling and does good to people!

But the words! The content of sermons and prayers and homilies in so much religion is tragic and terrible. Unintelligible language in juvenile theologies from modern cultures which have never been allowed to grow up. The prayers and hymns whose tunes are great but whose meaning is too obscure to fathom. The sermons in artificial voices on artificial themes. Much of the language of our liturgies, including the Creeds, is such that no ordinary person can understand them and the theologians still argue about the Creeds as they have for hundreds of years.

So people flock to fundamentalist Pentecostal churches or African Independent Churches, where at least the music makes sense. But again — the words! The prayers and sermons that bring Good News only to the indoctrinated in-group and say nothing to the people of the Earth!

So people leave the fundamentalist churches and AICs also and become agnostics because the shared joy and friendship and ubuntu experience of twenty-first-century Earthlings does not find expression in the thoughts and words of those still preaching and praying in the seventeenth century.

Ubuntu is not dependent upon religion: it is the other way around. Ubuntu signifies the natural approach to life, an attitude that runs through all primal society. Ubuntu, like the teaching of Jesus and most of the prophets, is focused on this world, not the next. Spirituality is a highly secular concern, a social attitude affecting the whole of living. Ubuntu is wholistic, not dualistic. Is does not understand or experience life divided into separate pieces like sacred or secular, human or divine, physical or spiritual, faith or politics, personal or social, my religion or your religion. It sees these as complementary, not competitive. Ubuntu is not merely personal and individualistic but communalistic, a social spirituality.

When you go into a room full of people in Africa you do not simply nod and say "Hi!" — you go around and greet each one. Human relations are a shared and corporate event. One practice always surprises visitors to a meeting where an African speaker has "delivered the goods," or a group has been welcomed. In the applause that follows, the speaker and everyone else joins in. It is a sharing. humbling, enriching experience for everyone.

The Methodist church at Tsomo in the Transkei was established among the Fingo people over a century ago, when for the first time people in that district were becoming Christians. In the church safe I found some carefully preserved pages torn from an old notebook which was the first Register of Baptisms, used long before the modern printed versions were produced with columns for the names of child, mother, and father. In those early pioneering days, baptism was a family matter. The records were lists of whole families being baptized together, father and mother, girls and boys, a sharing ubuntu occasion, a decidedly secular event with a deeply spiritual connotation.

8.5. The Prophets

The tourist agenda of the modern world is full of religions. Rome means the Vatican and St. Peter's; London says St. Paul's and Westminster Abbey; Paris spells medieval cathedrals; New York and Toronto feature modern cathedrals and synagogues; Geneva the World Council of Churches; Istanbul the great mosque of Hagia Sophia; Jerusalem the Wailing Wall, the Church of the Holy Sepulchre and Dome of the Rock; and so it goes throughout the world. Africa is also stuffed full of religious memorabilia from the pyramids of Egypt to the mosque at Jenne in Mali, and the great ruins of Zimbabwe.

But none of the great institutions behind these tourist attractions began as a religion. No one ever sat down and said: "Let's have a religion about souls and heaven." None of the inspiration behind the religions was initiated by priests or rabbis or imams. They were all started by prophets, laypeople with very secular jobs involved in the very secular world, who became concerned for the spirit of Earthlings as farmers and tradesmen, camel drivers and fishermen, scholars and statesmen, artisans and secretaries. Such were the prophets who led the Earthlings in the things of the spirit.

RELIGIOUS INSTITUTIONS

8.6. Christianity in Africa

Against the wall in the entrance foyer of the Howard Library at the University of the Witwatersrand in Johannesburg stands a high cross made of blocks of stone held together by ancient iron bands. The corroded state of the iron shows that the cross must have been buried for many years, and it was. In 1938, reading the records of the explorer Bartholomeu Dias, who rounded the Cape five hundred years before, Eric Axelson wondered what had happened to the cross that Dias brought from Portugal and planted on the dunes at Kwaai-hoek, by the Bushman's River in the Eastern Cape, to claim the new country for Christ. After some explorations with his students, they found it, and thus it came to Johannesburg.

When the explorers, traders, and colonialists arrived they saw no signs of religion as they understood it in European terms of churches and priests, Bibles and hymns — which gave rise to a twin approach to missionary work. Some saw it as a corollary of establishing a colonial presence to embrace every aspect of life — politics, economics, education, medical provision, and religion — all part of a remotivated commercial purpose.

Others, affected strongly by the rise of enlightenment and missionary concern that arose in the postslavery era, saw missionary work in terms of uplifting the locals from paganism, bringing light into darkness, and saving souls. Many colonials neither saw nor bothered about the difference: they came for the profit. The Dutch who arrived in Cape Town in the seventeenth century to escape persecution in Europe did not come to evangelize. Isolated attempts by Portuguese Catholics from 1488, Moravians in Ghana from 1737, and the Society for the Propagation of the Gospel, were all defeated by disease. Moravians and Lutherans began their work in the south at Genadendal and Namibia, and eventually the trickle of interest became a flood.

Christian religions poured into Africa, carried by utterly dedicated people, bringing with them colonial concepts of theology and religion, economics and politics: Portuguese (1488); Dutch (1652); Muslims (1658, 1694, 1780); Reformed (1665); French (1688); Catholics (1688, 1804); Germans (1737); Lutherans (1779); British (1795, 1806, 1820); Anglicans (1806); Methodists (1806); Congregationalists (1806); Presbyterians (1813); Jews (1834); Hindus (1860); Pentecostals (1908, 1914). Religion in Africa varied. It produced both oppression and liberation, justified many of the worst features of colonialism, supported slavery, and invented apartheid. But religion also played an important part in the liberation of slaves, the establishment of schools and hospitals, and, belatedly, the liberation struggle against apartheid. The church was divided.

Many modern people now recognize that the Christ-ianity exported to Africa and the rest of the world was far from the Way of Jesus. This had been usurped at an early stage by the requirements of the Roman Empire and for centuries became the tool of subjugation to the political and economic empires of Europe. The hijacking process has continued into our own age, so that Charles Villa-Vicencio writes of the church being "trapped in the dominant structures of oppression, controlled by an entrenched bureaucracy, conditioned by a history of compromise and impoverished by an inability to break out of the iron cage of history."[18] Christianity in Africa was, and still is, a site of struggle.

8.7. *The Missionary Era*

The call of the Christian gospel to "go into all the world and make disciples of the nations" (Matt. 28:19–20) had always been followed by the church to some extent, but the response in the eighteenth century, especially in Africa, introduced an unprecedented movement, an extraordinary two centuries of birth, life, and then euthanasia. It originated in three factors. First, the Evangelical Revival, often associated with John and Charles Wesley in the UK and the United States, produced a generation of people convinced that God promised eternal life to those who accepted Christ as their Lord and Savior and sought a life of love and compassion on Earth. The promise came with a warm personal assurance that called them from the cold formalities of the churches of England and Rome, constrained to share salvation with all the world. Second, the Evangelicals were also reacting to the horrors and guilt of the slave trade, anxious to set right the appalling suffering and death unleashed upon the "heathen world" and were being publicized by the abolitionists and their new media methods. Third, in the same period shipping exploded: ships, navigation, world trade, and political exploration suddenly made it feasible to reach the unreachable world, and colonialism burst into being.

These three factors were the springboard of the missionary movement. One result of the emancipation of slaves in the United States and the UK had been the establishment of Sierra Leone as a country for returned slaves on the West Coast of Africa, a process that the Clapham Sect in London also promoted at the height of the campaign against slavery. The Baptists (1795), Methodists (1796), London Missionary Society (1797), and Church Missionary Society (1800) all found their feet in Africa through Sierra Leone. By the middle of the nineteenth century, they had spread throughout the continent, as thousands of people in Europe and North America felt called to mission work.

There was a deliberate separation between church work and missionary work. The established churches of the Western world had followed the colonists to every part of the continent, but their concern was to minister to the settlers and the members of the established churches, not to convert the indigenous people. From its inception missionary workers realized the necessity of education and healing, making schools, hospitals, and medical work a major concern of their societies, and all missions sought improvements in agriculture. David Livingstone's famous appeal to the universities of Britain (1857) to join the movement to "spread Christianity and commerce" to Africa was entirely within the mind-set of the times, both for philanthropic and colonial reasons. Enabling African people to develop and enjoy their full human capacity and the positive benefits of civilization was felt to be the right thing to do — and also essential if the colonies were to be made more profitable.

There were links between church and mission, but for many years there was little functional contact between churches among whites and missionaries among blacks. The rapid growth of missionary societies was sometimes attributed to their freedom from ecclesiastical control and the employment of laity. The 1888 World Missionary Conference in London was attended by 1600 people from 139 missionary societies worldwide. But both funds raised and staff recruited for the missionary work were largely from Europe and North America. The clergy and leadership were white imports, and the other workers mainly black until well into the twentieth century. They still are in many U.S.-based fundamentalist churches.

Whites in both church and mission found it difficult to focus faith in a different cultural or political environment and to think in different terms than "West is best." Elliott Kendall writes that Westernism was not only the problem of imported churches: but "The missionaries failed to appreciate a culture other than their own and used their position of strength as spiritual leaders to impose a destructive and restrictive attitude toward local community life and culture.... So much that was African had to be discarded as the new European religion thrust its rigid concepts on a people who were at that time at a disadvantage" — including names, dress, song, dancing, customs, and culture.[19]

But Africa was reaching another stage. The demand for a role in economic and political affairs was paralleled in the ecclesiastical field but took an unexpected turn. As the church, education, and experience grew, Africans not only developed the skills and positions to run the colonial churches themselves, but brought their own experience of being Earthlings into the equation. There was no justification for excluding them from leadership positions in church or mission, but there was no way for such African thinking and expertise to emerge until Africans had liberated themselves from Western domination. A few churches had made a start by ordaining black clergy, which made the challenge of religious liberation even more obvious: but they knew they must stand on their own feet.

The notion that a moratorium be declared on importing missionary activity from the West still startles many today. It was set out in 1971 by Rev. John Gatu of Kenya, at the Mission Festival in Milwaukee. It was necessary because

> we in the Third World must liberate ourselves from the bondage of western dependency by refusing anything that renders impotent the development of our spiritual resources, which in turn make it impossible for the Church in the Third World to engage in the mission of God in their own areas. . . . The gospel will then have a deeper and more far reaching effect than our mission Christianity has provided so far.

He pointed out the negative connections between Christianity and the commercial exploitation of Africa inherent in Livingstone's comment at Cambridge, and he criticized the Western notion that income and acquisition had become a measure of position and prestige. "It is certainly not a New Testament idea, but an emanation of the thinking of the industrial society that can see value only in terms of money and statistics. . . . We cannot build the Church in Africa on alms given by overseas churches." He calls for the total liberation of the people by the Holy Spirit "not an extension of our personal, denominational, and historical connections. Let mission be the mission of God to the world, not of the West to the Third World."

The role of the church in Africa had been a major question at the formation of the first All Africa Conference of Churches (AACC) at Kampala in 1963, and the moratorium issue came strongly to the fore at AACC 3 in Lusaka in 1974, which set out the challenge both for and by African Christians:

> We must accept the challenges of the real meaning of salvation in Africa today, in the light of our own religious heritage which sees the whole of life as religious without the classical division between sacred and secular. We may then see the task of evangelism as the total witness in word and deed to whole persons and communities, leading to liberation and fullness of life. We have therefore to examine critically what we really preach. Do our sermons have any message and concern for the unemployed youth, people facing natural disaster, those fighting wars of liberation, tribalism, racism, or those in the growing refugee population?

Their search for identity was inspired by their sense of dignity in their ancestral past. "The God who visited the world in human form through Jesus Christ was the same God who revealed Himself to our forefathers."

But both churches and missions were dependent on funds raised and clergy recruited overseas, and they listed their progress by the number of churches opened and the number of converts made, a typical "market" report that many saw as a monstrous impertinence. You could count hospital beds, or school classrooms, but you couldn't measure spiritual progress by a head count. There was a growing awareness that Christianity in Africa was in the throes of forward movements that the West had never imagined.

8.8. Colonialism in Africa

All colonial Christianity developed on apartheid lines of separate development. Not only did the different religious institutions divide people between Christian, Muslim, Hindu, Jew, and African traditional, but Christian institutions at national and denominational level used the name of Jesus to divide people instead of following the Way of Jesus to unite them. In direct rejection of their founders and prophets, they focused on building huge national and international organizations bowing to the will of an elite, not local communities of disciples. The children of Abraham — Christians,

Jews, and Muslims — have been great oppressors for many centuries and, sometimes, liberators. This had several negative effects among African people, but the most serious was the insistence on emphasizing individual sin, personal salvation, and heaven rather than communal sin and the liberation of Earthlings.

According to Dwight Hopkins:

> The problem with the black churches was that they had uncritically swallowed the racist doctrines of the white Christian missionaries...and by directing the attention of black Christians to...petty sins white theology prevented them from comprehending a larger perspective on sin, i.e., a system of evil, a structural matrix in which whites lorded themselves above the black majority....They gave support to apartheid, instead of witnessing and struggling against it."[20]

Steve Biko saw the different dimension very clearly: "It is a sin to allow oneself to be oppressed."

◆ ◆ ◆

When I came into the ministry in mid-twentieth century, colonial religion still ruled — and for many it still does. True religion meant Christ-ianity of the denominational form in which we were brought up: those attached to Islam and Hinduism were pagans; those who followed African beliefs and customs were ignorant heathens; and they all had to be converted to our brand of Christ-ianity. Those who supported these colonial views were quite sincere about it, having been indoctrinated from childhood, and any other approach was not even considered feasible. Liberation from this attitude came mainly from African Christians who had been reborn through the awareness of black consciousness in the various liberation movements. Rediscovering humanity through the positive assertion of the aspect used to deny it — their blackness — led to a reassessment of much of the politics, economics, and culture they had learned from the West, and also of Western religion.

Many Africans who had genuinely become Christians or Muslims were well aware of the positive and socially nourishing effects of traditional beliefs and practices, especially in the sphere of the veneration of their ancestors. They did not worship them but, like people worldwide, they missed them and welcomed an institutionalized way to cherish their memory. Many believed that "upon death, the knowledge and experience that a person accumulates in life are taken with the deceased's spiritual essence into the less visible realms where the forces of the universe and other spirits exercise their powers over the living. Many Africans believe they can communicate with their ancestors and through respect and appropriate offerings have some influence in the less visible world."[21]

This concept of communicating with ancestors was totally rejected by the early missionaries of Christian churches, who suppressed what they considered to be pagan superstitious practices, but this began to change in the twentieth century, says Archbishop Buti Tlhagale. "There was a growing acceptance that African cultures embodied values of family, life, community, authority, moral norms, and ritual practices aimed at restoring peace, reconciliation, and well-being. An entirely new approach came into being." The archbishop goes on to suggest that this applies to both African Christians and African Muslims, and underlines a point he made in an earlier paper: "Humanity has a common origin that predates the diversity of faiths."

Precise statistics of the millions in Africa are not possible, but while approximately two-thirds of African people are Christian and a third are Muslim, a huge number in both these groups continue to give credence to African traditional beliefs as well. In a general but quite crucial contribution, this concerns the focus that African tradition places on the community rather than the (un-Jesus) modern Christ-ian emphasis on the individual and the church. In specific particular ways, tradition contributes much through African thinking on such questions as healing, polygamy, the role of women, and good neighborliness.

> African culture, like Islam and Christianity, gives Africans an identity. African culture therefore looms large as a solid basis for dialogue. African culture is the common gift both African Muslims and African Christians bring to both Islam and Christianity respectively. We ignore at our own peril the challenge of such a dialogue.[22]

8.9. *African Indigenous Churches*

One of the most significant events in Africa was the emergence of the African Indigenous or Independent Churches (AIC) among people who wished to become Christian but not Western, and to stand on their own feet without being treated as ignorant underlings by the imported white missionaries. Among of the first leaders of this movement were Rev. Nehemiah Tile, who founded the Thembu National Church, and Rev. Mangena Mokone and James Dwane, who became deeply involved in the Ethiopian movement. Today there are thousands of independent churches that flourish in every township and village. Like all religious bodies they have been seriously corrupted by oppressive forces from time to time, but they have within them unique possibilities of liberation. There is a sense of joy and overcoming in African people that runs counter to much that dominates the West, especially the influence of a media seeking to promote Western values. Africans demonstrate the ability of human beings to triumph over adversity. Elliott Kendall saw it as a major input from Africa to humanity: "Africans generally have discovered something which the world has failed to find: how to be happy in the midst of distress. In the long search for human happiness they have much to contribute."[23]

During the first year of President Thabo Mbeki's presidency in 1999 he met leaders and members of the African Independent Churches at a great gathering held in the arena at Ellis Park, Johannesburg. Thousands attended, dressed in their best for the occasion — sometimes an ancient best, which made it very clear that the AICs often represent the poorest sections of the community in desperate need of jobs, houses, education, healing, and advancement. There was much singing, earnest praying, sparkling preaching, and an earnest address from the president of which I remember not a word. My lasting memory is that after the last "Amen," when everyone expected to climb aboard the buses to go home, the whole congregation, led by the party on the platform, leapt to their feet, grabbed the hands of their neighbors, and began to sing and dance in whirling exuberant circles, with Thabo Mbeki singing and laughing with the rest, dancing from group to group in celebration of merely being alive together in a promising Earthling experience of liberation and ubuntu.

In the 1970s Adrian Hastings could say: "The authenticity of African Christianity today is found in a synthesis impatient with any setting up of barriers between the old and new, or between different Christian churches."[24] The synthesis is much further along in many places today.

8.10. Ecumenism

Ecumenism — the attempt to recognize and implement the world-wide nature of the church — was in part a reaction to the recognition that the church had totally failed humanity in both the First and Second World Wars. If the church was to be relevant it would have to solve its internal problems of denominationalism, linked to nationalism, and present a wider united approach to the problems of the world. This led to the establishment of the World Council of Churches in Amsterdam in 1948 and similar moves in many nations.

The challenges in Africa were complicated because many churches still depended upon Western churches for direction, leadership, and funding; because tensions still existed between the churches and the missionary societies, which still ran the mission churches as separate bodies; and because most of the white leadership had little grasp of the actual belief and behavior of African believers.

The first Assembly of the All Africa Conference of Churches (AACC) meeting in Kampala in 1963 declared:

> The tragedy of our situation is that...Christianity is still a foreign religion to us....Christian freedom demands a great deal of tolerance toward, and even a sympathetic listening to, those Africans who, while accepting the Christ, find it difficult to accept also the Western concepts of Roman-Greek origin which wrap Him up as He is handed over to us.
>
> By a miscarriage of purpose the Church has succeeded in preaching to and teaching Africans about a strange God whom they have somehow come to identify as the God of the white man. But what has happened to the God as known to their forefathers — the God who is the foundation of their traditional beliefs? He remains still with them. And so we have left them with two Gods in their hands, and thus made them people of ambivalent spiritual lives.[25]

That was 1963.

But ten years after the AACC first met, Malcolm J. McVie could write: "The God of African traditional religion and Christianity is in fact the same. God who revealed himself fully in Jesus Christ is none other than the one who has continually made himself known in African religious experience."[26]

Although some Christians and clergy in Africa became more colonial than the colonials and more conservative than many in the United States or Europe, there has been a growing awareness of spiritual truth among African people. Many have doubted the inherited notions of belief from both North and South, whether expressed in evangelical or agnostic terms, and there is a developing consciousness of a real and relevant component of Earthling spiritual life. There was a realization in the ecumenical movement — similar to the political democratic movement — that real change in Africa would not come through ecclesiastical or political pronouncements from outside or on high, but through mass mobilization and action of people on the ground. Beyers Naudé saw this too: "The true power of change and renewal always emanates from the grassroots, from the rank and file of the thousands and millions of those whose names never become known, whose commitments to justice and peace are never sung in praises, but without whose support and action no meaningful change ever takes place."[27] That quest for spiritual maturity in Africa kept on growing — as Earthlings would expect — not only deeper and deeper but wider and wider.

8.11. The Interfaith Era

Many of the world's religions now have followers on the African continent. Christ-ians are widespread, mainly as a result of colonialism and the missionary movement. Islam came first to the north of Africa by conquest, then to sub-Saharan Africa by traders, and to South Africa by the relocation of prisoners and slaves from Indonesia during the Dutch rule. Hindus came to Eastern Africa to trade, and to South Africa during the British era after 1806, which brought indentured labor from India to Natal to produce sugar cane when Zulu tribesmen resisted redeployment as farm laborers. Jews came from Europe to trade, to escape political persecution on racial grounds, or to take part in the spread of business.

For over a century people from different faith backgrounds throughout the world had been seeking to understand one another. This came to a head at a conference to establish a World Parliament of Religions in Chicago in 1893, as part of the celebrations of the arrival of Columbus five hundred years before.[28] During the twentieth century the African quest for liberation from colonialism and the struggle to overthrow apartheid became a nonracial, interfaith concern, endorsed by many people of all religious groups.

The Anti-Apartheid Movement (AAM), based in the UK, was a matter of common concern, and in March 1984 the United Nations sponsored a Colloquium in London to consider the matter. Archbishop Trevor Huddleston, whose early ministry had been in Johannesburg and was by then retired, took the chair. The Colloquium stated: "We met together from different religions of the world to respond from the viewpoint of faith to the fact of apartheid. We were united in concern at the suffering it causes South Africans and the affront it presents to the moral conscience of humanity."[29]

The delegation from South Africa included Hindu, Christian, and Muslim believers, led by Gerrie Lubbe, who upon returning home formed a South African chapter of the World Conference on Religion and Peace (WCRP-SA). For about a decade they formed a strong part of the liberation movement and were instrumental in ensuring there was an interfaith awareness in the new South Africa, which clearly figured in the new constitution. But the blunt fact is that while the concept of an interfaith Africa is on the agenda of Africa, America, and Europe, the establishment of an interfaith movement has stumbled, mainly through the continued colonial attitudes of the religious institutions committed to their patches. It is a matter of major concern, for if religions cannot work together, what good are they for Earthlings today?

8.12. Fundamentalism

Another major development of the past century in Africa has been the emergence and growth of the "fundamentalist" religions, which have been strongly promoted as U.S. policy during the Reagan and Bush presidencies. Consultations and publications have promoted the notion that the freedom-loving Western democracies promise peace and prosperity to Africa and are opposed by Islamic terrorism, from which the United States will come and save us. This arrant nonsense has been fed by the Western media for decades, but the truth is quite different. In hard fact, the three great world religions of Judaism, Christianity, and Islam are each infested by powerful right-wing groups all claiming to have the whole truth, each wanting power for themselves, and it is these factions that are threatening peace. The real struggle to liberate Earthlings is not between these religions, but within them. "What is taking place now in the Muslim world is an internal conflict between Muslims, not an external battle between Islam and the West," writes Reza Aslan in a comment that applies to all religions.[30]

Johan Cilliers writes: "Although Africans will probably always have this sense of belonging it remains an open question whether contemporary worship services are not straining under external influences such as globalization and Americanization, up to the point where the sense of community is fragmented by a spirit of individualism, consumerism, and privatization."[31]

The globalization of capitalist dictatorship presently contaminating Africa exhibits a commitment to violence, not compassion, to domination not cooperation, and has no vision but its own material gain. This barbarian empire, led in recent years by the United States, threatens the survival of Earthlings.

The violent warring history of Christ-ianity, totally opposed to the Way of its Founder, began with its fatal adoption as the official religion of the Roman Empire in the fourth century. Its subservience to political and economic objectives, the Crusades, the wars over the rise of Protestantism and national states in Europe, the pursuit of slavery and colonialism, its endorsement of the elite, and its reluctance to accept the insights of the Enlightenment all undermined the original concept of the people of the Way of Jesus.

From this faulty imperialist background, Christian fundamentalism emerged with the publication in the United States between 1910 and 1915 of twelve pamphlets entitled "The Fundamentals." Fundamentalists emphasized a literal interpretation of the Bible and engaged in major controversies with the proponents of higher criticism over theories of evolution and democracy. They pursued ecstatic forms of evangelicalism, witness, prophecy, superstition, and life after death, and later gained major support by funding through television. Right-wing fundamentalists in America, Europe, and Africa, with strong support from capitalist financiers, have moved into what many call Christo-fascism. They assert that the conflict between Christ-ian and Muslim indicates that Armageddon is near, the United States is God's instrument for Christ to come again and destroy its terrorist enemies, so Christians, worldwide, should support the United States. Such is the fundamentalist distortion of Christ-ianity that has been spreading throughout Africa for the past generation.

Zionism is in a similar position, claiming Israel as God's ancient promise to the Jews. Zionism was formally established in August 1897 by Theodor Herzl at the founding of the World Zionist organization. It received an array of contentious support from different groups, was supported by the British Balfour Declaration in 1917, and saw the state of Israel formally established in May 1948. It is a modern political and economic state, which some claim has a spiritual identity with the Tanach and the Talmud; others see it as a Western ploy on the edge of the oil in the Muslim world, and Palestinians see it as a totally unjust occupation of the homeland they have dwelt in for hundreds of years. Millions of Africans know exactly what this feels like.

Muslim right-wing fundamentalism, which threatens Africa, is also a modern invention that has nothing to do with the ways of Muhammad in the seventh century. The Prophet saw his task as spreading the way of peace, mercy, and spirituality, and focused particularly on the need to change the economic structures that were oppressing the poor. He recognized and supported the many common roots with Jews and Christians and had no basic conflicts with either (except for the claim that Jesus was God, on which the Church was also divided). Because the Prophet left no clear successor, different political and religious factions have sought precedence ever since, invariably claiming support from the Quran.

In its search for control of oil, the United States and its Western allies have constantly manipulated this Muslim disunity, switching from side to side with the political temperature. Many accuse U.S. and Israeli aggression for antagonizing the right-wing fundamentalism that developed in Islam.

All these distortions are idol worship, mounting a major initiative to embroil Africa in its tentacles, which is seen more clearly when we analyze the present flash point in the Jewish-Christian-Muslim conflict on the northern doorstep of Africa in the Middle East.

Most Africans know that the Middle East conflict is not between these religions, but between the right-wing fundamentalisms that misuse them. Neither the conflicts nor the twisted religions have any basis in the prophets of Judaism, Jesus of Nazareth, or the prophet Muhammad. They are deadly distortions of scripture providing fraudulent theological backing used to promote political and economic oppression. Fanatics are fanatical. Christians, Jews, and Muslims embrace a mistaken enthusiasm: they turn anti-Zionism into anti-Semitism; they corrupt Christ-ian theology with an anti-God, anti-Jesus, anti-abortion, anti-gay, pro-war thesis; they promote distortions of Islam and dub all Muslims suicide bombers; and they are all very sincere about it. Religious institutions carry much responsibility. They have often encouraged fundamentalism by their failure to embrace scientific and ecumenical realities on the one hand, and their cold cerebral presentation of spiritual reality on the other. The first precipitated agnosticism, the second led to emotionalism, and both were aligned to the idol worship of the inhumanity of power and money. These are the factors of the modern assault on Africa by various fundamentalist groups.

8.13. Have Religious Institutions Failed Earthlings?

Merely to ask if religious institutions have failed Earthlings in belief and in practice rouses a storm of horror and resistance, but this is precisely the challenge that the present situation compels. The religious institutions we inherited from the colonial era (still rampant in the West) continue to be identified with much suffering and death. It is running away from such considerations that has brought us all to the brink of disaster. With extinction looming we cannot play maybes with our spirituality anymore. The question is what are Earthlings of Africa — or the world — to believe?

The notion that there are a multiplicity of gods each calling us to the only true religion is absurd and untenable. So is the notion that one God is calling us to accept a variety of religions that are competing with one another. On the other hand, prophets have emerged in every place and age who have proclaimed a vision and values for ways of life that all Earthlings share: ways of cooperation and compassion, of love and justice for all — an ubuntu experience for this life. It is observable fact that it was the priests who came after the prophets that have led Earthlings into competitive religious institutions, who not only sought to have Jesus killed and were sure they were being godly in doing so, but have done similar things throughout history.

What African Earthlings and the whole world need and seek is the spiritual power to transform and liberate this life now, not a focus on suppositions and superstitions about a possible life after death. We need what Archbishop Buti Tlhagale calls "a visible mechanism or forum of exchange, mutual acceptance and support."

The life of human spirits has been focused by religious institutions on themselves and dominated not by spiritual unity and strength, but by maintenance of their own divisive structures, personnel, buildings, and finances, and the insistence that spiritual life depends on maintaining such institutional separation. We have been taught to understand "spirit" as if different religions are promoting their individual product of spirit at a supermarket. Versions of Christianity, Islam, Judaism, Hinduism, or traditional belief systems deny, and often oppose, the legitimacy of other systems, although we all know that the spirit of all Earthlings is one and the same.

This competitive motivation applied especially to Christians in Africa during the colonial period, when it was assumed that God was a Christian and all other claimants of divinity were false guides; and while British reserve naturally did not brag about it publicly, it was clear that Queen Victoria and her empire had a special relationship with the divine. The establishment of a particular sort of Christian body (whether Catholic, Protestant or Pentecostal) was seen as a legitimate and central part of the colonial mission.

When facing difficulties such as world wars and apartheid the institutions were capable of coming together, but this unity did not last. The major agnostic rejection of the church in Europe in the period of the First and Second World Wars instigated the growth of the Christian ecumenical movement, but the institutions today continue to promote themselves as distinctly and separately as ever. During the struggle against apartheid some people in all churches opposed it and supported the ecumenical South African Council of Churches (SACC). But only very slowly did the churches allow this commitment to trickle into their own ecclesiastical structures of racially divided congregations, clergy, training, and stipends. With the end of political apartheid in 1994, the institutions returned to ecumenical apartheid, so that John de Gruchy of Cape Town could say to the SACC in 1995: "It is tragically ironic that when the nation was divided by apartheid we found our unity in the struggle, and now at the precise moment when the new South Africa is seeking to achieve national reconciliation, the church seems to be going back into its denominational shells."[32] The same can be said of the interfaith movement. When the Cold War threatened the world, and when colonial oppression dominated Africa, there was interest in growth toward unity in interfaith movements like WCRP and the CWPR, but the moment these pressures were off, the various religious institutions reasserted their separateness and commitment to undermine the unity of Earthlings.

Increasing numbers of spiritual agnostics in Africa and elsewhere assert that the beliefs that many of the religious institutions cite as the reason for their competitive separate development are highly questionable, whether people reject them by human instinct or academic expertise. Many scholars today recognize that much that is acclaimed as truth by the religious institutions is not the original product of Earthling prophets who were hijacked by religious manipulators a few generations later.

The African continent, with millions of Christians, is told that Jesus is God and that other religions are false. It is a simple fact that nowhere in the New Testament does Jesus claim to be God: others may have thought so, but he never said so himself. The positive spiritual and social teachings of Jesus were sidelined during the first few centuries of the Christ-ian era, which were dominated by debates about his nature and the standing of the church in relation to the Roman Empire. The Good News of Jesus about the Basileia of the God of love on Earth was in contrast to the imperialistic type of God and his church presented by Constantine and his followers. The church became focused on the controversy that developed around the Creeds in the centuries following Jesus. Three hundred years after Jesus there was reluctant approval of the Creeds by the church. Instead of facilitating the spiritual evolution and growth of Earthlings in society, the church promoted a divine dictatorship, which turned their institutions into the allies and custodians of oppressive political and economic conflict.

Similar disruptive distortions occurred in all religions invading Africa. The shared beliefs that benefited the spiritual growth of all human beings were pushed aside by the precepts that emboldened divisive economic and political institutions.

Many enlightened Africans who are conscious of and seeking a full and powerful spiritual life therefore question the divisive notions that are thrust at them. They ask: Is it necessary to believe in the physical resurrection of Jesus of Nazareth to believe in the Good News of the spiritual values of the Basileia that he proclaimed for the growing evolution of the human community? Is it necessary to believe in Zionist theological or political dogmas, or join this or that Jewish community, to believe in the vision and values of the prophets of Israel? Is it necessary to be involved in conflict between Sunni and Shi'a to be blessed by the vision and teaching of the Shari'ah (pathway) of the prophet Muhammad in the Quran? Is it necessary to advocate and perpetuate divisive denominational systems within Hinduism in order to enjoy the Sanatana Dharma, or Way of Life? Is it necessary to spurn and reject the spiritual traditions of the African elders in order to find and follow their truth? Is it necessary to denounce the beliefs of atheists or agnostics who reject religion but are committed to discover the path to human reconciliation and renewal? Do we, in actual hard fact, worship idols?

Some will say this is a simplistic view: yes, indeed, let's keep it simple! Some will say this ignores the reasons for the great divisions that motivated our fathers of faith in the past: let's leave them in the past! We must put in their proper place religious institutions that commit us to beliefs that divide and weaken Earthlings, hastening us on the way to self-destruction, and welcome those that emphasize the spiritual life we share that unites and empowers us.

All Earthlings are spiritual creatures who receive and give the resources of spirit to one another, from love and faith to compassion and vision. The challenge is to find and respect the resources that empower us, not those that undermine and de-spirit us — and not to reject those who drink from other wells.

◆ ◆ ◆

One of the divisive factors in religious institutions is their focus on the afterlife. I have attended a number of deathbeds, when eyes no longer see, breathing stops, life no longer is, and we face the great mystery of what has happened to that person — in my case, to one of my own sons. Some people identify with the feelings of Bertrand Russell, who was quite sure that when we die it all stops, just like that.

But for thousands of years most people have felt that life goes on, though they don't know how. And it is here that religious institutions have promoted numerous divisive answers, none of which have any certainty and many of which are simply superstition. They, however, are presented with such power and emotional certainty that many succumb to such bewitchment whether it comes from traditional preachers, TV evangelists, politicians, or pop stars. That may seem to be a disruptive and supercilious comment, but it is exactly what happens every week in thousands of different religious institutions from the Cape to Cairo and Somalia to Senegal. It is no wonder that people wonder about the validity of the religious institutions we inherited from colonialism.

8.14. So Where Are We Going?

Many modern Africans — and others — believe it is time we pulled these spiritual concerns out of obscurity and deal with the factual, scary background of the spiritual life of Africa, which offers the same vision and value to all Earthlings. It produces one of four reactions.

One is to write off all religion as a waste of time, which is the attitude adopted by millions of emancipated educated agnostics: they reject anything that smacks of god (though not necessarily the spiritual nature of humanity) and think religion is simply not worth bothering about anymore.

The second response is seen in the massive growth of fundamentalist born-again prosperity-religion cadres, so persuasively promoted by the economic and political right wing. Fundamentalists have a long history in all religions of proclaiming that God will bring an end to the world and save them to live in heaven.

The third response is to stick with the religious apartheid of colonialism.

The fourth is to take the path that leads beyond the Kairos document and liberation theology stage to seek the spiritual revolution of a secular spirituality.

◆ ◆ ◆

One of the most surprising facts about the antiapartheid era in South Africa is that although many in the religious bodies were critical of apartheid, they never came together to say so. The South African Council of Churches brought together the opposition in the

Christian churches and became a strong vocal critic of the apartheid regime.[33] The Muslim Judicial Council was clearly opposed to apartheid, and some of its leaders became prominently outspoken. Many members of the Hindu community were strongly against apartheid as individuals though their various groupings never came together to reject it officially, nor did the Jews. But the religious movements never came together either to denounce apartheid or to support the liberation movements. Individuals did so; small groups did so; but there was never a united religious action. The religious institutions were controlled by economics and politics, not the spirit.

This failure of the religious institutions to take a united spiritual stand was just as evident in the newly liberated South Africa, and it was the Christ-ians who were the stumbling block. After the first nonracial democratic election, President Nelson Mandela invited the leaders of all the South African religious communities to meet together to discuss the situation. Twenty-seven groups attended on June 24, 1997, at the ANC headquarters, which was then in Shell House in Johannesburg. In his address President Mandela supported the separation of religious and state structures in modern South Africa — but also drew them together.

> Religions must not control the government, and government must not run the religions. But this does not imply antagonism between religion and state. It does not separate political integrity from spiritual integrity. Morals and truth are indivisible. Politicians have spiritual responsibilities, and religions have political responsibilities — and each is concerned with society and those who belong to it. The transformation of our society requires the greatest possible cooperation between religious and political bodies, critically and wisely serving our people together. Neither social nor religious objectives can be achieved in isolation. They are held in creative tension with common commitments. We are partners in the building of our society.[34]

There was an enthusiastic response, which centered around the desire to establish a structure for the religious institutions to work together for the transformation of society. At a further meeting it was agreed to form a National Religious Leaders Forum (NRLF.) Since the great majority of South Africans are Christian, it was proposed by Chief Rabbi Harris, seconded by a representative of the Muslim Judicial Council, that the South African Council of Churches be asked to chair the forum. The SACC flatly refused. The secretary of the SACC gave no reasons; she simply said no and was supported by other members of the Christian community. They needed a revolution of spirit to even think of working together with other religions, and it is this that has dragged down the building of the new South Africa ever since.

Listening to that discussion in 1997, I was transported in a trice to Chicago in September 1893, when the religions of the world were invited to the inaugural meeting of the World Parliament of Religions. The archbishop of Canterbury, E. W. Benson, leader of the world's Anglicans, refused to attend. He said that his difficulties rested

> on the fact that the Christian religion is the one religion. I do not understand how that religion can be regarded as a member of a Parliament of Religions, without assuming the equality of other intended members and the parity of their position and claims. . . . While I quite understand how the Christian Religion might produce its evidence before such an assembly, a "presentation" of that religion must go far beyond the question of evidence, and must subject to public discussion that faith and devotion which are its characteristics, and which belong to a region too sacred for such treatment.[35]

He needed a revolution of spirit.

Organized religions have had great potential to continue and enhance the insights of the prophets in theory, but in fact they have allowed themselves to be hijacked by institutions that have other objectives, often derived from their submission to divisive secular priorities. Spiritual disunity is closely linked to political and economic rivalry. Throughout Africa are those who recognize the need for a common liberated, compassionate, cooperative, interfaith approach, but attempts to bring religious *institutions* together to say so have not been successful.

Looking at the situation in Africa in this twenty-first century, it seems clear that there are some issues on which all the religious bodies in Africa, America, and Europe could come together to act against the widespread cause of human hurt:

- to expose and refuse to support bribers, corruptors, and the oppressive quest for wealth

- to publicly explore a positive economic agenda to change the system that keeps most people poor into a system which ensures that everyone has enough

- to set out a positive ecological agenda

- to confront the antihuman factors in the media and advertising industry and run a collective positive media

- to pursue a program to outlaw and replace the oppressive conditions imposed on the people in the townships, shantytowns, and neglected rural areas of Africa

- to explore and develop the vision and values of African traditional spirituality

They have failed to do so and the results we see around us. They need a revolution of spirit. The BBC Reith Lecturer of 1970 said:

> Organizations are dynamically conservative: that is to say they fight like mad to remain the same. This is such a pervasive characteristic of social systems that it may be used in effect to define what a social system is: namely, a social entity which has the property of preserving its integrity and boundaries in spite of too many internal and external threats to both. . . . We discover the depth and complexity of organizational resistance to change when we seek to change it. . . . Organizations resist change with an energy that is roughly proportional to the radicalness of the change that is threatened.[36]

It needs a revolution of spirit.

Earth has been brought to an intolerable position in that its future is threatened by the selfishness and violence of institutions controlled by elite groups which threaten the end of human life in this century. Many of the secular killers are supported by religious institutions whose failure to provide relevant leadership in the spiritual field has prompted fundamentalist superstition to undermine, and in much of the world to usurp, the spiritual energies of Earthlings.

Liberated Earthlings are well aware of the conflict in their community and in their own being: between good and evil, collective, and self. Religions would often speak the language of the prophets but follow the actions of the kings and merchants. They would preach peace and pray for the success of war. They would proclaim the Gospel and practice apartheid. They would promote the Bible and the Quran from pulpits built on the profits of slavery. What we need to save Africa is a spiritual revolution. So does Earth.

Afterword

One of the names his followers used for Jesus was "the Light of the World," and many have found the same luminosity in their prophets, even if their religious structures have been part of the darkness. Many believers today are being converted, leaving their idols, and discovering what Jesus and Muhammad and other prophets were actually saying. The stars shining in the darkness have been the small groups with vision driven by faith, love, hope, and joy who shed light around them.

Chapter 9

The Crux of the Matter

Synopsis

The crux of the matter is that much of Africa today has been bought out and corrupted by the West. Basic change is required in every sector of society to empower and save Earthlings, which we recognize is fundamentally a deep challenge to our spirits. Many in the West share the belief of many Africans that a new postreligion secular spirituality is crucial for Earthlings. But how can it happen?

9.1. The Need of Spiritual Revolution

9.2. The Common Ground of the Spirit of Earthlings

9.3. Liberation from Colonial Religion

9.4. The Secular Influences

9.5. Challenge to the Church — The Kairos Time

9.6. The Liberation of Religion Today

9.7. Postreligion

9.8. But What Has Actually Happened?

Paying lip service to spiritual values will not do. The emphasis must be on realizing them in the given social, political, economic, and cultural context. Spirituality is a paradigm of engagement, and engagement is the dynamic of transformation.
— Swami Agnivesh speaking in Pretoria, May 2006[1]

9.1. The Need of Spiritual Revolution

The world has seen political revolution, industrial revolution, colonial revolution, national revolution, and economic revolution, but today we know we need a spiritual revolution. Every challenge we face shows the need to renew the vision and values of the spirit in which Earthlings tackle the matter of living. Many have been aware of this and have explored the way ahead through calling Christ-ians to an ecumenical approach, or all religions to interfaith discussions, but neither has worked. There are one-shot conferences from time to time, but no intention to come together to forge a united approach to the spiritual problems facing humanity. There is not the slightest sign of the religious institutions uniting to influence the challenges and impending collapse of Earthlings. At local and national levels, religions are primarily interested in promoting their own institutions. Indeed, their separation and antagonism toward one another, the steady growth of agnosticism, and the clear failure of religious institutions to address the problems means they do not figure in the councils of the world or the hopes of Earthlings. Religions will not save us.

The crux of the matter is how to recover the spiritual roots of Earthlings before these developed into religious institutions, before humans began to promote religious patches designed to compete with other religious patches. Our spiritual roots and the growth of human spirits long predate the attachment to ideas about God and the dogmas and practices of religious structures. To what extent do our religions help or hinder Earthlings to rediscover together the essential roots of spiritual power? These questions start bells ringing in every Earthling, and they ring very clearly in Africa. It is one reason why Africa matters.

Our problem in Africa today is not centered on the oppressive colonial attitudes in the United States, Europe, Russia, China, or Asia, but in Africans who have the same attitudes right here at home. We liberated ourselves from colonialism in some obvious ways, but the oppressive powers have wormed their way beneath the surface to seduce our own community. The merciless dictators of finance, the systems of suffering and delusion, those who dominate and diminish our spiritual and cultural concerns are in Nairobi and Johannesburg, in Libya and Lesotho, in Ghana and Ethiopia. From our cabinets to our kitchens, our board rooms to our beaches, our sanctuaries to our brothels, the Five Horsemen of the Apocalypse have colonized much of Africa today, and it is here that we must confront them. What are the crucial issues, and does the African insight help to liberate the West?

9.2. The Common Ground of the Spirit of Earthlings

In the lead up to its first democratic election in 1994, the South African branch of the World Conference on Religion and Peace (WCRP) issued a pamphlet entitled *A Liturgy for Interfaith Prayers for Peace and Unity*. It was divided into seven meditations headed:

The Unity of Our Human Being

The Struggle of Good against Evil

The Personal Experience of Spiritual Power

A People Discovering Unity Together

A Tolerant People

A People of Justice

A Transforming People

Each section included quotations from the major scriptures, which made clear that all religions are doors to the same spiritual energy. The secret of human liberation and transformation, the crux of the matter, is in rediscovering the spiritual energy in all Earthlings, the vital force within everyone everywhere. It is the uniting shared spirit of human community in all its patches, in which the prophets of all religions concur, the common ground—whatever name they use for spiritual energy. One key fits all the locks.

A surgeon once told me of his fascination as a student with the fact that whatever the color, shape, or size of a person on the surface, when you put a scalpel in at a certain point there was the blood vessel or nerve or sinew you were seeking. Psychologists learn to do the same with the minds of Earthlings, and it is true of our spirits. Go to any patch of humans, probe any scripture, hear any prophetess or prophet, be loved or laughed with or made peace with by anyone, and you are sharing the same Earthling spiritual experience. All Earthlings are rooted in the same spirit.[2] All prophets speak of love, joy, and peace, of patience, kindness, and generosity, of loyalty, humility, and self-control as the Way for the human spirit (Galatians 5).

Whatever our particular personal religious profile, there is a way of being human that all people recognize, including millions who do not claim to be religious at all. Love is not Christian or Hindu; peace is not Muslim or Jewish; generosity is not religious or atheist;

compassion and cooperation are not Communist or Democratic: these qualities are human. This central reality of spiritual maturity in all development and religions has been given many names, from holiness to the harvest of the spirit, but they all refer to the same Earthling quality, which is why all religions call themselves the Way of life. They are all on the same track.

Some people find this hard to accept. They are so stuck on promoting the priority of their patch of religious assertions, inhibitions, prejudices, and fears (to say nothing of obeying the conservatism of their religious superiors) that they seem unable to capture the truth of our common grounding. But many other Earthlings in Africa and elsewhere have evolved their vision and values beyond the stage of asking if a person is Christian or Jewish or Muslim or Buddhist or agnostic. They have left the patches behind, with their sense of superiority and conflictual pronouncements, and are seeking an awareness of spirituality that is the common experience of all Earthlings. This is what Mahatma Gandhi was asserting when he said he was Hindu, Christian, Buddhist, Confucian, Muslim, and Jew. He could have said "agnostic" as well.

This sometimes seems to come more easily in Africa. David Mosoma says that "most traditional African societies view religions as a source of bondedness . . . African indigenous religions accommodate other religions rather than exclude or antagonize them. . . . Religion is not simply a department or compartment of life, rather, it is life."[3]

Western theologians seek the same understanding. W. Cantwell Smith asserts that "God has been at work in all faith communities, . . . but we are the first generation of Christians to see this seriously and corporately, . . . to discern God's mission to humankind in the Buddhist movement, in the Hindu, in the Islamic, as well as in the Jewish and the Christian."[4] Swami Saradananda of Durban agrees: "The ethics and morals of all religions of the world are fundamentally the same."[5]

This is the context in which we begin to understand Africa's traditional concept of vital force, of a secular spirituality as a way of life for all people, and to recognize ubuntu as the common ground of all successful community. The recent rapid urbanization of Africa and the spread of Westernism, does not necessarily destroy the attachment to traditional roots for everyone. Dele Jegede writes:

In Nigeria, a university professor seeking promotion may not hesitate to supplement his Christian or Islamic devotions with a visit to the diviner, who consults with his oracle and advises that a sacrifice be offered to some supernatural forces believed to have mediatory powers to positively affect the outcome. A legal practitioner and respected member of the society is at once active at church and at the lodge of the local "reformed" fraternity, considered by devout Christians as a euphemism for a secret society. On purchasing a car, an urban Yoruba business executive first takes a "traditional" insurance policy: he seeks protection from the wrath of Ogun, the god of iron, by summoning community elders to pour libation and ask for ancestral guidance. The car is then taken to the local church, where the minister is implored to bless it. A young Christian couple anxious to have a child seek help from the traditional healer, who also doubles as *imam* at the local mosque.[6]

It is a comprehensive awareness that can be expressed in many different ways worldwide and should be respected, not denigrated.

9.3. Liberation from Colonial Religion

The religious institutions that bestraddle Africa today have inevitably been heavily influenced by colonialism, and the spiritual life of the continent is engaged in a major liberation struggle. Many Earthlings rejoice in looking beyond both their primal spiritual origins and subsequent colonial developments.

During the two hundred years of the missionary movement, Western Christians were convinced that their duty and delight under God was to spread the Christian churches to the whole Earth, and especially to Africa. That has changed for two reasons. First, local African churches have taken their own initiatives in leadership and content. Second, the Western churches have begun to fail. Huge efforts, including repeated Evangelical campaigns, have failed to stop people moving away from traditional Christianity into agnosticism or to the superstitions of heretical fundamentalist escapisms. Western people had been seriously questioning their inherited Christ-ian institutions ever since the Enlightenment, and especially since the First World War, but the spiritual life of Earthlings needed to be liberated from religious oppression, not consigned to oblivion. Colonialism sometimes got it wrong, but that did not mean giving up religion altogether: there are plenty of liberated religious people.

Even fewer suspected that the main liberating thrust would come from the primal believers on Earth, many of whom were Africans. Africa today is looking for a new type of spirituality in the secular world. Human beings are creatures of body, mind, and spirit living in community, and spiritual life is an essential part of their makeup. There were, however, very good grounds for rejecting colonial religions. European missionaries were palpably in association with the overseas administrators and were part of the whole European invasion of Africa. "Victorian missionaries in Africa inclined to the view that British civilization and Christianity were almost identical. They thought of African culture as heathen, the work of the devil, to be rooted out as soon as possible."[7] Jesus had been coopted by the empire, and liberation from oppression included salvation not by Jesus, but salvation from Jesus.

This was very clear in the address by John Gatu of the AACC in Milwaukee. "The imperialistic attitude of the West, that you have something to share with your fellow man, must be challenged in this context. For we know only too well that behind such good and sentimental sayings there is a cruel sense of the wish to continue the past images and a therapeutic satisfaction for those who do not wish to face the challenge of mission in their own countries and on their own doorsteps." "There was no concept of respecting deeply the religious experience of others. . . . The missionaries failed to appreciate a culture other than their own and used their position of strength as spiritual leaders to impose a destructive and restrictive attitude toward local communal life and culture."[8] A generation later Steve Biko had the same understanding: "The Church made it plain that everything African was heathen and superstitious barbarism. Conversion to Christianity meant rejecting traditional forms of dress, authority, social organization, culture, marriage, and medicine. The black people were made to believe not that salvation was in Christ alone, but that salvation is in accepting the new white ways of living."[9]

Similar challenges surfaced in all religions, and as the years of liberation and postliberation have passed many Africans in many places have begun to take serious note of liberating Jesus from

Christ-ianity, liberating the Prophet from Islamophobia, liberating Hinduism for modern Africa, and liberating Judaism from aggressive Zionism.

One of the most fascinating sites in the world is the wall of Herod's Temple in Jerusalem, which I visited once with three other South Africans — a Christian and two Muslims.[10] Jesus must have known the wall well, and it still towers many meters over the thousands who go there to pray. Up above, the wall supports the Temple Mount, dominated by the great mosque the Dome of the Rock. It is a place of reflection and unity of which the late chief rabbi of South Africa, Cyril Harris, once wrote: "On Fridays, when thousands of Muslims attend the Mosque on the Temple Mount, the prayers to Hashem of the Jewish worshippers below mingle with the prayers to Allah of the multitude of Muslims above. The same G-d understands and receives both sets of prayers."[11]

9.4. The Secular Influences

Many of the compelling factors in the spiritual development of Africa have secular origins. Perceptions that initiated the pursuit of prophetic practices did not usually come from meditating on the Bible, the Quran, or the Upanishads, but from meeting face to face with poverty, hunger, disease, cruelty, racism, hatred, and oppression, or love and laughter. Because civilization had imposed a spiritual apartheid on the world by divorcing religious and secular activity, much of the spiritual and ethical learning in the human community has been initiated through secular rather than religious inspiration.

Relevant theology has always arisen from social action. The truth that Jesus promised would make people free came "if you follow my commandments" (John 8), which meant action. The social protest against slavery was a crucial factor in the deeper spiritual understanding of the missionary era. It was Bishop John William Colenso's concern for the well-being of the people that led him to question many theological positions of the nineteenth-century church. Kendall writes that although "his controversial career was debated within the theological thought terms of the period, in essence he was forced to more radical thinking in order to achieve justice for the Zulu people."[12] Visiting black colleagues in their homes and feeling their suffering led Beyers Naudé of the Dutch

Reformed Church and many others to a new theological approach to colonialism, racism, and apartheid in the formation of the Christian Institute of Southern Africa. It happened to me too: when the church sent me to minister to African, Indian, Colored, and White people, the secular realities forced me to remint the spiritual realities and become involved in the political sphere.

Liberation theology arose among people who were convinced that the motives of political and economic liberation were correct, became involved in that struggle, and sought to understand and promote it theologically. Liberation theology was highly subversive of colonial theology and disturbed the comfort zones of oppressors. It "arms itself with the necessary theological daring and with a good dose of creative imagination in order to tackle previously unknown questions posed today by the continents under oppression."[13] Leonardo Boff writes:

> The historical roots of liberation theology are to be found in the prophetic tradition of evangelists and missionaries from the earliest colonial days in Latin America — churchmen who questioned the type of presence adopted by the church and the way indigenous people, blacks, mestizos, and the poor, rural and urban masses were treated. . . . They are the source of the type of social and societal understanding that is emerging today.[14]

Vaughan Jones of Britain had a similar understanding:

> Liberation Theology is not merely a political theology. Liberation Theology has one essential starting point that there is a historical movement toward liberation. It is not identifying a dream but a reality. The question it is posing is this: If there is a movement to overthrow colonial domination, military dictatorship, and United States Imperialism, what does that mean for people of faith?[15]

That is precisely the question raised in the African situation. Moral and ethical considerations that led to the vision and values espoused by the liberation movements in Africa were deeply spiritual, but did not originate in the religious communities. They were frequently not endorsed by the religious leadership until great pressure was brought to bear, because the church was too submissive to the colonial ruling elites. Many who were uncomfortable with obvious oppression in Africa were far too scared to act in support of liberation movements and justified themselves by the dictum of keeping religion and politics apart. The pronouncements at Chorlton-cum-Hardy, the life and work of Nkrumah, Nyerere, Kenyatta, Lumumba, Luthuli, Biko, Mandela, and a thousand others; the policies of the various political parties; the Freedom Charter, the Black Consciousness Movement, the United Democratic Front, and numerous other groups seeking the fulfillment of their human heritage throughout the continent, all walked the talk of the prophets. Yet none of these movements arose from religious institutions. No Christian, Muslim, or Hindu organizations attended the Freedom Charter rally at Kliptown. The University Christian Movement, which helped to launch the Black Consciousness Movement in South Africa, was heavily criticized by the church, as were the Christian Institute, Call of Islam and Jews for Justice when they gave support to the liberation struggles. Individuals and small groups who were already identified with the struggle worked out the theology, but they were frequently either ignored, ostracized, or deliberately opposed by the ecclesiastical authorities. Religion became a site of struggle. This was very clear in the drama of the Kairos document.

9.5. Challenge to the Church — The Kairos Time

Fax machines had become all the rage by the 1980s, and in September 1985 I sat with Ian Linden, director of the Catholic Institute of Race Relations in London, as a thirty-page document spilled slowly onto the floor, fed page by page from seven thousand miles away in Johannesburg. It had been prepared in secret lest the apartheid authorities ban it before it was released, and that same day it was being taken from the printing press and mailed to hundreds in plain envelopes throughout the land. It was issued by a small ecumenical, multiracial group in Soweto that was concerned at the failure of the Church to respond to the apartheid situation that was causing such injury and death to the people, and called for the Church to become involved in the liberation struggle. The document was called *Challenge to the Church*, and almost as an afterthought, subtitled the Kairos document — kairos being a New Testament Greek word to indicate "the time is now."[16]

Reading it today, many still believe it to be one of the most important documents of recent centuries, far surpassing many official
pronouncements issued from Rome, Canterbury, Geneva, or other
shrines. While it emerged as a critique of the apartheid situation,
its analysis of state theology, church theology, and prophetic theology applies to the world situation of most religions today. It is a
Gospel for the Poor.

State Theology is "simply the theological justification of the status quo, with its racism, capitalism, and totalitarianism. It blesses
injustice, canonizes the will of the powerful, and reduces the poor
to passivity, obedience and apathy," which it does by "misusing
the theological concepts and biblical texts for its own political purposes." Much of what it says about state theology still applies to the
world at large, and the false god behind these beliefs is denounced
as an idol.

The term "church theology" describes the attitudes and opinions
of many religious leaders who are guardedly critical of oppression,
but misuse the concepts of reconciliation, justice, and nonviolence
to justify them in avoiding any conflict with evil. This comes from
the false type of faith, which has turned spirituality into the "otherworldly" affair that has dominated the church for centuries and
leaves so many Christians and church leaders, when faced with crisis, in "a state of near paralysis." Both of these positions describe
perfectly the despair felt throughout much of Africa today when it
faces the world situation.

The Kairos document then examines what it calls "prophetic theology" and calls for a bold and incisive response that is prophetic
because it speaks to the particular circumstances of the crisis; it
"does not give the impression of sitting on the fence but is clearly
and unambiguously taking a stand." From its social analysis Kairos
shows that the struggle is against oppression and tyranny, which
cannot be reformed but must be removed and replaced. It concludes by asserting a message of hope because God sides with the
oppressed. It calls on the church and all people to participate in the
moral duty of resisting oppression and to struggle for liberation and
justice, not only in its sermons and statements, but also through
its actions, programs, campaigns, and divine services.

The response was immediate, impressive, and significant. Several hundred men and women clergy from every denomination
signed it; there was massive support from ordinary oppressed

people, especially the youth, who insisted that their clergy preach about the Kairos document "or else we're not coming to church"; many supported it but kept quiet; Prime Minister P. W. Botha demanded that the church repudiate it; some church leaders like Peter Storey of the SACC and Desmond Tutu criticized it because they had not been consulted first. Six years later, when apartheid laws were being turned into history, David Mosoma saw the Kairos document as a product of "a new African and black epistemology that sought to be honest and realistic in the African context...and...unmasked the forces of both political and religious deformation."[17] Ground out in Soweto under the crucifying pressures of apartheid, which left no room for sentimental assertions and superstitious make-believe faith, the Kairos document is still a vital witness of Africa to Earthlings.

There are plenty of black colonials in Africa who, for various reasons, endorse the priorities of the political, economic, and religious empires set out by both West and East, but these will not liberate Earthlings. Many of our compatriots have been taken in by such powerful protestations and have earned the sobriquet "lackeys of Western imperialism," or "black exponents of white power." Many sincere and persuasive people are offering us political, economic, and religious reasons for staying exactly where we have been under colonial and Western domination, except a step or two higher on the ladder, but that is not liberation. What we require is a new prophetic vision and empowered values, a new kairos vision, however unlikely, weak or small it may seem, because, in the womb of Africa, we know life means growth.

The essential matter is simple: it is to produce secular Earthlings with power in their spirit, people driven by faith, hope, and love, who can recognize the kairos moment of today, communities that can resist and face the Five Horsemen of the Apocalypse and chase them away. The kairos time is not the liberation time, but sees it coming, acts in anticipation of it, and is part of the struggle for it. It is the vision and commitment that we saw in Africa and look for in the wider world now.

9.6. The Liberation of Religion Today

Liberating religion is not new, and many see the need of it today. Altering the focus from past history to present understanding, dumping dogmas designed in a previous age, to determine a new direction, and sweeping aside the corruptions that have crept in to clear a path for the faith of a living age, has happened constantly. Jesus and Muhammad were major liberation theologians in their day, and spiritual revolution is coursing through Earth now. The central factor is its concern and good news for the needy and to free those still trapped in colonial religions.

Christ-ianity is a huge problem for Christians all over the world and one that Earthlings must solve. The problem is not in the relevance and importance of Jesus the Nazarene, but in the competitive and cantankerous religious institutions that came after him. The Light of the World has been fogged out. We have been so pressured to believe that the doctrines and practices of our particular denominations have the authority of Jesus-God behind them, and that it imperils our eternal life to question them, that what many claim to be Christianity is often anti-Jesus. The colonial attitudes still rule many whites and blacks who need liberating. There is a vast difference between the teachings of Jesus, which are focused in the Gospels, and the teachings of the church, which are focused on the Creeds. The Nicene, Apostles', and Athanasian Creeds emerged several centuries after Jesus, as products of the struggle for political and economic power when the Roman empire was seeking the support of the emerging churches. The factual horror stories of the Creeds and the churches that produced them are a fearsome account of corruption, politicizing, maneuvering, persecution, torture, and death built around some desperate sanctity, yet many people are still taught that if we do not believe the Creeds are truly God-talk we shall go to everlasting torment in hell when we die. This has not an ounce of Jesus-talk behind it. This was the message of fear and damnation which the colonial Christians carried around the world, claiming that the only way to avoid hideous everlasting punishment by a God of righteousness and love was by attending the church and its sacraments.

The Creeds make no mention of the central teaching of Jesus about the Basileia, the ruling power in the community to liberate Earthlings. They say nothing about his teaching that Matthew summed up in the Sermon on the Mount (Matt. 5–7). They ignore the qualities of spiritual Earthlings that Paul called the harvest of the Spirit (Gal. 5:19). Yet many churches insist that their congregations stand and recite the Creeds on a weekly or daily basis. The Way of Jesus is far simpler and deeper than the superstitious fundamentalist religions of today and the conventional comments on political and economic matters still nurtured in the competitive elitist terms of colonialist empires.

Jesus proclaimed the Good News of a ruling power, a Basileia in the Earthling community (*malkuth* in Aramaic, the language he spoke). Basileia was the Greek word for ruling power, a spiritual "force of gravity," a driving force of care and compassion, a bias to justice, love, and peace, a nuance of evolution and liberation, a ruling power that is operating among Earthlings here and now. Being a Jew, Jesus saw this ruling power in terms of God, and the early Christians, being Romans, translated it as the "kingdom of God," though the Basileia has nothing to do with empires imposed by elitist men — or kings or presidents or elitist women either!

Some find it helpful and instructive to spell out this proclamation of the ruling power in the Earthling community in terms of the liberating revolution among women and youth. Men seem to find it much easier to lay down the law as benign oppressors than to be liberated persons building human community, so the insight and leadership of women and young people are a crucial part of the postreligious age of secular spirituality.

In Cape Town fourteen women in the Circle of Concerned African Women Theologians have written of their experiences. "All these stories are lived theologies. Their footprints speak of a sturdy engagement with life," writes Denise Ackermann.[18] "One thing we women have learned is that you cannot separate the private from the public sphere. . . . If religion is relegated to the private sphere it can . . . result in an excessive preoccupation with personal morality at the expense of a social conscience." Isobel Phiri raises a fundamental issue in her comment on the deconstruction of patriarchy: "The deconstruction of patriarchy is a fundamental concern for African women's theologies. Patriarchy is evident within cultural, political, religious, social, and economic systems and structures. It involves men dominating women and thereby hindering authentic growth within the society. Patriarchy is a concern because Africa cannot reconstruct adequately while patriarchal ideology persists to inform and influence the fabric of society. This concern should be shared by all contextual theologies in Africa."[19]

James Cochrane, also of Cape Town, examines the meaning behind Jesus saying to his disciples: "Only those who receive the basileia [kingdom] as a child will enter it."[20] The child has a deep sense of a "justice culture," a sense of fairness, which means that children experience the freedom to make decisions, to deepen their integrity, meet other persons' integrities, to stand up for justice for someone else, and to experience themselves as a power with people. Adults, so often nurtured in cynicism and wounded by fighting oppressive systems, need to be ministered to by young people to regain recognition of a sense of justice and fairness in the depths of human nature and community. David Tacey, working among Australian young people, found their grasp of spiritual potential impressive. "Religion is often dumbfounded and astonished by their assumption that the world is good, that creation is graced by the presence of the divine. . . . Both religion and youth spirituality are possessed of valuable truths, and each can learn something important from the other."[21] Similarly, the Cape Town multiracial "Interfaith Initiative" in February 2004, observed that "The most important sign that interfaith relations were maturing was found in the way in which young people were taking leadership."[22]

The true role of religious concern is to liberate people into developing spiritual power (faith-love-joy-peace) in both individuals and communities. We need liberating *from* oppressive religious institutions confining their attention to individuals, *into* progressive spiritual communities.

The Christian Institute of Southern Africa under the leadership of Beyers Naudé, which played a decisive role in the struggle for liberation, began when Beyers met some of his black colleagues and their families in their own homes and saw and felt their cruel and impoverished circumstances. For many years the Christian Institute and the South African Council of Churches had offices in the same building in Braamfontein, Johannesburg, with plenty of clergy, Bibles, and hymn books around, but the driving force came from the constant stream of needy people, political activists, students, detainees, and their families — and visits from the Security Police. The ANC had been banned for years and no contact with its structures was permissible, but I well remember visiting Beyers in his garden[23] and being shown a scrap of paper smuggled through in an overseas visitor's cigarette case — a note from Oliver Tambo, the exiled leader of the African National Congress. (It just said thanks for all you are doing.) Steve Biko of the Black Consciousness Movement was another secular leader who fueled the spirit of the CI; we used to see him regularly, flying down to meet him at a deserted airstrip near his home in Kingwilliamstown. Professor C. W. Du Toit writes that "Biko was the eagle who kicked out his nestling so that it could learn to fly; he was Zarathustra's prophet who encouraged the student to surpass his master; he was a Bonhoeffer who told human beings to take responsibility for themselves without hoping for divine intervention. For all these reasons black consciousness may be regarded as a beacon of African renaissance, comparable to the scientific revolution of the Enlightenment and the French and American revolutions."[24]

The highly educated and Westernized Kenyan leader Jomo Kenyatta revealed his roots by dedicating a book to "... all the dispossessed youth of Africa: for perpetuation of communion with ancestral spirits through the fight for African Freedom, and in the firm faith that the dead, the living and the unborn will unite to rebuild the destroyed shrines."

9.7. Postreligion

Many religious communities show great reluctance to admit that today we live in a postreligious age, when religions seem to have lost influence, but they should welcome it. The phrase came up when church attendance went down, and many empty churches in Europe were sold off, but it was the strongest possible demonstration that the churches were missing the mark and needed salvation and liberation. Postreligion is a good and godly movement: the rediscovery of primal spiritual emphasis, with all the wealth of spiritual experience since, seeing the meeting points of colonial religions and going beyond them, the desire to replace a spent force with a vital force, which both believers and unbelievers recognize. Wilfred Cantwell Smith believes "we have entered into a period in which we must speak of a common religious history of humankind. We now have to think on a global scale of what men and women everywhere have to learn from all the religious traditions."[25] The Muslim scholar Reza Aslan has a similar approach. "What is most desperately needed is not so much a better appreciation of our neighbor's religion, as a broader more complete understanding of religion itself."[26]

The "postreligion age" was named after the World Wars when people rejected the church, but the phrase has now moved from despairing regret to an exciting emancipation. "Postreligion is a godly initiative," says Elizabeth Harris of British Methodism. Our inherited religions have often been seen as "good stuff for kids," but people today are seeking a grown-up secular spirituality. This accepts many earlier beliefs, it warms to much in them, but seeks spiritual adulthood. It is the dynamic thrust of the Life Force of the Spirit in human community—a secular spirituality.

9.8. But What Has Actually Happened?

Despite the grounding in primal values, the vision and commitment of so many, the lives of generosity and deeds of self-sacrifice and devotion, the era of African independence has led to unending stories of atrocities. Extravagance and starvation, genocide and crime rule. A thousand herded into a church and a thousand throats cut. Twenty-seven years in prison for being right and good. Thousands starved to death. Books and Constitutions written and ignored. Money from bribes: money for bribes. Murder, retaliation, and retribution. Murder and forgiveness. Corruption rules, corruptors worshiped, corruptors sacked. Compassion, cooperation, commitment crucified. Spiritual vision and values vanquished to worship idols. Political idols, economic idols, ecological idols, media idols, religious idols. Feet of clay.

Throughout Africa the civilization that colonialism brought to the continent has broken down the secular-spiritual life of African Earthlings instead of developing it. Democracy brought political independence but sidelined ubuntu and rejected economic justice. The economy largely remains in the hands of oppressors who have manipulated and corrupted support. The worship of wealth and power has become an idol that has usurped the place of every other god. Justice and integrity have not been liberated, and money is routed to leaders and their political supporters. In every country numerous "oppressed" have become "oppressors," and the quest for a renaissance of Earthling community in Africa has been met with ineptitude and rejection from religious bodies, governments, and the African Union. They have been wasted years, not because of the string of wicked people from Amin to Mugabe and Thatcher to Bush who have laid the land waste, but because the good people have been unable to transform the impetus of liberation into implementation, and white Western influence and wealth has continued its oppression through black surrogates.

Forty years after African countries began to throw off colonialism many are still wracked by violence and war, killed by armaments supplied by the rest of the world at ruinous cost. Time and again civilian rule has been taken over by military rule, with force. There was no justice in the massacres of Tutsi and Hutu in Rwanda, and the only ones who gained from the genocide were the arms manufacturers. Sudan has hosted years of warfare between Muslim, Christian, and traditional believers. Hundreds of thousands of people were crammed into refugee camps in Darfur, the Congo, and many other places. Chad is a horrible story of corruption, destruction, and death. Thousands were murdered to remove opposition parties in Zimbabwe, where the economy has been looted, shattered, and a large proportion of the whole population has fled violence and starvation to seek some form of survival in neighboring countries. The huge population of Nigeria, the people of the Congo, Malawi, Liberia, Guinea, Mauritania, Burkina Faso, Sierra Leone, and Madagascar are among those who have suffered the decimation of their societies by war, and in Somalia, the Sudan, Egypt, and several Francophone countries religious conflict has added to the horror.

In every country money is now god, whether measured in dollars, pounds, shillings, or rands. The pursuit of wealth rules, affecting not only work, housing, and health, but religion, education, sports, family life, the media, and politics. The prime need for the development of industrial and agricultural capacity and skills within Africa is thwarted by external demands for our raw materials and quick cash profits, with everything occurring to the benefit of farmers, factories, and finances of West and East. The just distribution of wealth internally is fatally distorted by the bribery and corruption that take place in government and business in both West and East and are growing every day in Africa. The liberation that we used to see as freedom from oppression by whites in political terms has now been changed to liberation from oppression by the wealthy class over the poorer class in economic terms, whatever their pigment.

◆ ◆ ◆

The "liberation" of Africa from colonial rule during the closing decades of the twentieth century inaugurated a new era of oppression that throws light on both the collapse facing the Earthling community in the twenty-first century and Africa's contribution to the way forward. This insight can be considered under three headings: the role of wealth, internal conflicts, and the failure of religions.

The Role of Wealth

Despite the impression of being a dried up desert of poverty, huge quantities of wealth are sloshing around Africa like the swirling waters following tropical downpours, looking for outlets. The wealth comes from minerals under the ground and seas, crops, a mass of available labor, government expenditure, grants and aid, and investment from overseas. It is widely known that much of the wealth disappears into the pockets of corrupt African politicians, government servants, and influential individuals, but this conceals the real problem — which is not the bribed but the bribers, not the corrupt but the corruptors. The simple fact is that the civilized world is corrupt through and through: it is the way it does business. These are the agents of corruption in Africa.

Building large dams is a highly skilled, expensive, and lucrative operation, and there is stiff competition among Western companies for these profitable contracts, often costing far more than necessary because of the bribery. The cost of the Turkwel Gorge Dam built in Kenya in the late 1980s for $270 million by French contractors is said to have been double the original estimate because of bribes. British, Canadian, German, and Italian contractors were all found guilty of bribing public officials to secure contracts in the multi-billion dollar Lesotho Highlands Water Project of the 1990s. The Owen Falls Dam Extension Project of 1992 in Uganda was riddled with controversy over bribery, as was the Bujagali Hydropower Project on the Nile, near Jinja. Similar stories abound in other countries, the excuse always being that "this is how business is done these days."

The massive contracts for the provision of identity documents in Africa have also figured in bribery scandals throughout the continent, including the case of Nigeria, with its huge population, involving French, British, and Israeli firms. Soon after its first democratic election, in 1994, South Africa, under pressure from the manufacturers of killing machines in the West, decided to update its defense force including warships, fighter aircraft, and numerous other military materials provided mainly by Britain, Sweden, and Germany. Fifteen years later the scandals involving corrupt kickbacks are still raging. It is a similar story throughout the continent. The secrecy employed in military matters makes it easy to conceal the deals behind the scenes, but enough leaks out to show the widespread duplicity of Western companies. They know it in the West, and we feel it in Africa.

The gravest concerns at the moment are focused on coal and oil, which are filling Earth's atmosphere with the poison of carbon dioxide. The handful of coal-financed directors who control Eskom, the national producer of electricity, have pressured the South African government to continue being the biggest polluter on the continent, instead of developing quicker, easier, cheaper, alternatives that will provide work for thousands.

Africa's resources of oil are small compared with the Middle East, but are nevertheless significant. U.S. companies are in Algeria, Mauritania, Chad, and the Sudan in the north, and in Nigeria, Angola, Equatorial Guinea, Gabon, and São Tomé and Príncipe in the West. France and much of Europe are also involved. The new kid on the block is China, with activity in the Sudan, including the new Chad-Cameroon pipeline. India is establishing links from the East and Brazil's eyeing the prospects from the West. Many commentators assert that the oil boom in Africa has been for the benefit of the elite class and their foreign partners, but has not benefited the people of Africa. "It feeds into corruption and violent conflict, rather than the development of society."[27]

A morass of concern surrounds the Western extension of so-called property rights to include the production of genetically modified seed and plants. Despite scientific doubts about long-term benefits and legal doubts about the claim to genuine originality, these products are taking over large-scale markets for export business and pushing out the millions of small-scale farmers who feed the hundreds of millions of African people living on the land.

The postcolonial misuse of Africa to promote foreign interests rather than the development of its own people extends to agro-fuels, forestry, fishing, the textile industry, trade, militarism, politics, democracy, and much of academia and the religious world. Liberation from political colonialism enabled international economic oppression to proceed, leaping and bounding into the civilized obsession of separating spiritual, ethical, and moral responsibility from secular interests, which is why Earthlings face extinction.

Internal Conflict

The division of Africa with artificial boundaries drawn by the Congress of Berlin in 1884–85 with no Africans present was already a recipe for tension, and the colonial insistence on following Western priorities of competition and conflict rather than ubuntu principles of cooperation led to major disruptions of society in due course. The "divide and rule" policy was the death certificate for thousands of totally innocent people. It still is. Promoted by former colonizers, arms manufacturers, and mercenaries, the quest was for profits, not the principles of successful Earthlings.

The Failure of Religions

Despite the leadership of vision and values offered by the prophets in every sector of society, the religious institutions, worldwide, either ignored them or killed them. The long submission to political and economic elites promoted divisive conflicts that they brought with them to Africa. The declining interest and support indicates that our inherited colonial religions are not capable of handling the current world situation.

Africans recognize that attempts to bring religious *institutions* together to liberate humanity have not been successful in either ecumenical or interfaith affairs. The institutions are playing games of power-for-themselves and are determined to keep themselves separate and worship their own idols. Many religious communities today have simply withdrawn from the real world into their colonial cocoons and have little to do with bringing spiritual transformation to social affairs. Many who consider themselves guardians of the morals of individuals are themselves the protectors of collective systems of immoral economic oppression and political violence. Many "believers" who embraced liberation and rejoiced in the overthrow of oppression a few decades ago seem to have deserted the God involved in the liberation of society and gone back to running religions that languish in the oppressive status quo. They have forgotten the words of the Upanishads and the Gita, of Gautama the

Buddha, of Isaiah and Amos and Zoroaster, of Jesus and Muhammad, and devote themselves to promoting traditions "which make the Word of God of no effect." We need to rediscover a secular spirituality: "the mystery of life which lies beyond everything that humans have encapsulated in systems."[28]

Increasing numbers of people in Africa know that the time has come for change. The grip of the oppressive economic regimes must be broken. There is no alterative to throwing out the idols that have usurped the message of the prophets. There is no alternative for Earthlings but to recover the care and compassion and cooperation of ubuntu. There is no alterative way to do it than by small groups of Earthlings working from the bottom up. There is no alternative to real democratic change, worldwide.

The Crux of the Matter

Ecology, economics, and theology have always been very closely integrated in human development, leading each other forward and from time to time demanding revolutionary changes in Earthling development. One of the earliest was the first agricultural revolution about three thousand years ago, when new methods enabled people to grow more food than they needed for themselves, and trade with the surplus built up their wealth. This led to the first civilizations, which in turn demanded progression from the concept of spirits focused in local cults to the emergence of the great confessional faiths of China, Buddhism, and Hinduism and eventually Judaism, Christianity, and Islam.

The industrial revolution that developed from the seventeenth and eighteenth centuries onward made similar demands. As Karen Armstrong puts it, "All over the world people are finding that in their dramatically transformed circumstances the old forms of faith no longer work for them: they cannot provide the enlightenment and consolation that human beings seem to need. As a result men and women are trying to find new ways of being religious."

The Earthling community has continued to evolve; unprecedented ecological and economic developments have totally changed our way of life. Education and science, reading, writing, and printing demand an enlightenment that neither the great confessions of faith of the medieval religions nor the colonial political and economic empires of the twentieth century can provide. People know in their deepest being that the Earthling community is capable of better than the suicidal violence of nations, and the self-centered greed of both capitalism and socialism. These "do not work for us anymore," and the conflicts of interest between the religions offer no solution at all.

One possibility is atheism, which is spreading rapidly throughout the world, but does not provide a new way forward. Atheism does not mean that something has gone wrong with people, but that something has gone wrong with religions. The second possibility is fundamentalism, which is also spreading widely in all religions, but also offers no way forward. We need something new.

Afterword

Spirituality is secular. It has no existence in a vague ethereal realm. The heart of the matter is not a set of commandments but the rediscovery of spirituality as the stuff of secular life — the human experience of living a belief in care and goodness. That revolution of the spirit, of ubuntu, is the crux of the matter.

Chapter 10

Something New Out of Africa

Synopsis

Africa asserts that the time has come for Earthlings to emerge from their long childhood in the patches and go over into adulthood. We can take our true selves seriously and enact a way of salvation/liberation. It comes from the bottom up not the top down and is a turning from (repentance) and turning to (faith). Small liberated groups are emerging in Africa, America, Europe, and Asia.

10.1. Beyond Patches to Earthlings

10.2. Empires Collapse

10.3. From the Bottom Up

10.4. Small Groups

10.5. A Postreligion Theology

10.6. The New Era

10.7. Going Over

Perhaps the time has come for the emergence of a united movement of the people of the world that would come together to work for the creation of a new world order.

— Thabo Mbeki

10.1. Beyond Patches to Earthlings

Homo sapiens took its first naked steps in Africa many millennia ago but has long been fitted with colonial boots in a world where the "civilized" nations dominate Africa. They often seem to have taken over not only our gold and diamonds but our minds and souls as well, making the whole Earth a disaster area headed for collapse. But two thousand years ago, as we have seen, the elder Pliny said there was "always something new out of Africa" and many descendants of Mrs. Ples think something new is coming out of Africa today: a new understanding and approach to humanity is emerging.

As the world has sought to gobble Africa up by colonization, globalization, and liberation-without-transformation, many people in Africa know we must recover the vision and values of Earthlings, which means un-learning much. We must revisit square one and rediscover the priorities that existed when Earthlings first emerged. The Earth cannot be saved by civilization: it has the brains and brawn but not the spirit for it. The social spirituality of ubuntu helps both West and East to appreciate the things that matter in transforming life on Earth today.

The civilization of the globe has failed Africa, and now we seek to read Africa into the globe. The primary concern of Earthlings must be to seek mature community for the whole Planet, not to pitch patch against patch. Our spiritual nature long predates the invention of ungodly disputes about idols by the elites of national and religious institutions that play such havoc with humanity. Like the chameleons on the shrubs in our garden that take on the color of their surroundings, we tint our Earthling vision to favor the viewpoint of our own colonial inheritance. As Christian, Muslim, Hindu, Jew, or agnostic, or as American, British, or Chinese, we talk of tolerance, but actually wish to convert others to our point of view. Real progress means recovering the primal spirituality that all Earthlings enjoyed before they left Africa to become civilized. Our basic spiritual nature, like walking on our back legs and having huge brains, is deep in the makeup of all of us humans, and unity and strength come from reembracing this basic vision and these values.

Some people are middle-ditherers. They have lost confidence in their patches, but have not yet found faith in being Earthlings. They recognize there is something beyond being Christian, Muslim, Hindu, Jew, or atheist; something beyond being British, Xhosa, German, or American; white or black; but they have no firm sense of being whole humans of Earth. The true faith of being a community of human beings who are Earthlings has not yet made them free (John 8:31–32). They are currently rootless, with a sense of lost-ness, which makes them susceptible to exploiters with boodle or bombast. In the struggle to save the planet we are oppressors or liberators whether we like it or not, and we must liberate ourselves. It demands a decision to un-think our inherited divisive views, and rethink Earthling society, recovering the common good of life, the sacred-secular approach that chases away the Five Horsemen with their abuse of politics, economics, religion, the media, and ecology, and puts us into the business of liberation, not apocalypse.

The agenda for Earthlings to save humanity this century follows closely on the hard facts learned in all liberation struggles in Africa and worldwide. We must choose to liberate ourselves from our patches and their leadership, claiming life together rather than death separately. Earthlings are engaged in an epic secular-spiritual revolution to rediscover ubuntu in the face of the peril of human extinction. As long ago as 1974, the All Africa Conference of Churches meeting in Lusaka said: "African traditional religion with its firm belief in both a transcendent and immanent God and the conception of man as having no separate existence from his Creator, from the living dead, or from the community, provides us with the roots on which a firm and permanent faith can survive in Africa."

Many people, globally, are looking for the dawn, ready for the rising sun, believing in the vital force of the Basileia or whatever they call this dramatic movement of evolution and transformation. "Space is open . . . for the development and consolidation of a global progressive movement encompassing all sections of society including both progressive governments and progressive social movements, and progressives in the religious and cultural movements too. It must be broad in scope, but organized and galvanized along principled lines," said Aziz Pahad.[1]

Fellow spirits are emerging everywhere with the vision and competence to free themselves from the manipulation of the imperialist elites. Evolution has seen industrial revolution, agrarian revolution, scientific revolution, democratic revolution, economic revolution, and now a global revolution of spirit is thrusting forward. The characteristics considered to be African tradition are actually human tradition. The vision and vigor encapsulated in ubuntu is available to us all to save one another and our planet.

10.2. Empires Collapse

It encourages many of us, in despondent moments, to realize that the empires of the patches always collapse. Throughout history, the great empires of the past have come — and gone. The quest to retain power in state, money, or religion has always been built on self-centered desire and delusion, which have collapsed. It happened in China, India, Egypt, Greece, Rome, the Middle Ages of Europe, the rise and fall of the British Empire, the swift sweep of Soviet Communism, and the current traumas of the United States and globalized capital. Our gods are idols.

The evolution of Earthling spiritual concerns has seen a succession of religious patches, including those in Africa, from Traditional to Christian, Jewish, Muslim, Hindu, and Buddhist. All have seen constant change and development. Postreligious global realities are emerging in what Martin Prozesky calls "a voyage of moral discovery." It begins with

> the creation of a global morality. Science and technology are already global realities. So are the market, electronic communications, jet travel, some prominent sporting codes [rules] and pollution. Each of these is fraught with ethical problems, and there is no way these will be overcome by the fragmented, backward-looking moral sense that continues to define the ethical landscapes of the planet. . . . We need a new global ethics agenda in which ethics consciously seeks the involvement of practicing technologists in a shared quest for a more powerful ethic and even more successful science as the two defining features of the 21st century.[2]

It hurts when we get it wrong. The quest for change brings empires down like buildings tumbling when earthquakes move beneath them, and it brings much suffering. The pain of millions in the tragic competition of the patchwork empires guides us to what is wrong and right, and this is happening now. Suffering is the pattern of the patchworks, and their inability to sustain life in the twenty-first century will continue until people free themselves to be reborn as Earthlings. In a situation of overpopulation, aggressive warfare, greed and poverty, ignorance, superstition, twisted information, and captivity by a secular life that excludes spiritual power and a spiritual life that focuses on heaven instead of Earth, collapse is the way to new life. It is the story of Africa.

Anguish awakens many of us to reality and urges us forward, and is doing so now. Humanity crumples because we have got it wrong, and we must expect warfare and hunger, sickness and death, the crunch of corruption and ignorance, the pangs of poverty, fear, and superstition to run amok until we get it right, liberate ourselves, and learn the ways of community. The deadly grip of the patchwork empires of our countries, religions, economies, and cultures brings confusion and catastrophe as they collapse around us, and as Earthlings continue to evolve.

Struggle is the stuff of evolution all over the world. It is to this that Kgalema Motlanthe speaks when he says: "The fundamental transformation of our social values requires an engagement in struggle every bit as determined and relentless as the struggle to deepen democracy, to eradicate racism and other forms of discrimination, and to build a better life for all our people."[3]

The struggle against suffering insists that Earthlings go down or up: there is no standing still. Either we submit to the perpetual suffering of oppression or we liberate ourselves to become free, healed, secular-spiritual Earthlings. In this twenty-first century we must become Earthlings and leave behind the view of the world with faith corrupted and hope confined by patchwork gods whose day is over.

10.3. From the Bottom Up

Change comes from the bottom. I have had an interesting life. Living "between the times" when the world has been turning upside down has meant knowing many people and going many places, but the formative meetings have not been those with presidents and archbishops and professors, the wealthy and endowed, the parliaments and high profile religious celebrations. The pointing finger has been in shacks in townships, with displaced farm laborers and their families, in shanty towns, talking in hospital wards and waiting rooms with HIV/AIDS families headed by teenagers, students sprawled in overcrowded rooms in hostels, revolutionaries "on the run," those out of work, the weak and ailing aged in rural huts, and those seeking new ways of being. Many may be depressed, but always there are people with an enlightened, independent, postreligious vision seeking the spiritual maturity of the human community. And it is so good to be together.

Such groups enable the reflection and action that move humanity forward. Their efforts can be highly academic, writes Paul Gifford, but not necessarily. "It is essentially a popular thing, done by ordinary people reflecting on their own experience. . . . People with little formal education can articulate their experiences, analyze their situation, recognize structures, make connections, see imperfections, and propose alternatives."[4]

During the struggle for freedom in Africa it seemed as if all the cards were stacked against us. We had no money, no vote, little education, and no media, and religions were run by people who might occasionally criticize oppressive regimes but had no intention of taking the risk of joining the struggle against them. But down at the bottom the people had faith in the struggle; we believed that liberation was built into the structure of humanity and would overcome the oppression. We knew that change comes from below, not from above, and it would come from us.

The words of Beyers Naudé of the Christian Institute bear repeating: "The true power of change and renewal always emanates from the grassroots, from the rank and file of the thousands and millions of those whose names never become known, whose commitments to justice and peace are never sung in praises, but without whose support and action no meaningful change ever takes place."[5] Earthlings evolve from the bottom upward, not the top downward.

10.4. Small Groups

Small groups that prompt a postcolonial vision with the verve and values to lead the world to maturity are the crucial activity at the moment, not vast national or international conferences or the prominent people the media promote to sell their wares.

We often make mistakes about it. People concerned for liberation issues become enthusiastic and set up study groups, consultations, and conferences to examine the issues involved as if they can lead change from the top and later mourn the fact that their efforts seemed to fade away. The main problem was that we met in the wrong places, in austere and privileged religious, political, or academic centers in cities or universities or the premises of big financial houses, far from the haunts of the needy. We sought the support of "people of influence" instead of "the influence of the people." The way forward is to recover the practice of regular small group living and sharing and supporting. Because we hurtle around in cars and aircraft, watch television, and talk on telephones, many families and neighbors don't actually meet together anymore. The transformation experience of meeting has been commercialized and individualized out of us. The dead weight of self-justifying politicians, business people, labor and religious leaders worshiping the idols of themselves in the media always inhibits the impetus of liberation from below.

I was very fortunate that my introduction to the real things of Basileia life was not ruined before it started by high powered religious or political meetings, funded by business interests. I came to know plenty of that; but I learned the trade of Jesus and Muhammad and the prophets of the East in the homes of penniless evangelists, clergy and lay preachers, political prisoners who had served their terms, impoverished students, struggling school teachers, overburdened housewives, farmers, professors, and doctors who "wanted to do the best they could," black and white, young and old, male and female, in unheard of places like Umbogintwini, Gqogqora, Sotondoshe, Langa, Sekhukhuneland, Mahlabatini, and Soweto (which sounds very African, but is an acronym for the SOuth WEstern TOwnships of Johannesburg). Talking with Steve Biko and his colleagues in his mother's home in Ginsberg Location; Joe Slovo at home trying to tune my antiquated guitar; taking the Dalai Lama to meet Walter Sisulu in his house in Orlando; the young students planning Mashwabada Myatula's funeral with Frank Chikane — change came from small groups of people who knew nothing of the word "Basileia," but knew more of the experience of the ruling power of ubuntu than a thousand books and sermons.

Jesus' conviction about a ruling power among Earthlings proclaims a positive evolutionary movement in human society that we can recognize and go with, the life force coming to harvest (Mark 1:15). The Basileia was not to establish a church institution, not to provide a way to life after death, not to make Jesus into a god, not based on great leaders. The Basileia was *among you*, full of promise, known in small groups of Earthlings.

Followers of Jesus walking on the postreligious path today and studying their scriptures find that some of the notions of earlier Christian empires played no part in the actual teaching of Jesus. Traditions about the Trinity, original sin, hell, apocalypse, Pentecostal-type fundamentalist superstitions, the quest for money, and interesting practices about smells and bells do not figure in Jesus' concern for the Basileia on Earth.

Many people are aware that their deepest being reaches beyond the popular expectations of the media or religion. They are often troubled, feeling a strength and comfort just beyond them that alarms them, scares them, may make them lonely and restless, but fascinates them, calls them, and fires them with faith and hope.

The Jesus people were not rooted in doctrines and institutions, but in community that arises from small groups, the sense of ubuntu, of compassion and cooperation in caring for one another, in following the Way of the prophets, the values of love, joy, and peace, in the vision of shared ownership and responsibility for the Earth. This is the liberation struggle to which we are called.

The elites and empires had never heard of Jesus and Muhammad, the Buddhas and the Gandhis, the Darwins and the Dunlops, the Wright Brothers and the Wesleys, the suffragettes and the socialists, the Shakespeares and the Bunyans who came in from the cold — but they are the ones who wrote change on the pages of history. New life began to grow: new ways of doing politics and economics, new ways of industry and agriculture, news ways of sociology and culture, new ways of learning and using our spirituality. Every advance in liberation in Africa, from the small states around the Bulge, through the massive countries in central Africa, right down to those in the south, came from small groups of people who met in their homes, at work, at play, and began to spread a new view. Earthlings have often been driven by elites, but they are not led by them. The great and powerful may seem to rule, and think they rule, but new life comes from below or it does not come at all. The caesars, kings, and dictators give way to the people; popes and potentates and priestly impresarios see people turn to lonely crucified prophets; the rich see the masses follow the poor; the oppressors see the powerless liberate themselves.

Evolution is a bottom-up business, a do-it-yourself concern that emerges among small groups learning to establish a common liberated, compassionate, cooperative postreligion unity. We certainly need good leaders, women and men with vision and courage and charisma to lead us forward, to haul the Horsemen off their mounts and change direction, "Courageous visionary leaders at all levels of society are critical to success," says Mamphela Ramphele. But the greatest immediate need is the leadership of small local groups who know where they are going and will spur their leaders on. Throughout Africa — and the world — small groups are coming together of their own volition on their own grounds, part of the great move forward by evolving Earthlings in this century.

Just recently, while writing this book, I have come across the following:

- students in a university town have set up a small organization to assist impoverished young people to find education and jobs;
- nine local clergy from several Christian, Muslim, and Hindu backgrounds meet regularly in a country town to talk theology and politics, anchored in a project to change the living conditions of the needy in their local township;
- a dozen people from different backgrounds said: "Twenty years ago we thought we had won the liberation struggle, but look at Africa today. It has not worked. Where have we gone wrong? How do we get it right?"
- clergy, academics, and students in a provincial town meet several times a year to explore the religion and politics of the society in which they live, breaking through the secular-spiritual barriers of civilization;
- a handful of people from different language and racial backgrounds, concerned about the failure of institutional religion and politics to address the needs of those discriminated against on grounds of race, sexual orientation, lack of education, or poverty, are now exploring these issues;
- another totally mixed group is focused on the environment, with constant use of the Internet, meetings, and putting pressure for change on authorities in business and government;
- several groups of just "ordinary people," Christian, Hindu, Muslim, and agnostic, meet regularly in their homes over supper and explore their spiritual and secular experience.

Small dissatisfied, questioning, liberating groups with new thinking are arising in the trade unions, among women, fishermen, reformed Jews, educators, socialists, politicians, financiers, and the media. And if I have learned of these just recently, imagine the mass of concerned people in such small groups across the continent and across the world. From such small groups Earthlings emerge to organize, liberate, and save the planet.

10.5. A Postreligion Theology

Theology is the science of spirituality indicating where the human community is going, but it is not a Do-It-Yourself kit for getting there.

Christopher Wren, the architect who designed St. Paul's Cathedral in London, lived in a small house on the south bank of the Thames, where he could see how the work was progressing. He was an architectural genius, with a magnificent concept, a grasp of design and construction far beyond his peers, the ability to negotiate the problems and conflicting interests of builders, ecclesiastics, governments, and financiers for forty years to ensure the cathedral was built — but he would have been useless with hammer and chisel. Similarly, theology may envision an emancipated human community, but the actual building will be done by scientists, environmentalists, unionists, economists, politicians, educators, the media, religions, and many practicing Earthlings. Theology can provide the vision, purpose, and design of a spiritually alive community: others have the expertise to turn it into bricks and mortar. "This imaginative anticipation of an alternative society is now more urgent than ever," writes Johan Cilliers.[6]

The South African Institute of Contextual Theology, set up in the closing years of the liberation struggle, stated:

> Theology has been thought of, for far too long, as a highly specialized, intellectual, and abstract study reserved for academic experts and students of theology. Today more and more people are beginning to feel the need to liberate themselves from theologies that are determined and thought out by an academic and ecclesiastical elite. They are discovering that theology, like so many things, can be done, and very effectively done, by themselves.[7]

We have discovered that Earthlings do not have to adhere to any specific beliefs about God or become this or that sort of Christian, Muslim, Jew, Hindu, or agnostic in order to believe in the spiritual vitality of Earthlings. Theology can launch humanity into spiritual adulthood with a new vision that chases away the Five Horsemen of the Apocalypse with hope for humanity. People are relearning how to be Earthlings together without laying down any requirements about religion. The real treasures of what you believe or do not believe about a supreme being, or heaven, or your ancestors, or your guru, can be taken into this transformed awareness of what life is about.

Many groups in the South and West and East pick up the same vibrations of the enlightened theology of transformation emerging in Africa today. They proclaim with glad assurance that there is a ruling power (Basileia) among Earthlings

+ that works through ubuntu in care, compassion, and cooperation;

+ that endows a new vitality and poignancy on the whole of life;

+ that moves the emphasis from the afterlife to this life and from the individual to the community;

+ that enlarges the concern of the spiritual to include the secular and the secular to include the spiritual;

+ that moves concentration from individual self-centered religious communities to seeking life, health, and peace for Earthling communities;

+ that turns away from old notions of merely personal repentance to new visions and values for repentance and faith in society;

+ that brings to people the assurance that they are on the right track.

It is best to let people give their impressions in their own words.

Tinyiko Sam Maluleke describes his early life in a remote rural village where the people enjoyed traditional exuberant African religion during the week, and on Sundays footed six miles together to the mission chapel.

The real and lived experience of the people was unorthodox, rich, varied, and untidy — borrowing, taming, radicalizing, bending, deflecting, and reflecting thoughts and experiences from many traditions...in a coherent conjunction that has produced and continues to sustain African Christianity....I am suggesting that in African Christianity we have a new religion — new in relation to pre-colonial African religion and new in relation to colonial Christianity....We need to begin looking at this new religion on its own terms and not constantly judge it against either conventional Christian doctrine or conventional African religion. African Christianity is a dynamic young religion which we have not yet begun to appreciate....This means rethinking many of our inherited analytical categories. We can meet this challenge only if we are prepared to relinquish some of our long-held methodological starting points.[8]

Stephen Bantu Biko, of the Black Consciousness Movement, who was killed by the Security Police, said:

Ours is a true human centered society whose sacred tradition is that of sharing. We must reject, as we have been doing, the individualistic cold approach to life that is the cornerstone of the Anglo-Boer culture. We must seek to restore to the Black man the great stress we used to lay on human relationships, the high regard for people, their property, and for life in general; to dwarf the triumph of technology...and to reduce the materialistic element that is slowly creeping into our society.[9]

Louise Kretzchmar takes it further:

The involvement of moral leaders with communities beyond their own small church group or social location, is vital.... Those who have crossed the racial and class lines and formed deep and trusting relationships with individuals and communities different from their own have developed a theology less determined by the ideology of their own social group.[10]

There is no way of counting the millions of people throughout the world who have liberated themselves from the superstitious and fanciful inventions of their religious patches and laid hold of a lively faith in the sacred-secular approach of Earthlings. **Martin Prozesky** calls them "freelance believers."

Secular spirituality is not limited to religious institutional practices, says **Celia Kourie** of UNISA:

> Post modern spirituality in many instances can be described as secular spirituality.... Religion no longer holds meaning for large numbers of women and men today, yet there is a deep desire for true spirituality.... Clearly, a non-religious path which contributes to society and enhances human life is to be esteemed.[11]

Fidel Castro records that throughout his upbringing Jesus Christ was one of the most familiar names to him although he never really acquired religious faith:

> I never saw any contradiction in the political and revolutionary sphere between the ideals I upheld, and the idea of that symbol, that extraordinary figure, that had been so familiar to me ever since I could remember.[12]

Joe Slovo was a major figure in the South African liberation struggle, a minister in Mandela's government, and the leader of the South African Communist Party. He wrote:

> It is my contention that there is a major convergence between the ethical content of Marxism and all that is best in the world's religions. But it must also be conceded that in the name of Marxism and religion great damage has been done to the human condition. Both ideologies have produced martyrs in the cause of liberation and tyrants in the cause of oppression. Let us [socialists and believers] stop concentrating exclusively on the debate about whether there is or is not a paradise in heaven. Let us work together to build a paradise on Earth. As for myself, if I eventually find a paradise in heaven, I will regard it as a bonus.[13]

All these are indications of the postreligious theology that is emerging in Africa, as elsewhere, but cannot be confined to previous concepts. Earthlings are doing something new.

10.6. The New Era

One of the fascinating experiences of living in the bush, as we do, is the dawn. You never quite know what it will bring. The sun is coming up: that is for sure. A new era is dawning and will present itself to you in due course. One morning on an early stroll we met fourteen breakfasting giraffes who suspended operations to stare at us, as we stared at them. Or it might be twenty mongooses sitting up and staring over the grass, or zebras, or wildebeests tossing their heads, or kudus with their beautiful horns, a chattering, tumbling, leaping crowd of vervet monkeys, or a snake suspending itself from a branch to the ground — and those still abed see none of it. Day is coming, and with it new life and adventure.

That is how we are as the New Era dawns on Earthlings. It is coming, but we don't know the details. The old empires are collapsing but we don't know what demise the headlines will show today. Nor do we know clearly what the next great strides will be, because the unity and collective life of small groups is emerging day by day. But for sure yesterday is gone, and a new day is dawning.

There is a ruling power, a vital force, operating in the Earthling community: driving ecology, economics, politics, the media, and spirituality. Positive developments are happening within the Earthling community as it becomes aware of the need and imminence of new birth and knows it has the spirit to overcome the problems. People, not power groups of empires, are the stuff of Earth to whom theology says we should bend an ear. Earthlings are chasing away the Five Horsemen of the Apocalypse with a new hope.

10.6.1. Ecology

Earthling theology prompts the spirit to move the environmental agenda to a positive vision for which science and technology are rapidly providing the tools. Sustainable practices and renewable energy can replace the crises of infanticide and extinction with human survival and enjoyment. There is plenty of land in Africa for agriculture to provide food for its people and also for export if food, not profits, is given priority. There is ample room for forestry and scope for fish farming and preserving water, if these are done for the benefit of all people and not for the private profit of a few companies. Limitless supplies of electric power are available in Africa by harnessing the power of sun, wind, and tides. Additional dams on the Congo alone have potential to supply electricity to the whole of Africa and to phase out the ecological destruction of coal-burning power stations. Many cars, trucks, and aircraft can be replaced with eco-friendly vehicles, buses, trains, and ships. Educated, cultured, and prosperous families will handle the birth rate, and good town planning and building construction can accommodate the rapid urbanization. It is a new ecological era.

10.6.2. Economics

The postcolonial economic agenda counsels a movement away from the economic systems designed by the rich on the basis of ruthless competition and greed to an ubuntu economic system, based on compassion and cooperation, to provide peace and prosperity for all. The agenda is not set by the capitalism vs. socialism debate of the eighteenth- and nineteenth-century West, but a development economy arising in the majority world, putting the provision of work and income for all before financial profit for some. It comes from a new attitude to stewardship and possession and community. It demands an economic system that focuses on well-fed, healthy, well-educated, cultured Earthlings, who have banished poverty and ignorance, not on acquiring excessive wealth for a few. It is not served by inserting black people into the colonial system designed to promote an oppressive class that was formerly white, nor by corrupt fundamentalist so-called "Christian" theologies promising wealth now and heaven later to those who support their churches: the new economic era is essentially an ethical struggle to facilitate good things for all. Its spiritual resource of concern for others explores new developments, new concepts, new structures, and new economic opportunities to use capital to liberate instead of oppress.

10.6.3. Politics

Earthlings are moving beyond the concept of nation-states toward an international cooperative and supportive community. It is hard going, but that is the vision. The theological pattern for Earthlings is where and *how* our political path should lead, taking the place of *to whom* current greed-hugging priorities are directed. Our politics are being rethought and replaced by a postcolonial political agenda that knows the reality of history, but also recognizes that Earthlings today reject antagonistic political patches led by people whose agenda is to secure personal profit. The politics of Earthlings demands politicians of integrity, free from bribers and corruptors and position seekers. It requires reviewing the role of political parties in serving the democratic purposes of thousands of families and tribes with common ubuntu aims in the developing world. One key to this renewed political dispensation is clearly to unlock the vision of democratic objectives to tackle the vast social transformation required to save the world, but of equal importance is to unlock the credibility of politicians.

10.6.4. Proclamation

The theology of Earthlings needs proclaiming both orally and visually, media to tell out the good news of transformation. Print and electronics have replaced the pens of those who championed the prophets in earlier ages. A new culture mediates a new vision of truth and freedom, providing information rather than propaganda and inspiration rather than indoctrination. The great media future lies in proclaiming and enabling the ubuntu culture. People on Earth want compassion, cooperation, and commitment. The people do not want brutality, cynicism, and corruption, which is what much of our media proclaims. The media can produce a democratic choice of alternatives. An honest investigative media is highly informative about the values and methods to challenge evil and liberate community. The challenge of the spiritual revolution is for groups to take the media seriously and mediate together interfaith and intersectoral developments for rebuilding humanity. It means turning away from much of the present media, which is controlled by the economic and political agents of human extinction. Liberation movements have always been fortified by small, alternative, independent media, and new ventures in the world of text messaging, email, and websites make anyone's finger tips a pulpit or a platform for broadcasting change.

10.6.5. Spirituality

One of my favorite daydreams takes place in the large living room of a home in Africa, which may be a commodious circle under the thatch of a rural hut, or a large spread like the living room in our old house in the suburbs of Jo'burg. Our hostess is black and busy, a highly articulate academic, but on this occasion, she is aiding her children to be sure that everyone has tea or wine or water, *wors* (sausage), salads or cakes. Our children and grandchildren are in my daydream too, including Eddie, who has Down syndrome, although he is so cheerful and chatty you would hardly notice. Perhaps the company has got to him.

For Jesus is there in my daydream, only thirty years old, sitting next to his friend Mary of Magdala, telling a story to Gautama the Buddha on one side with Isaiah the statesman and Amos the shepherd on the other. Muhammad is locked in talk with Karl Marx, whenever they can get a word in, because the former's wives and the latter's daughter are very loquacious. Confucius and Lao Tse are having a great time, nodding away in agreement with Zoroaster and Abraham, as one of the African women gives a little exposition of ubuntu.

When the conversation becomes general, not one of these prophets in my daydream refers to the religious and political institutions that claim their names: it seems a painful subject of conflict and confusion that they all prefer to avoid. The focus of the conversation is Earthlings today. The prophets from the past are discussing the people of the present, the spirit of the communities and comrades now, and how things are going. They reveal a similar analysis, similar hopes, and a similar vision, espousing the same values, and asserting the same powers in the depths of human community. They do not harp on the oppressors and corruptors (they have seen so many fail), but on the transformation brought about by groups formed by compassion, caring, and cooperation; they talk about going forward to do new things together; they clearly all believe in a positive power operating in the Earthling community to drive away our fears and guide our progress; no one mentions heaven. And then, just as I am about to ask questions, the daydream ends and I realize again that we have to do some of it ourselves.

The struggle for a postreligion agenda is not simply polite inquiries about doctrines, kosher, halal, dress, and the ways and days of religious celebrations. It is about the struggle to release the spirit in humanity committed to expound and explore together a postreligion spiritual revolution. It is the recognition that at the root of all our religions lies the fact of our spiritual nature, the power to reject the oppressors of division and violence.

Methodist President Ivan Abrahams says, "Bound together on our journey by common values and a strong moral consciousness, we should draw upon all the resources of the human spirit, organized religion, spiritual movements, and other institutions to act and speak from a position of love and respect."[14]

Spiritually alert people are moving beyond protecting the institutions and doctrines of the patches that divide us, emphasizing the hyper-reality of life on Earth here and now, rather than hypothetical life after death, rediscovering the ruling power of love and joy and peace that all the prophets proclaim in every aspect of life.

The role of theology is to take the vision, values, presence, and cooperation into the democratic processes of politics, economics, and religion. Religions "must take seriously their duty to understand the special role religion inevitably plays, and should educate their members on this issue," writes Paul Gifford.[15] It calls parents and teachers, clergy and politicians, business and the media, managers and workers, employed and unemployed to consider how to do compassion and cooperation together in the modern suffering world. True spiritual presence "needs comprehensive and sustained participation in the political community . . . in the full process: setting the agenda, making the rules, and critically examining the outcomes," says Russel Botman.[16]

"The fundamental transformation of our social values requires an engagement in struggle every bit as determined and relentless as the struggle to deepen democracy, to eradicate racism and other forms of discriminination, and to build a better life for all our people," says Kgalema Motlanthe.

The new era is a new era: whether in reluctance or relief it has left behind the old ways of doing religion, politics, and economics. Earthlings are growing up.

10.7. Going Over

> There is always a way for those who must go over
> When from the known the mind revolts and despairs
> There lies the way, and there we must go over.
> — Ruth Pitter, *The Bridge*

I have often been to places of worship that were strange to me and some come easily to mind: a carpet-floored mosque in Hebron; a synagogue in Jerusalem; Catholic churches in Rome and Winnipeg you could hardly see for the incense; the circle of a Canadian

Indian congregation in Regina; the loaded altar of a Hindu Temple in London; the massive congregation packed into the Church in Khartoum; from stained glass with a choir and organ to a stone under a tree in South Africa.

There are two reactions. The first is to check the differences: shoes or no shoes, pews or carpets or kneeling stools, altar or communion table or tabernacle, cross or crucifix, the bowls and plants and stones and objects around the altar, the pulpit and the imam's chair, the treatment of walls and windows, the vestments, the smells and sounds of it all. The second reaction, behind all these things, senses the common Earthling awareness of spiritual presence and power wherever you have come from yourself. You want to take the shoes from off your feet because, like Moses, this is a place where Earthlings like you do their human holy thing together. This is what it is all about, and the viewing like a visitor to a museum melts into the satisfaction of quietness, sitting or standing or kneeling to contemplate the wonder of Earthling spiritual union and communion. It is a unity that runs underneath all the tensions and conflicts and hopes in Africa.

This book seeks to proclaim a new vision, not a detailed program. The proclamation comes first: the manifesto comes later from people-in-community: the need for jobs, for health care and education, for a reordering of resources and a development economy, for a spiritual-secular approach to the world, a representative government beyond the patches of national states, and the liberation of Earthlings from ecological suicide — all needs to be worked out by us all. But the first essential is to liberate our heads and hearts: to freshen the debate, catch the vision, stir the faith that invigorates action as Earthlings.

The actual experience of going over to believe in a renewed Earth, the truth that liberates us, the faith that frees, often crystalizes in a specific moment of awareness that can come in a hundred different ways, from a political rebirth to a religious conversion or an intellectual awareness. (I know exactly where and when it first came to me — in a forest — and other special moments of awareness since.)

The prophets in all walks of life call us to repentance and faith, and there is much sense in this in Africa and everywhere else. Repentance means *turning away* from negative ways of life, and faith means *turning to* positive ways. Traditional evangelical campaigns see repentance only in terms of personal sin (anything from theft and drunkenness to sexual or religious aberrations — which is a switch-off for the millions who aren't involved with these things anyway). It demands a turning to new beliefs and behaviors (anything from joining a different religion to accepting that Jesus let himself be killed to bargain his life with God to obtain forgiveness for your sins — or so they seem to put it!). But both repentance and faith move with the times. Religious believers today often need to be liberated from indoctrination by the individualistic-colonialist-imperialist-missionary religions they inherited, or from the superstitions of the poppycock fundamentalists and turn to the postreligion secular-spirituality world.

Many Earthlings seeking new life in Africa today know that both repentance and faith are far wider than the personal desire to go to heaven when you die. That concern does not preclude a responsible concern for what happens to humanity while we are alive. Repentance cannot be confined to personal sins; it includes the collective sin that prompts anti-Earthling economic, political, and religious systems. Millions who live good and upright personal lives suffer perpetually from our poverty-stricken sinful society. Africa knows well that our present religious, political, and economic systems don't work for Earthlings, and we shall get nowhere by trying to be good in bad systems, as if you could throttle people kindly. Repentance begins by admitting that personal goodness and hopes of heaven are not sufficient to transform the secular systems leading Earthling communities astray. Whatever we have done about religious institutions, we must bring the spiritual and secular together again. Evil systems are not handled by reforming them but by transforming them.

This is an area where the African message of liberation and ubuntu seems crucial to Americans and Europeans seeking to "go over" to the Earthling experience.

Faith and intellect walk hand in hand and side by side. To live by faith does not mean living as if something is true when it is not, but living in the confidence that evolution and liberation are real. Faith is a hard-nosed experience of believing in positive powers operating in the community, an intellectually satisfying concept based on wisdom gleaned in earlier theological periods but pointing onward, an expectant realization of positive happenings in life. Faith is not an object of belief, but the experience of believing. Faith does not say, "The Basileia will come tomorrow if you are good" but "We're on our way." Faith means living in the process of discovery, not in the process of denial. Faith is the act of swimming, hope is where you are swimming to, and the energy for swimming comes from love. Faith and hope and love empower the quest for liberation and transformation of society today — but are not necessarily religious.

Africa matters because Africa is Good News about faith. It knows that the problems the Earthling community faces are essentially matters of spirit, of vision and values to move the community forward, not of brain and muscles and doctrines. Many ordinary people of Africa know that civilization has to be liberated from the horrendous purposes of elites and empires by rediscovering the truth that small is beautiful and liberation comes from the bottom up, not the top down.

◆ ◆ ◆

Evolving beyond where we are does not mean throwing away all our earlier religious beliefs in order to grasp the new truth, any more than it is necessary to renounce our race, our sex, or our history to dispense with racism, sexism, or nationalism. Many have been reared in a spirit of antagonism between patches of believers and unbelievers. Atheists believe there are neither good nor bad gods. Agnostics believe that the case for or against god is not proven and keep their minds open. Believers are legion. But the conflict between believers and unbelievers was not a major issue for the prophets in their quest for liberation from the elite of the political-religious systems of their day. We learned the same in the African liberation struggles: liberation from oppression brought us all together: you did not have to belong to this or that political party or religious group or race. Liberation was an Earthling thing, like evolution. Believers and unbelievers can both be extremely moral and ethical people, totally committed to the liberation of Earthlings, and willing to put their lives on the line for it. People from many different backgrounds had a common agenda to unite with atheists, agnostics, and different believers, races, and classes, not to antagonize them. We all have a good case.

We are no longer dominated by the clamor of the Horsemen of the Apocalypse. Rather we hear the call of the Earthling community turning the world around with ubuntu, the care and compassion of a global revolution of secular spirituality.

"A person can be good in a bad world, but a bad world cannot be made better unless those who value good unite, organize, and mobilize in a struggle to change the world," said Kgalema Motlanthe. "We dare not abandon the struggle, either through timidity, or complacency, in the belief that we can hope a new set of values into existence. Like every other form of transformation, we can only hope to achieve our values through struggle. And more struggle."[17]

It is an interfaith, interdisciplinary, bottom-up, meeting-people initiative to proclaim the Basileia vision and values. It takes spiritual guts to join the struggle to take humanity from extinction to transformation.

◆ ◆ ◆

Bill Bryson, contemplating the uniqueness of Earthlings in space, finds it "an unnerving thought that we may be the living universe's supreme achievement and its worst nightmare simultaneously," seeking both extinction and transformation. "What we do know is that there is only one planet to do it on, and only one species capable of making a considered difference.... To attain any kind of life at all in this universe of ours appears to be quite an achievement.... It is a trick we have only just begun to grasp."[18]

Beneath and beyond our inherited and exhausted colonial packages groups of transforming people share a sacred space of wisdom, strength, and hope with no footing for the horsemen of the Apocalypse. A uniting human ethical spirituality to turn the world upside down is available to us — and to our grandchildren. Women and men, young and old, poor and rich, believers and nonbelievers are responding to the primal ubuntu thrust to take the evolution of Earthlings together to its next stage. It is from them that we can expect something new out of Africa to change the world.

And we are all Africans.

Afterword

The challenge that the people of Africa present to the people of America and Europe is a very practical, down-to-earth spiritual business: to liberate themselves from the oppressive economic, political, and religious systems holding them back and to enter the era of Earthlings. We need one another.

And in Conclusion

Writing a book in South Africa for a publisher in North America at the end of this first decade of the twenty-first century without mentioning the names of Barack Obama and Jacob Zuma seems almost irreverent! If precedents hold, both are likely to be in office for several years. Both have roots in Africa. Both were elected by the mobilization of ordinary people; both came in advocating change; both are facing criticisms and objections. It is a most exciting and promising time. Good and bad will emerge, but it is a most promising time to be alive when people reach for the ubuntu way ahead.

◆ ◆ ◆

How can Earthling communities transform the future by reflection and action? Consider:

- In what ways is humanity threatened with destruction?
- What practical things can you urge — and on whom — to build alternatives?
- In the liberation struggle we discovered that reform was the enemy of transformation: How does this apply?
- How can the corruption of power and wealth be exposed, removed, and replaced?
- Whom can you work with to promote the Earthling revolution where you are?
- What vision and values can you build on?
- What can you offer a secular-spiritual age? Whom can you talk to?

How can your religious community bring people together:

- to proclaim their commitment to a liberated Earthling political community?

- to establish Truth and Reconciliation commissions on the economy?
- to insist that their governments embrace ecologically sound policies?
- to empower the media to serve the vision and values of humanity?

Notes

Introduction

1. Martin Prozesky, *Frontiers of Conscience: Exploring Ethics in a New Millennium* (Pietermaritzburg: Equinym Publishing, 2003), 27.

Chapter 1. The Five Horsemen of the Apocalypse

1. Martin Rees, *Our Final Hour: A Scientist's Warning: How Terror, Error, and Environmental Disaster Threaten Humankind's Future in This Century — on Earth and Beyond* (New York: Basic Books, 2003).

2. David Tacey, *The Spirituality Revolution: The Emergence of Contemporary Spirituality* (Sussex and New York: Brunmer-Routledge 2004), 85.

3. Joerg Rieger, *Christ and Empire: From Paul to Postcolonial Times* (Minneapolis: Fortress Press, 2007), 278.

4. Albert Nolan, *Jesus Today: A Spirituality of Radical Freedom* (Maryknoll, N.Y.: Orbis Books, 2006), 31.

5. Al Gore, *The Assault on Reason: How the Politics of Blind Faith Subvert Wise Decision-making* (London: Bloomsbury Publishing, 2007), 9.

6. Jakobus S. Krüger, *Along Edges: Religion in South Africa: Bushman, Christian, Buddhist* (Pretoria: UNISA, 1995), 4.

7. Gert Theissen, *On Having a Critical Faith* (London: SCM Press, 1979), 76.

8. Albert M. Luthuli, *Let My People Go* (Glasgow: Collins Fount Paperbacks, 1989).

Chapter 2. The Earthling Matter

1. Bill Bryson, *A Short History of Nearly Everything* (London: Black Swan Books and Doubleday, 2003), 573.

2. Life may have developed somewhere else in the universe but is so far out in space, or of such a different form, that it is beyond our life or knowledge. Earthlings seem pretty unique as human beings.

3. Brian Swimme on Teilhard de Chardin in *What Is Enlightenment?* (Spring–Summer 2001), *www.EnlightenmentNext*.

4. Aleksei Leonov, "The Home Planet," in *Towards Gondwana Alive* (Pretoria: Gondwana Alive Society, 1988), 15.

5. Bryson, *A Short History of Nearly Everything*, 548.

6. Jakobus S. Krüger, Gerrie Lubbe, and H. C. Steyn, *The Human Search for Meaning: A Multireligious Introduction to the Religions of Humankind* (Hatfield, Pretoria: Van Schaik, 2009), 15.

7. S. A. Thorpe, *Primal Religions Worldwide: An Introductory, Descriptive Review* (Pretoria: UNISA, 1992), 3.

8. Poster on wall of "Carry the Kettle" community, Ontario, Canada.

9. Kofi Appiah-Kubi and Sergio Torres, *African Theology en Route* (Maryknoll, N.Y.: Orbis Books, 1979), 167.

10. Albert Nolan, *Jesus Today: A Spirituality of Radical Freedom* (Maryknoll, N.Y.: Orbis Books, 2006), 63.

11. One of the most foolish things the patches ever did was to deny one another the insights and benefits of the other patches.

12. Steven Bantu Biko, *I Write What I Like* (Aelred Stubbs) (London: Bowerdene Press, 1978), 47.

13. Mercy Oduyoye, *The Value of African Beliefs and Theology for Christian Theology* (Maryknoll, N.Y.: Orbis Books, 1979), 110–11.

14. Krüger, Lubbe, and Steyn, *The Human Search for Meaning*, 55.

15. Nelson Mandela, *Long Walk to Freedom* (Johannesburg: Macdonald Purnell, 1994), 316.

16. Jean Marc-Ela, *African Cry* (Maryknoll, N.Y.: Orbis Books, 1986), 48.

17. Joe Teffo in correspondence with author.

18. Buti Tlhagale in correspondence with author.

19. Arno Peters projection of 1967 is far more helpful, but until space travel is a little cheaper — go for a globe.

20. Global warming has already changed the snowy peaks of Africa.

21. "The polecat does not know it stinks."

22. "The Kairos Document" (1985), quoted in full in *Between Christ and Caesar,* ed. Charles Villa-Vicencio (Grand Rapids, Mich.: William B. Eerdmans, 1986), 251.

23. Desmond Tutu, *No Future without Forgiveness* (London: Random House, 1999), 34.

24. It can be, of course. *Ubuntu* is what the great saintly writers of many religions are portraying, despite the huge problem of relating their experience and writing within the spiritual apartheid of their inherited religious institutions, which separate sacred from secular.

25. Joseph G. Donders, *Non-Bourgeois Theology* (Maryknoll, N.Y.: Orbis Books, 1985), 157.

26. Des Van der Water, *Towards an Agenda for Contextual Theology* (Pietermaritzburg: Cluster Publications, 2001), 35.

27. D. Westerman, *Africa and Christianity* (Oxford: Oxford University Press, 1937).

28. Donders, *Non-Bourgeois Theology,* 156.

29. Gwinyai H. Muzorewa, *The Origins and Development of African Theology* (Maryknoll, N.Y.: Orbis Books, 1985), 91.

30. When I questioned the validity and viability of the present economic system at an interfaith conference in Africa, one of the Americans was incredulous, saying: "But that *is* the way the world works."

31. *A Decade of Interfaith Dialogue: World Conference of Religion and Peace,* ed. Gerrie Lubbe (Johannesburg, 1994), 3.

32. Thorpe, *Primal Religions Worldwide,* 122.

Chapter 3. The Liberation Matter

1. Julius Nyerere in *Africa since 1910*, ed. A. A. Mazrui (Pretoria: Ministry of Education, 2004), 11.

2. Letter to satyagraha organization from Justice Albi Sachs.

3. Nelson Mandela, *Long Walk to Freedom* (Johannesburg: Macdonald Purnell, 1994), 281.

4. David Lamb, *The Africans* (London: Methuen, 1985), 140.

5. L. Wilson in *The Legacy of Stephen Bantu Biko*, ed. C. W. Du Toit (Pretoria: UNISA, 2008), 117.

6. Ibid., 157.

7. Bokwe Mafuna in Chris Van Wyk, *We Write What We Like: Celebrating Steve Biko* (Johannesburg: University of the Witwatersrand Press, 2007), 87.

8. Just as many in the West supported colonialism and apartheid well into the Thatcher/Reagan era.

9. Elliott Kendall, *The End of an Era: Africa and the Missionary* (London: SPCK, 1978), 27.

10. Lamb, *The Africans*, 146.

11. Albert Nolan, *Jesus Today: A Spirituality of Radical Freedom* (Maryknoll, N.Y.: Orbis Books, 2006), 31.

12. Neville Alexander in *The Legacy of Stephen Bantu Biko*, ed. Du Toit, 52.

13. Thabo Mbeki to the Nelson Mandela Foundation, 2006.

14. Kendall, *The End of an Era*, 68.

15. John Gunther, *Inside Africa* (London: Hamish Hamilton, 1955).

16. Quoted in Jeff Guy, *The Heretic: A Study of the Life of John William Colenso, 1814–1883* (Johannesburg: University of Natal, Ravan Press, 1983), 79.

17. Jean-Marc Ela, *African Cry* (Maryknoll, N.Y.: Orbis Books, 1986), 3.

18. Gwinyai H. Muzorewa, *The Origins and Development of African Theology* (Maryknoll, N.Y.: Orbis Books, 1985), 9.

19. C. W. Du Toit in *The Legacy of Stephen Bantu Biko*, ed. Du Toit, 226.

20. See Kendall, *The End of an Era*, 95.

21. Manas Buthelezi, *Church Action in the South African Crisis* (Johannesburg: SACC, 1988).

22. Reza Aslan, *No God but God: The Origins, Evolution, and Future of Islam* (London: Arrow Books, 2006), xix.

23. Tom Nairn in a note to the author.

24. Anne Yates and Lewis Chester, *The Troublemaker: Michael Scott and His Lonely Struggle against Injustice* (London: Aurum Press, 2006), 305.

25. Guy, *The Heretic*, 72.

26. Richard Holloway, *Godless Morality: Keeping Religion out of Ethics* (Edinburgh: Canongate, 1991), 11.

27. AACC cited in Kendall, *The End of an Era*.

28. Ibid.

29. Basil Moore, ed., *Black Theology* (Johannesburg: University Christian Movement, 1972).

30. Henning Melber, *African Liberation Movements and the End of History* (Uppsala, Sweden: Dag Hammarskjöld Foundation, 2008).

31. Address to the ANC Commission of Religious Affairs, June 12, 2007.

Chapter 4. The Ecological Matter

1. Geoff Davies, South African Faith Communities' Environment Institute, Cape Town, 2009.

Chapter 5. The Political Matter

1. Nelson Mandela, *Long Walk to Freedom* (Johannesburg: Macdonald Purnell, 1994), 21.

2. Russel Botman as cited in Mongezi Guma and A. Lesley Milton, *An African Challenge to the Church in the Twenty-first Century* (Johannesburg: South African Council of Churches, 1997), 75–78.

3. Jean-Marc Ela, *African Cry* (Maryknoll, N.Y.: Orbis Books, 1986), 48.

4. Brigalia Bam as cited in Guma and Milton, *An African Challenge to the Church in the Twenty-first Century,* iv.

5. Molefe Tsele as cited in ibid., 84.

6. Sol Plaatje and Pixley ka Isaka Seme as cited in Francis Mele, *South Africa Belongs to Us* (Harare: Zimbabwe Publishing House, 1988), 38.

7. "The African National Congress has a long history of association with the Church. Our founders were church men and women. Throughout our years that link has never been broken" (O. R. Tambo, "South Africa at the Crossroads," lecture at the British Defence and Aid Fund, London, 1988).

8. I was ordained at the Methodist Conference in 1958 in Pietermaritzburg. By coincidence, that great Christian chief Albert Luthuli of the then unbanned African National Congress was billed to speak at a meeting of the then unbanned Liberal Party while we were there. So my father and I ducked out of the conference and went to hear Luthuli. We discovered that half the conference had done the same, but it would have been unheard of for the white leadership to have invited Luthuli to address the Methodist Conference in 1958.

9. Mandela, *Long Walk to Freedom,* 354.

10. When I first became involved in the ministry the wife of one of my senior ministerial colleagues, a devout and leading church lady, told me that the danger was in our own households. The moment liberation came, it was our "garden boy" and "housegirl" who would cut our throats.

11. Charles Villa-Vicencio describes the long quest for human rights in his chapter in *Africa since 1910,* ed. A. A. Mazrui (Pretoria: Ministry of Education, 2004).

12. Sipho Buthelezi in ibid., 2.

13. Stephan de Beer in *The Legacy of Stephen Bantu Biko,* ed. C. W. Du Toit (Pretoria: UNISA, 2008), 173.

14. Claire Robinson as cited in *Africa,* ed. Phyllis M. Martin and Patrick O'Meara (Bloomington: Indiana University Press, 1995), 328.

15. Andre Odendaal in *Africa since 1910,* ed. Mazrui, 190.

16. John C. McCall, "Social Organization in Africa," in *Africa,* ed. Martin and O'Meara, 188.

17. Owen Sichone in *Africa since 1910,* ed. Mazrui, 50.

Chapter 6. The Economic Matter

1. *Beyond Poverty* (Johannesburg: South African Council of Churches Poverty Summit, 1998).

2. Ulrich Duchrow and Franz J. Hinkelammert, *Property for People, Not for Profit: Alternatives to the Global Tyranny of Capital* (London: Zed Books, 2004), 157.

3. Ecumenical Association of Third World Theologians (EATWOT), *Doing Theology* (1985), 186.

4. Nelson Mandela, *Long Walk to Freedom* (Johannesburg: Macdonald Purnell, 1994), 279.

5. Julius Nyerere, *Ujamaa: The Basis of African Socialism* (Dar es Salaam: 1962).

6. Tom Mboya in *Transition* 8 (March 1963).

7. Kwame Nkrumah, president of Ghana, Pan Africa, Nairobi, April 1963.

8. George Padmore in *African Socialism*, ed. William H. Friedland and Carl G. Rosberg (Stanford, Calif: Stanford University Press, 1964), 228.

9. Friedland and Rosberg, eds., *African Socialism* 4–5.

10. Owen Sichone in *Africa since 1910*, ed. A. A. Mazrui, (Pretoria: Ministry of Education, 2004), 51.

11. See Tsele in *An African Challenge to the Church in the Twenty-first Century.*

12. Thabo Mbeki in an address to the Mandela Foundation, Johannesburg, July 29, 2006.

13. Duchrow and Hinkelammert, *Property for People, Not for Profit*, 1.

14. Bishan Singh, "Economics without Ethics," PCD Forum, Bangkok, 1996.

15. ANC, Commission on Religious Affairs, 2007.

16. Martin Prozesky, *Conscience: Ethical Intelligence for Global Well-being* (Pietermaritzburg: University of KwaZulu-Natal, 2007).

17. S. de Gruchy, "Of Agency, Assets and Appreciation," *Journal of Theology for South Africa* 117 (2003): 20–39.

18. Sara Berry in *Africa*, ed. Phyllis M. Martin and Patrick O'Meara (Bloomington: Indiana University Press, 1995), 372.

Chapter 7. The Media Matter

1. Elliott Kendall, *The End of an Era: Africa and the Missionary* (London: SPCK, 1978), 42.

2. Palagummi Sainath, *Johannesburg Star*, October 29, 2008.

3. Al Gore, *The Assault on Reason: How the Politics of Blind Faith Subvert Wise Decision-making* (London: Bloomsbury Publishing, 2007), 99.

4. Joerg Rieger, *Christ and Empire: From Paul to Postcolonial Times* (Minneapolis: Fortress Press, 2007), 294.

5. Russel Botman in Mongezi Guma and A. Lesley Milton, *An African Challenge to the Church in the Twenty-first Century* (Johannesburg: South African Council of Churches, 1997), 78.

Chapter 8. The Spiritual Matter

1. Institute for Justice and Reconciliation, *Interfaith Solidarity*, Cape Town, 2004.

2. Jakobus S. Krüger, *Along Edges: Religion in South Africa: Bushman, Christian, Buddhist* (Pretoria: UNISA, 1995), 173.

3. Diarmuid O'Murchu, *Ancestral Grace* (Maryknoll, N.Y.: Orbis Books, 2008), 79.

4. Jakobus S. Krüger, Gerrie Lubbe, and H. C. Steyn, *The Human Search for Meaning: A Multireligious Introduction to the Religions of Humankind* (Hatfield, Pretoria: Van Schaik, 2009), 54.

5. J. S. Mbiti, *African Religions and Philosophy* (London: Heinemann, 1969).

6. S. A. Thorpe, *Primal Religions Worldwide: An Introductory, Descriptive Review* (Pretoria: UNISA, 1992).

7. Luke L. Pato as cited in *Spirituality in Religions*, ed. C. W. du Toit (Pretoria: UNISA Press, 1996), 112, quoting D. M. Tutu, *An African Prayer Book* (London: Hodder and Stoughton, 1995), xvi.

8. D. J. Mosoma, "Religious Liberty: An African Perspective," in *Religious Freedom in South Africa* (Pretoria: UNISA, 1993), 56.

9. C. W. Du Toit and Cedric Mayson, eds., *Secular Spirituality as a Contextual Critique of Religion*, a compilation of papers presented at the Forum for Religious Dialogue Symposium of the Research Institute for Theology and Religion held at the University of South Africa, Pretoria, May 11–12, 2006 (Pretoria: University of South Africa, 2007), 61.

10. O'Murchu, *Ancestral Grace*, 36.

11. John S. Mbiti, *Introduction to African Religion*, 2nd ed. (Oxford: Heinemann Educational Publishers, 1991), 13–15.

12. N. B. Pityana in *Bounds of Possibility: The Legacy of Steve Biko and Black Consciousness*, ed. N. B. Pityana et al. (Cape Town: David Phillip, 1991), 255.

13. Nelson Mandela, *Long Walk to Freedom* (Johannesburg: Macdonald Purnell, 1994).

14. A. A. Mazrui, *Africa's Pro-Democracy Movement* (London: Random House, 1999).

15. Desmond Mpilo Tutu, *No Future without Forgiveness* (London: Rider, 1999), 34.

16. John S. Pobee, *Who Are the Poor?* (Geneva: WCC, 1987), 55–56.

17. See also chapter 2.

18. Charles Villa-Vicencio, *Trapped in Apartheid* (Maryknoll, N.Y.: Orbis Books, 1988), 201.

19. Elliott Kendall, *The End of an Era* (London: SPCK, 1978), 56.

20. Dwight Hopkins in *Bounds of Possibility*, ed. N. B. Pityana et al., 195.

21. Patrick R. McNaughton and Diane Pelrine, "African Art," in *Africa*, ed. Phyllis M. Martin and Patrick O'Meara (Bloomington: Indiana University Press, 19950, 251.

22. Buti Tlhagale, Catholic archbishop of Johannesburg, unpublished paper, 2009.

23. Kendall, *End of an Era*, 42.

24. Adrian Hastings, *African Christianity* (New York: Macmillan, 1976), 52.

25. As quoted in Gabriel M. Setiloane, *The Image of God among the Sotho-Tswana* (Rotterdam: A. A. Balkema, 1976).

26. Malcolm J. McVie quoted in Gwinyai H. Muzorewa, *The Origins and Development of African Theology* (Maryknoll, N.Y.: Orbis Books, 1985), 9.

27. Beyers Naudé quoted in *Living Spirituality News*, London (Spring 2009).

28. Marcus Braybrooke, *Pilgrimage of Hope: One Hundred Years of Global Interfaith Dialogue*(London: SCM Press, 1992).

29. *A Decade of Interfaith Dialogue: World Conference of Religion and Peace*, ed. Gerrie Lubbe (Johannesburg, 1994).

30. Reza Aslan, *No God but God: The Origins, Evolution, and Future of Islam* (London: Arrow Books, 2009), 248.

31. Johan Cilliers, "Worshipping in the Townships," *Journal of Theology for Southern Africa* 132 (November 2008): 83.

32. John de Gruchy, "Becoming the Ecumenical Church in South Africa Today," background paper for SACC/WCC Conference, March 1995.

33. The Dutch Reformed Church had withdrawn from the South African Council of Churches many years before.

34. *Phakamani*, magazine of the ANC Commission of Religious Affairs, Johannesburg (April 2004): 7

35. Benson as cited in Braybrooke, *Pilgrimage of Hope*, 12.

36. Donald Schoon, BBC Reith Lecture, 1970.

Chapter 9. The Crux of the Matter

1. Swami Agnivesh, "A Spiritual Vision for the Dialogue of Religions," in *Secular Spirituality as a Contextual Critique of Religion*, a compilation of papers presented at the Forum for Religious Dialogue Symposium of the Research Institute for Theology and Religion held at the University of South Africa, Pretoria, May 11–12, 2006 (Pretoria: University of South Africa, 2007), ed. C. W. Du Toit and Cedric Mayson, 185.

2. I used to have a "teasing" sermon in which I quoted many scriptural passages and asked the congregation where they came from? Is it Mark? Luke? Paul? Old Testament or New? Isaiah or Amos? In fact, the texts were from the Upanishads and Quran, the words of the Buddha, Lao Tse, or Zoroaster, and I usually threw in a bit of Marx and Che Guevara as well.

3. D. J. Mosoma, "Religious Liberty: An African Perspective," in *Religious Freedom in South Africa* (Pretoria: UNISA, 1993), 50.

4. W. Cantwell Smith, *Religious Diversity* in *Mission Trends*, 229, quoted in Kenneth Cracknell, *Towards a New Relationship* (London: Epworth Press, 1986), 81–85.

5. Swami Saradananda, *Believers in the Future* (Johannesburg: WCRP, 1991), 63.

6. Dele Jegede, "Popular Culture in Urban Africa," in *Africa*, ed. Patrick R. McNaughton and Diane Pelrine (Bloomington: Indiana University Press, 19950, 274.

7. Canon Peter Hinchcliffe, *The Church in South Africa* (London: SPCK, 1968), 68.

8. Elliott Kendall, *The End of an Era* (London: SPCK, 1978), 56.

9. Biko in *Black Theology*, ed. Basil Moore (Johannesburg: University Christian Movement, 1972) viii.

10. Two of whom are now in the South African government, and one an archbishop.

11. Cyril Harris, *For Heaven's Sake: The Chief Rabbi's Diary* (Johannesburg: Union of Orthodox Synagogues, 2000), 325.

12. Kendall, *The End of an Era*.

13. Leonardo and Clodovis Boff, *Introducing Liberation Theology* (Maryknoll, N.Y.: Orbis Books, 1986), 38.

14. Ibid., 66.

15. Vaughan Jones, *What Is Our Theology of Liberation?* (London: Christian Socialist Movement, 1985).

16. *The Kairos Document: Challenge to the Church*, drafted by the Kairos Theologians in Johannesburg and published in London by the Catholic Institute for International Relations and the British Council of Churches, 1985.

17. Mosoma, "Religious Liberty: An African Perspective," 56.

18. Denise Ackermann, *Claiming Our Footprints: South African Women Reflect on Context, Identity, and Spirituality* (Matieland, South Africa: EFSA Institute for Theological and Interdisciplinary Research, 2000).

19. Introduction to her paper at the Consultation on Contextual Theology at Pietermaritzburg, September 2008.

20. James A. Cochrane, "To Dream the Impossible Dream," *Journal of Theology for Southern Africa* 129 (November 2007): 27.

21. David Tacey, *The Spiritual Revolution* (New York: Routledge, 2004).

22. *Interfaith Solidarity*, Institute for Justice and Reconciliation, Cape Town. February 2004.

23. Which was illegal because we were both "banned."

24. Du Toit in *The Legacy of Stephen Bantu Biko*, ed. C. W. Du Toit (Pretoria: UNISA, 2008), 209.

25. Smith as cited in Kenneth Cracknel, *Towards a New Relationship* (London: Epworth, 1986), 58.

26. Aslan, *No God but God*, xvii.

27. Cyril I. Obi in *A New Struggle for Africa*, ed. Roger Southall and Henning Melber (Pietermaritzburg: University of KwaZuluNatal Press, 2009), 199. This is a valuable commentary on current developments in Africa.

28. Jakobus S. Krüger, Gerrie Lubbe, and H. C. Steyn, *The Human Search for Meaning: A Multireligious Introduction to the Religions of Humankind* (Hatfield, Pretoria: Van Schaik, 2009), 15.

Chapter 10. Something New Out of Africa

1. Aziz Pahad, formerly of the South African Ministry of Foreign Affairs, paper on "Building a Global Progressive Movement," Pretoria, October 6, 2005.

2. Martin Prozesky, *Frontiers of Conscience: Exploring Ethics in a New Millennium* (Pietermaritzburg: Equinym Publishing, 2003), 74.

3. Kgalema Motlanthe to ANC, Commission on Religious Affairs, June 2007.

4. Paul Gifford, *The Religious Right in Southern Africa* (Zimbabwe: Baobab Press and the University of Zimbabwe, 1988), 95.

5. Beyers Naudé quoted in *Living Spirituality News,* London (Spring 2009).

6. J. Cilliers, "Worshipping in the Townships," *Journal of Theology for Southern Africa* 132 (November 2008): 84.

7. Report of ICT, *Ten Years of Theology and Struggle* (Johannesburg: Institute of Contextual Theology, 1991), 25.

8. T. S. Maluleke, *African Christian Theology in Transformation* (Cape Town: EFSA, 2004), 190.

9. S. B. Biko, "Black Consciousness and the Quest for True Humanity," in *Black Theology,* ed. Basil Moore (Johannesburg: University Christian Movement, Ravan Press, 1973), 25.

10. Louise Kretzchmar, "The Formation of Moral Leaders in South Africa," *Journal of Theology for Southern Africa* 128 (2007): 34.

11. Celia Kourie in *Secular Spirituality as a Contextual Critique of Religion,* a compilation of papers presented at the Forum for Religious Dialogue Symposium of the Research Institute for Theology and Religion held at the University of South Africa, Pretoria, May 11–12, 2006 (Pretoria: University of South Africa, 2007), ed. C. W. Du Toit and Cedric Mayson, 80.

12. Frei Betto, *Fidel and Religion: Castro Talks on Revolution and Religion* (New York: Simon and Schuster, 1987), 227.

13. Joe Slovo, *The Unfinished Autobiography* (Johannesburg, 1995), 192.

14. *Secular Spirituality as a Contextual Critique of Religion,* ed. du Toit and Mayson, 150.

15. Gifford, *The Religious Right in Southern Africa,* 110.

16. Russel Botman in Mongezi Guma and A. Lesley Milton, *An African Challenge to the Church in the Twenty-first Century* (Johannesburg: South African Council of Churches, 1997), 78.

17. Kgalema Motlanthe was the secretary general of the South African National Congress and served as president of South Africa between Thabo Mbeki and Jacob Zuma. The quotations in this book are from his address on Vision and Values given to the ANC Commission of Religious Affairs Consultation in Soweto, Johannesburg, in 2007.

18. Bill Bryson, *A Short History of Nearly Everything* (London: Black Swan Books and Doubleday, 2003), 573.

Index

Abrahams, Ivan, 23, 191–92
Ackermann, Denise, 165
Africa
  agricultural potential of, 103–4
  Christianity in, 130–35
  coastal areas, knowledge of, 52–53
  colonial attitudes within, 154
  communal approach in, to liberation, 43
  conditioned to the struggle for change, 40
  continued exploitation of, 90
  cultures of, 28
  democratic revolutions in, 3
  development economy and, 108–9
  distorted image of, 113
  diversity of, 2–3, 4
  driving routes through, 112
  economic architecture of, designed by the West, 104
  economic problems of, 108
  effect on, of Europeans' return to, 29–30
  Europe's division of, 73–74
  focus in, on the community, 23–25
  geography of, 27
  humans first appearing in, 16
  independence of nations in, 54
  indigenous religions of, accommodating other religions, 156
  inferiority complex in, 46
  internal conflict in, 172
  languages in, lacking word for "'religion,'" 31
  liberated testimony of, 36–37
  liberation in, struggle for, 4

Africa (continued)
  liberation movements in, 77–78, 80–84, 160–61
  looking in the correct direction, 38
  media in, dominated by Western interests, 112, 113
  missionary expansion into, 53–54, 131, 132–35
  moratorium declared in, on importing missionary activity, 134–35
  need of, to establish an ubuntu economy, 107
  people of, 28–29
  perception of, as heathen or pagan, 30
  political liberation of, spiritual power for, 76
  postliberation environment of, 168–74
  primal spirituality of, 121–22
  quest of, for liberated united continent, 93
  religion in, 28
  religious tolerance in, 123–24
  resources of, 2–3
  rivers of, 27–28
  role of, in media history, 110
  secular-spiritual life in, breakdown of, 168–74
  seeing, through Western eyes, 1
  seeking new political era, 93
  self-delusion in, 62
  spiritual awareness in, ecumenical nature of, 122
  spiritual development of, secular influences on, 159–61

Africa (*continued*)
  spirituality in, 18, 120
  threefold revolution in, 102–3
  traditional religion of, 32
  understanding religion in political
    terms, 76
  view of violence in, 84
  wealth's role in, 170–72
Africa and Christianity (Westerman),
    34
African Indigenous (Independent)
    Churches, 137–38
African National Congress, 4, 77–78,
    166–67
  dealing with the Black Con-
    sciousness Movement,
    42
  Program of Action, 81
African-ness, 103
African socialism, 99
  foundation and objective of, 101
  ideals related to, 102
African traditional beliefs, among
    Christians and Muslims, 137
African Union, 91, 93
afterlife, 147–48
ahoto, 124
Akan, concept of blessedness for,
    124–25
Alexander, Neville, 51–52
All Africa Conference of Churches
    (AACC), 28, 56, 61–62, 134–35,
    139, 177
ancestors
  communication with, 137
  veneration of, 25, 96
Ancestral Grace (O'Murchu), 122
Anderson, John, 14
Anti-Apartheid Movement (AAM),
    87–88, 141
apartheid, 33–34
  churches' role in, 62
  declared a crime against humanity,
    86

apartheid (*continued*)
  defeat of, 80
  ecclesiastical, 33–35
  ending of, leading to political victory,
    85–88
  opposition to, 81
  political victory of, 81
  religions' response to, 148–49
  religious, 56, 76
  See also South Africa
Appiah-Kubi, Kofi, 19
Armstrong, Karen, 173
Aslan, Reza, 56, 142, 167
atheism, 174
Atlantic Charter, 79
authority, questioning of, 57–59
Axelson, Eric, 130–31

Baartman, Ernest, 126
Bam, Brigalia, 76
Bambata, 77
Banjul Charter, 91
Bantu Education Act (1955), 81
baptism, as ubuntu occasion, 130
Basileia, 165, 166, 181–82
belongingness, 18–19
Benson, E. W., 150
Berry, Sara, 109
Bevin, Ernest, 79
Biko, Steve, 23, 42, 46, 59, 82, 123,
    136, 158, 167, 186
black consciousness, 136
Black Consciousness Movement, 42,
    46, 82, 90
blessedness, 124–25
Boesak, Allan, 37
Boff, Leonardo, 160
Boraine, Alex, 126
Botha, P. W., 83, 163
Botman, Russel, 75–76, 116, 192
bribery, 170–71
Bryson, Bill, 16, 196
Burke, Edmund, 88

Bush administration (G. W.), 59–60, 141
Bushmen, religion of, 17–18
Buthelezi, Manas, 56, 99
Buthelezi, Sipho, 90

Call of Islam, 161
capital, lack of, preventing Africa's political freedom, 103–4
capitalist empires, collapse of, 106–7
Castro, Fidel, 187
Challenge to the Church (the Kairos document), 161–63
change, coming from the bottom up, 179–80, 182–83
Christian Institute, 161, 166
Christ-ianity, 36–37, 54, 131–32, 136, 143, 164
Christianity
  corruption of, 54
  developing along apartheid lines, 135–36
  in missionary era in Africa, 131–35
Christo-fascism, 142–43
churches
  Africans' increasing role in, 134
  independent, 137–38
  role of, in Africa, 134–35
church growth, missionary focus on, 61
Churchill, Winston, 79
church theology, 162
church work, separate from missionary work, 133, 139
Cilliers, Johan, 142, 184
Circle of Concerned African Women Theologians, 165
civilization
  debacle of, 29–30
  development of, 173
  religious apartheid of, 33–35
  separating spiritual from the secular, 30–31, 32
civil wars, 90

climate change, 8, 66–67
coal, 171
Cochrane, James, 166
Colenso, John William, 54, 58–59, 159
colonialism, 50–51, 132, 135–37, 145
  influence of, on religious institutions, 157–58
  redrawing the map of Africa, 53
colonization, 131
community, African focus on, 23
community values, traditional African societies running on, 105
creation stories, 121
Creeds, Christian, 164–65
Cronin, Jeremy, 109

dance, 110
Dart, Raymond, 16
Dartmouth, Lord, 48
Davies, Geoff, 70
de Beer, Stephan, 90
Defiance Campaign, 81
De Klerk, F. W., 83
development economy, Africa and, 108–9
Dias, Bartholomeu, 130–31
dictatorships, 90
Dinizulu, 77
discipleship, political, 76
Discovery, museum for, 15
diversity, unity in, 121–22
Donders, Joseph, 32, 35
Du Bois, W. E. B., 80
Duchrow, Ulrich, 98, 107
Du Toit, Cornell, 55, 122, 167
Dwane, James, 138

Earthlings
  belongingness as trait of, 18–19
  lostness of, 25–26
  obsessed with patches, 17
  primal reality of, 24–25
  production of, 14

Earthlings (*continued*)
  representing the height of humanity,
    16
  self-awareness of, 13–15
  spiritual nature of, 17, 20, 21–22, 25
  See also humans
ecological systems, pressures on, 8
ecology
  new era in, 188–89
  issues in, 66–70
economic communities, becoming a
  law unto themselves, 34
economic oppression, liberation from,
  47–52
economics, 7
  different approaches to, in primal
    Africa and the West, 47–48
  domination of, by international
    powers, 8
  new era in, 189
  restoring ethics to, 107
economic system
  as cause of poverty, 35
  compared to the beast of the
    Apocalypse, 98–99
ecumenism, 139–40, 145, 150–51
education, purpose of, 91
Einstein, Albert, 124
Ela, Jean-Marc, 24, 54, 76
elite, 68–69, 106
empires, collapse of, 178–79
Esack, Moulana Farid, 37
Evangelical Revival, 132
evolution, 15–16
exploitation, economic, liberation
  from, 105–6
extinction, possibility of, 8, 66, 109,
  172

faith, 193–95
false assumptions, liberation from,
  47
financiers, Western, relying on bribery,
  104

forests, depletion of, 67
Freedom Charter, 81
fundamentalism, 59–60, 141–44,
  174
Gandhi, Mahatma, 44, 81, 156
Gatu, John, 134, 158
genetically modified seed and plants,
  171
Ghana, 92
Gifford, Paul, 180, 192
globalization, 51–52, 107, 142
global morality, 178
God, questions about, 21–22
going over, 192–95
Goldstein, Richard, 86–87
Gondwana, 15
Gore, Al, 9, 113–14
greed, 68–69, 100, 114
Gruchy, John de, 145–46
Gruchy, S. de, 108

Harare Declaration, 83
Harris, Cyril, 150, 159
Harris, Elizabeth, 168
Hastings, Adrian, 138
Herod's Temple, 159
Herzl, Theodor, 143
Hopkins, Dwight, 136
Huddleston, Trevor, 141
human rights violations, social
  experience of, 43
humans
  agenda for, 176–77
  common way of being, 155–56
  development of, 173–74
  spiritual energy in, 123
  See also Earthlings
hydroelectricity, 68

independence, dates of, for African
  nations, 88, 89
individualism, effects of, 127–28
interfaith era, 140–41
interfaith movement, 146

Islam
fundamentalism in, 143
internal battle in, 142

Jegede, Dele, 156–57
Jesus
cooptation of, 158
importance to, of identifying with
the poor and needy, 97
liberation of, 158–59
social teachings of, sidelined, 146
teachings of, varying from the
teachings of the church, 164
Jews for Justice, 161
Jones, Vaughan, 160
justice culture, 166

Kairos document, 31, 57, 161–62
kairos time, 163
Kendall, Elliott, 61, 113, 133, 138, 159
Kenya, 92
Kenyatta, Jomo, 80, 167
Kleinschmidt, Horst, 42, 127
Kourie, Celia, 187
Kretzchmar, Louise, 186–87
Krüger, Jakobus S., 10, 119

Lamb, David, 46, 49
land
becoming a personal possession,
34–35
belonging to the community, 101
possession of, 24
Leakey, Louis, 16
Leakey, Mary, 16
Leopold (king), 50, 53
Levellers, 100
liberation
bringing secular and spiritual
together, 31
from economic oppression, 47–52,
105–6
experience of, in Africa, 41–42
from false assumptions, 47

liberation (*continued*)
from imperialist elites, 177
often followed by disasters, 88–90
as ongoing process, 45
from political oppression, 52–54
from religious hostility, 60
from religious oppression, 54–57
social aspect to, 42–43
spiritual aspect of, 43–45
struggle for, Africa conditioned to,
40
as two-way process, 40–41
liberation economy, 99
liberation movements, 77–78, 80–84
liberation theology, 160
liberators, becoming oppressors, 62
Linden, Ian, 161
*Liturgy for Interfaith Prayers for Peace
and Unity, A* (World Conference
on Religion and Peace), 155
Louw, Lionel, 37
Lubbe, Gerrie, 141
Luther, Martin, 106
Luthuli, Albert, 10

Mafuna, Bokwe, 47
Makarovm, Oleg, 14–15
Malawi, 92
Maluleke, Sam, 185–86
Mandela, Nelson, 101
on church-state relations, 149
falling into apartheid mind-set,
45–46
on leadership, 74
on structure of early African
societies, 24
on Xhosas' religion, 123
Mansfield, Lord, 49
maps, misleading nature of, 26
Mazrui, A. A., 123–24
Mbeki, Thabo, 52, 106, 138
Mbiti, John S., 121, 123
Mboya, Tom, 101–2
McVie, Malcolm J., 139–40

media, 7
    Africa's connection with, 110
    destructiveness of, 9
    influence of, 113–14
    lack of trust in, 113
    liberated agenda of, 115–16
    misleading nature of, 112
    objective of, to undermine
        understanding, 114
    presence in, of struggle to liberate
        society from oppression, 112
Melber, Henning, 62
Mercator, Gerhard, 26
Meredith, Malcolm Ivan. *See* Padmore,
    George
Middle East, conflict in, 143–44
military takeovers, 92
missionaries, 53–54, 131–35
missionary movement, problem of,
    61–62
modernization, working out, in African
    terms, 41
Mokone, Mangena, 138
Moore, Basil, 62
Mosoma, David L., 122, 156, 163
Motlanthe, Kgalema, 63, 107, 179,
    192, 196
Mugabe, Robert, 62
Muhammad, preaching benevolence
    and care for the poor, 97–98
Muslim Judicial Council, 149
Muslims, liberation of, from officially
    sanctioned corruption, 56
Muzorewa, Gwinyai H., 36, 54–55

Nairn, Tom, 57
National Religious Leaders Forum, 149
native Americans, reflecting African
    beliefs, 18
Naudé, Beyers, 140, 159–60, 166, 180
neo-liberal capitalism, 9
new era, 188–92
Nigeria, 92
Nkrumah, Kwame, 80, 91, 102

Nolan, Albert, 9, 19, 51
noninterference, principle of, 90–91
Nyerere, Julius, 43, 101, 104

Odendaal, Andre, 93–94
Oduyoye, Mercy, 23
oil, 171
O'Murchu, Diarmuid, 119–20, 122
one-party states, 92
oppressed, interdependence of, 100
oppression, emergence of, following
    liberation, 62
oral tradition, 110, 111–12
Organization of African Unity, 91
Organization of African Unity Charter,
    90

Padmore, George, 102–3
Pahad, Aziz, 177
Pakenham, Tom, 53
Pan-African Federation, 80
Pass Laws, 81
patches, 17
patriarchy, deconstruction of, 165
Phiri, Isobel, 165
Pityana, Barney, 82, 123
Plaatje, Sol, 78
Pliny the Elder, 176
Pobee, John S., 124–25
political communities, becoming a law
    unto themselves, 34
political oppression, liberation from,
    52–54
political vision, search for, 93–94
politics, 7
    arising in context of change, 74–75
    based on tradition, 74
    control of, by globalized economic
        powers, 9
    dynamics of, viewing in context of
        other disciplines, 75
    misuse of, 91
    new era for, 189–90
    relation of, to religion, 75–76

population growth, 66
possessions, moral use of, 105
postreligion, 167–68, 184–87, 191
postreligious development revolution, 107
poverty, 68
power, distribution of, 92
primal belief, 32, 75, 121–22
primal people, shared belongingness appearing among, 18
proclamation, 190
progress
    constant spirit to, 45
    key indicators of, 109
prophets, 19
    rejecting unjust distribution of social wealth, 98
    as source of spiritual matters, 130
prosperity religion, 56–57, 59
Prozesky, Martin, 107, 178, 187

Ramphele, Mamphela, 82, 90, 183
Reagan administration, 59–60, 141
rebellions, 90
rebirth, 63
Rees, Martin, 8
Reflections on the Revolution in France (Burke), 88
religion, 7
    absence in, of ubuntu, 128–29
    colonial, 133–37
    colonial, liberation from, 157–59
    fundamentalism, 141–44
    interfaith era of, 140–41
    liberation of, 163–67
    missionary era of, 131–35
    responses to, 148
religions
    authority of, courage to question, 57–59
    avoiding calling for spiritual rectitude in economic affairs, 69–70
    competition resulting from, 20–21
    conflicts among, 20

religions (*continued*)
    corruption and oppression of, 57
    divisiveness of, 9–10
    establishing, as separate entities, 30
    failure of, 172–73
    focus of, on institutional order, 25
    institutional forms of, destroying Africa's soul, 34
    invention of, 19–20
    as mixed blessing, 20–21
    perpetrating antihuman behavior, 25–26
    possibilities of, for coming together, 150–51
    priorities of, 20, 33
    promoting the Apocalypse, 10
    separation of, from each other, 60
    separation of, from life, 35
    as source of bondedness, 156
    use of, to support oppressive political and economic power, 10
religious hostility, liberation from, 60
religious institutions, failure of, 144–47
religious oppression, liberation from, 54–57
repentance, 193–94
resistance, political, 77
revolution, spiritual, need for, 150, 151, 153–54
Rhodes, Cecil, 53
Rieger, Jeorg, 9, 114
Robertson, Claire, 92
Robinson, Mary, 86
Roosevelt, Franklin D., 79
ruling power, Good News of, 165
Russell, Bertrand, 147

Sachs, Albie, 44
salvation, 63
    bringing secular and spiritual together, 31
    for the world, 24

Saradananda, Swami, 156
SASO, 46
satyagraha program, 44
science, 7
Scott, Michael, 57–58
Scott, Robert Falcon, 15
Scramble for Africa, The (Pakenham), 53
secular spirituality, 56, 63, 156, 168, 173, 187
Seme, Pixley ka Isaka, 78
shipping, effect of, 132
Sichone, Owen, 94
sincerity, seduction of, 114-15
Singh, Bishan, 107
slave trade, 48–49, 53, 132
Slovo, Joe, 86, 187
small groups, importance of, 180–84
Smith, Wilfred Cantwell, 156, 167
smog, 67
socialism, 100–105
    as an attitude, 101
    requiring capital, 104
solar power, 67–68
solitary confinement, 127
Solomon, Gassan, 37
South Africa, 4
    antiapartheid movement in, 80–84
    boycott of, 87–88
    liberation of, 86–88
    retaining aura of uniqueness, for political maturity, 93
South African Council of Churches, 145, 148–50, 166
South African Institute of Contextual Theology, 184
South African Native National Congress, 77–78. *See also* African National Congress
spirit
    consciousness of, 119–20
    revolution of, 150, 151

spiritual communities, progressive, 166–67
spiritual energy, rediscovering, 155
    African approach to, 123–24
    false, 57
    new era for, 190–92
    postreligious approach to, 55
spiritual revolution
    challenge of, 190
    need for, 150, 151, 153–54
spiritual success, related to handling of the economy, 98
state theology, 162
Storey, Peter, 163
struggle, against suffering, 179
sunset clause, 86
Suppression of Communism Act (1950), 81
sustainable transformation, 109
Swimme, Brian, 14

Tacey, David, 8, 166
Tambo, Oliver, 42, 78, 166–67
Tanzania, 92
Teffo, Joseph Lesiba, 24, 122
Teilhard de Chardin, Pierre, 14
Theissen, Gert, 10
theology
    arising from social action, 159
    postreligious, 184–87
    role of, 192
Thorpe, S. A., 37–38
Tile, Nehemiah, 138
Tlhagale, Buti, 25, 137, 145
tradition, effect of, on politics, 74
Treason Trial, 81
Truth and Reconciliation Commission, 86–87
Tsele, Molefe, 76, 105
Tutu, Desmond, 21, 163
    on African worldview, 122
    on ubuntu, 31–32, 124

ubuntu, 3, 23
  aligned with the prophets, 98
  appreciating, by experiencing its
    opposite, 126
  economic system based on, 96–97
  experience of, 24, 124–26, 128–29
  not dependent upon religion, 128–29
  as response to vital life force, 122
  word for, absent in European
    languages, 31
ubuntu economic system, 108
Uganda, 92
Ujamaa, 99, 101
Umkhonto we Sizwwe, 82
United Democratic Front, 83
Universal Declaration of Human
  Rights (1948), 85–86
University Christian Movement,
  161
Upper Volta, 92

values, liberation of, 63
Van der Water, Des, 33
Villa-Vicencio, Charles, 10, 132
violence
  African perspective on, 84
  role of, in political discussion, 84
vital force, 122–24, 156–57

war, 67
  ubuntu fulfilled during, 128
wealth
  pursuit of, 169
  role of, 170–72
Wesley, Charles, 132
Wesley, John, 132
Westerman, D., 34
Western civilization, designed for care
  and promotion of the elite, 69
Westernism, 133
World Conference on Religion and
  Peace, 28, 141, 155
World Council of Churches, 139
world government, 94
World Parliament of Religions, 28,
  140–41, 150
world wars, ending of, 84–85
worship, communal, 128
Wren, Christopher, 184
writing, precedence of, 111

young people, grasping spiritual
  concepts, 166

zakat tithe, 97
Zimbabwe, 92
Zionism, 143